Working Positively with Personality Disorder in Secure Settings

DATE DUE

2 8 NOV 2014		
− 8 JUN 2015		
2 4 AUG 2017		
0 2 JAN 2018		
1 9 MAR 2018		

Demco, Inc. 38-293

Wiley Series in Personality Disorders

Series Editor: Professor Eddie Kane – Personality Disorder Institute, University of Nottingham

The Wiley-Blackwell Series in Personality and Mental Health publishes both single-authored and multi-authored books. The aim of the series is not merely to present critical findings and commentaries based in excellent science but also to ensure they are grounded in the realities of day-to-day practice and service delivery. The series seeks to draw together work from across the wide spectrum of professional disciplines that are essential to the development of well-balanced theoretical perspectives and truly holistic service delivery. Books in this series will be useful to clinical practitioners, lawyers, policy makers, ethicists, services users, carers and those who fund and manage the complex systems of health, social care and criminal justice.

Published

Using Time, Not Doing Time: Practitioner Perspectives on Personality Disorder and Risk
Allison Tennant and Kevin Howells

Working Positively with Personality Disorder in Secure Settings: A Practitioner's Perspective
Phil Willmot and Neil Gordon

Forthcoming

Forensic Care for Personality Disordered and Psychopathic Offenders
Mark Freestone

Working Positively with Personality Disorder in Secure Settings

A Practitioner's Perspective

Edited by Phil Willmot and Neil Gordon

A John Wiley & Sons, Ltd., Publication

This edition first published 2011
© 2011 John Wiley & Sons Ltd.

Wiley-Blackwell is an imprint of John Wiley & Sons, formed by the merger of Wiley's global
Scientific, Technical, and Medical business with Blackwell Publishing.

Registered Office
John Wiley & Sons Ltd, The Atrium, Southern Gate, Chichester, West Sussex, PO19 8SQ, UK

Editorial Offices
The Atrium, Southern Gate, Chichester, West Sussex, PO19 8SQ, UK
9600 Garsington Road, Oxford, OX4 2DQ, UK

350 Main Street, Malden, MA 02148-5020, USA

For details of our global editorial offices, for customer services, and for information about how to
apply for permission to reuse the copyright material in this book please see our website at www.
wiley.com/wiley-blackwell.

The right of Phil Willmot and Neil Gordon to be identified as the authors of the editorial material in
this work has been asserted in accordance with the UK Copyright, Designs and Patents Act 1988.

Library of Congress Cataloging-in-Publication Data

Working positively with personality disorder in secure settings: a practitioner's perspective / edited
by Phil Willmot and Neil Gordon.
        p. ; cm.
    Includes bibliographical references and index.
    ISBN 978-0-470-68380-4 (cloth) – ISBN 978-0-470-68379-8 (pbk.)
    1. Personality disorders–Treatment.   2. Prisoners–Mental health services.   I. Willmot, Phil.
II. Gordon, Neil, 1959-
    [DNLM: 1. Personality Disorders.   2. Forensic Psychiatry.   3. Hospitals, Psychiatric.
4. Mentally Ill Persons–psychology.   5. Prisoners–psychology.   6. Security Measures.   WM 190]
    RC554.W67 2010
    616.85′820086927–dc22

                                                    2010027874

A catalogue record for this book is available from the British Library.

This book is published in the following electronic formats: eBook [9780470973127]; Wiley Online
Library [9780470973110]

Set in 10 on 12 pt Galliard by Toppan Best-set Premedia Limited
Printed & Bound in Singapore by Ho Printing Singapore Pte Ltd.

01   2011

To the patients and colleagues who inspired this book.

Contents

About the Editors and Contributors

The editors

Phil Willmot is a Consultant Forensic and Clinical Psychologist with the Personality Disorder Service at Rampton Hospital, Nottinghamshire and a Senior Fellow of the Institute of Mental Health. He has over 20 years' experience of working with forensic clients with personality disorder, albeit for most of that time he was unaware of it. He worked for 14 years as a forensic psychologist in HM Prison Service in a number of establishments and as an Area Psychologist, and specialized in the assessment, treatment and management of high risk offenders and programmes for sexual offenders. In 2002 he moved to the Personality Disorder Service at Rampton for a new challenge and was surprised to find that his patients there were remarkably similar in presentation to the clients he had worked with in the prison service.

His areas of specialism include assessment and the treatment of sexual offenders with a diagnosis of personality disorder. His research interests include the links between personality disorder and sexual violence; forensic service users' perspectives on treatment; and the process of therapeutic change. He is currently studying for a PhD with the School of Community Health Sciences, University of Nottingham.

Neil Gordon is a psychotherapist working as a senior clinician and supervisor in a high secure forensic setting. He has conducted research into the client's view of psychotherapy and has also explored how psychotherapists in high secure settings adapt their therapeutic style in a context-sensitive way. Neil provides clinical supervision and organizational consultancy inputs to individual practitioners and forensic teams, and has conducted a wide range of consultancy interventions in both the public and independent sectors, focusing on the relationship between organizational culture and team behaviours. He is a Fellow of the Higher Education Academy and an Honorary Teaching Fellow at Sheffield Hallam University. He is also a member of the course team of the Metanoia Institute, London, Doctorate in Psychotherapy Programme. Previously he has held posts as a Senior Lecturer in Higher Education where he has developed and led mental health educational programmes from undergraduate to doctoral level.

Over the last 25 years Neil has worked as a psychotherapist in forensic, community and inpatient settings. He is a member of the International Society of Schema Therapy and is an accredited schema therapist. He developed and now leads the schema therapy group programme at Rampton Hospital and was formerly responsible for multidisciplinary training and workforce development within the Personality Disorder Service. He is currently seconded as a Senior Fellow to the Institute of Mental Health, Nottingham University, where he is Head of Doctoral Programmes and leads the Masters Programme of the National Personality Disorder, Knowledge and Understanding Framework (KUF), recently commissioned by the Department of Health and Ministry of Justice.

Neil has published articles on a wide range of topics, including personality disorder, organizational change, mental health education and qualitative research.

The contributors

Kerry Beckley is a Consultant Clinical Psychologist with Lincolnshire Partnership Foundation NHS Trust. She previously worked for several years in the Personality Disorder Service at Rampton Hospital and was a Senior Clinical Tutor on the Trent Doctorate in Clinical Psychology. She currently works across low secure and community forensic services in Lincolnshire. She has a particular interest in the use of schema therapy in forensic settings and is an accredited therapist with the International Society of Schema Therapy.

Jason Davies is a Consultant Forensic and Clinical Psychologist and Lead Psychologist for Rehabilitation/Recovery and Low Secure Services with Abertawe Bro Morgannwg University Health Board. He worked for a number of years in the Personality Disorder Service at Rampton Hospital, and has also worked in DSPD services, as a clinical lecturer at the University of Sheffield and as Lead Psychologist in a medium secure hospital. He is a Senior Fellow of the Institute of Mental Health and Honorary Senior Clinical Lecturer at the University of Swansea. His areas of specialism include working with complex needs (including offending behaviour, dual diagnosis and personality disorder), engagement and readiness, staff training and supervision, service development and individual and service evaluation. Other research interests include psychometric measurement and the assessment of sadistic attitudes and behaviour.

Andrea Daykin is a Forensic Psychologist in the Nottinghamshire County Community Forensic Service. Over the last ten years she has worked in various settings, including DSPD and the Personality Disorder Service at Rampton Hospital, low secure and community services, and prison. Her clinical interests include personality disorder, clinical supervision, clinical boundaries, the long-term effects of childhood trauma and fire-setting. She is currently assisting with the implementation and evaluation of a pilot outpatient clinic for clients with personality disorder within the community forensic service and is undertaking the Association for Cognitive Analytic Therapy North Practitioner-level training.

Sue Evershed is Lead Psychologist in the Men's Personality Disorder and National Women's Service at Rampton Hospital and a Senior Fellow of the Institute of Mental Health. She worked for 17 years with high secure male prisoners and young offenders as a forensic psychologist in HM Prison Service where she was part of a team responsible for the development of a Special Unit to manage disturbed and dangerous prisoners. She moved to Rampton Hospital in 1997 to work with learning disabled and personality disordered high secure patients. Her areas of specialism include working with complex needs (including offending behaviour, personality disorder and comorbid mental illness), clinical supervision, clinical boundaries and staff training, and treatment standards development. She has research interests in treatment evaluation, therapeutic engagement and therapeutic processes.

'James' spent seven years as a patient in the Personality Disorder Service at Rampton Hospital. Since writing his chapter he has been transferred to a medium secure unit.

Gopi Krishnan is a Consultant Forensic Psychiatrist and Associate Medical Director of Forensic Services with Nottinghamshire Healthcare Trust. He was previously Clinical Director of the Personality Disorder Service and The Peaks Dangerous and Severe Personality Disorder Service at Rampton Hospital.

Kath Lovell is currently Managing Director of Emergence, a new organization which incorporates the existing work of Borderline UK, which was the oldest PD service user-led organization in the UK, and Personality Plus, also a service user-led organization established to challenge the stigma surrounding personality disorder through celebrating creativity. Kath led Borderline UK through the development phase of the new national Knowledge and Understanding Framework for Personality Disorder, and now leads for emergence in the subsequent delivery and roll-out phase

Kath has been involved in a number of service user involvement initiatives, which draw on her personal experience of living with a diagnosis of Personality Disorder and of accessing mental health services. Her experience of accessing a variety of services in different settings has afforded a unique perspective from which to train and work with professionals and fellow service users, with the aim of improving the experience and effectiveness of services for all. This includes working as Expert By Experience with the Henderson Hospital, assisting in the provision of training and consultation for a diverse number of recipients, such as CMHTs and Non-Statutory Organizations, and teaching on the Postgraduate Certificate in Personality Disorder, in conjunction with the Cassel and Henderson Hospital. Kath has also worked as a service user researcher at St George's University of London, Tooting, working on a project to improve 'The Lived Experience of

Detained Patients'. In addition to her role with Emergence, Kath is also a Director of the National Survivor User Network.

Graham Lowings is a chartered Clinical Psychologist. After a brief spell working with a child and adolescent service, Graham moved to the Dangerous and Severe Personality Disorder Service at Rampton Hospital. He is currently working within Mental Health Services at the hospital on a project to expand neuropsychological assessment and rehabilitation services to patients.

Jenny Marshall is a Trainee Forensic Psychologist in the Personality Disorder Service at Rampton Hospital. She has worked in HM Prison Service and has worked at Rampton for five years. Her area of interest is in arson treatment. She completed her Master's degree in Applied Forensic Psychology at the University of York.

Andrea Milligan is a Clinical Nurse Specialist and works within the Dangerous and Severe Personality Disorder Unit at Rampton Hospital. She qualified in 1994 and has worked within a high secure environment since 2000. She has delivered a range of educational programmes for staff and is involved in both group and individual therapeutic treatment interventions. Her current clinical work focuses on the delivery of dialectical behaviour therapy. She has undertaken further degree-level study, including a BA (Hons) in Mental Health Care Practice and completed an MSc in Personality Disorder in 2008.

Louise Sainsbury is a Consultant Clinical and Forensic Psychologist. She has worked at the Personality Disorder Service, Rampton Hospital for over 10 years and has also worked in medium secure service. Her areas of specialism include schema therapy, integrating treatments for personality disorders and offending, working with complex needs, entrenched difficulties and 'unmotivated' patients, using a developmental perspective and adapting and implementing the Violence Reduction Programme for personality disorder. Her predominant interests include attachment theory, its contribution to understanding personality disorder and informing individual and group therapy, working with patients who have been labelled untreatable and patients' experiences of engaging in treatment.

Amanda Tetley is a Research Fellow in the Institute of Mental Health at the University of Nottingham. Her current work focuses on issues associated with treatment engagement in people with personality disorder. Her previous work has explored the transition from high to medium psychiatric secure services for offenders with personality disorder and has also included the evaluation of therapeutic approaches for this group. Prior to joining Rampton Hospital, she completed her PhD in Psychology at Loughborough University, Leicestershire.

Series Preface

The Wiley-Blackwell Series in Personality and Mental Health publishes both single authored and multi-authored books. The aim of the series is not merely to present critical findings and commentaries based in excellent science but also to ensure they are grounded in the realities of day-to-day practice and service delivery. The series seeks to draw together work from across the wide spectrum of professional disciplines that are essential to the development of well-balanced theoretical perspectives and truly holistic service delivery. Books in this series will be useful to clinical practitioners, lawyers, policy-makers, ethicists, services users, carers and those who fund and manage the complex systems of health, social care and criminal justice.

Over the past 20 years there has been growing interest in the interrelationship of personality and mental health and particularly in personality disorders. A number of diverse theoretical clinical approaches have emerged, and internationally very different policy and legislative approaches have been adopted to underpin individual country's attempts to recognize the social complexities presented by and to people with personality disorders. New perspectives continue to emerge and significant human, scientific and financial resources have focused on challenging existing traditional ideas and seeking a more coherent theoretical framework for interventions based on well-researched empirical evidence.

For many years personality disorders were, and often still are, regarded as untreatable, and wrongly identified as synonymous with dangerousness. In fact, people with a personality disorder who pose a high risk of harm to others are a tiny minority, whereas this group often self-harm and take their own lives. Recent figures from the Department of Health indicate a range of 47–77% of suicides have a personality disorder. The diagnosis has frequently been used as an informal or formal criterion for exclusion from services which others with mental health issues take for granted, as well as from ordinary life opportunities such as decent housing and employment.

Personality disorders are not something we catch or are born with, but are 'a way of being', which develop as we grow up. To have a personality disorder means to have some aspects of your personality that will cause you repeated problems, particularly with relationships. Personality disorders affect people across their lifespan and often across generations. People with a personality disorder will often have experienced abuse, trauma, neglect or disrupted care in childhood. In addition to the exclusion they so frequently experience, people with a personality disorder appear more likely to have diagnosable mental illnesses, such as depression, panic attacks and addictions (including poly-drug abuse).

New approaches in clinical and social interventions, coupled with a more benign policy and legislative environment in some countries, are leading to real innovation and enhanced life chances for people diagnosed with personality disorder. At the same time, a refreshed understanding of the aetiology and development of personality disorder is coming from behaviour genetics and developmental psychology. The developmental explanations of personality disorder are being enhanced by increased understanding of biological and developmental mechanisms. These new approaches and understandings challenge traditional theories about the origins of the diagnoses and the life outcomes that should be expected.

Set in this exciting context of new research enquiry, ethical, social, policy and legislative challenges, this book offers an insight into the practical realities of constructing and delivering treatment to some of the most complex and excluded people anywhere. The national personality disorder programme in England is an integrated initiative among a number of government departments. The aspect of the programme which is central to the issues described in this book is the Dangerous and Severe Personality Disorder Programme, established in 1999. The model described in 1999 was designed to test, research and further develop intervention programmes in selected high security prisons and hospitals in England.

The authors of this book are current and former members of the Personality Disorder Service at Rampton High Security Hospital, where they have led the way in the treatment of high risk individuals with personality disorders. This book brings together that experience in an easily readable and often inspiring exposition of the critical issues that are the day-to-day challenges for staff and patients in these complex environments. The book is usefully conceptualized in a number of related but distinct sections that will be attractive to readers who come from different starting points and interest groups. The sections present a description of the work context, describe how the population has evolved in complexity and deals with some of the critical issues at the interface with step-down facilities. It moves through very effective descriptions of the treatment processes and deals with the absolute core of the work's philosophical underpinning, the critical importance of the therapeutic relationship. In this section is one of the most interesting approaches to examining this relationship in a secure setting in recent years – the chapter in which 'James' discusses his therapeutic journey and his psychologist reflects on that journey. This is powerful and different and will attract a good deal of interest. It deserves to be used as a model more generally. The examination of the development of an aware and supported workforce, and the initiatives taken to improve capacity around these fundamental areas, are clear and the messages direct. The section on outcomes and measuring change rightly gives a focus to an area that is current and important, but is often sidestepped; some useful insights emerge. The book concludes with some excellent views about what may shape this field in years to come for practitioners, policy-makers and funders alike.

Professor Eddie Kane
Director
Personality Disorder Institute University of Nottingham

Preface

This book is unapologetically about a single service, the Personality Disorder Service at Rampton, a high secure hospital. It describes the service, its context, ethos, treatment pathway and workforce issues, and how these have developed over the past decade. However, in writing we have aimed to make it relevant and of practical use not just to practitioners and service managers in other health settings who are working with patients with personality disorder, but also to the much larger group of staff in prisons, the Probation Service and other forensic settings who are likely to be working with offenders who exhibit a wide range of (usually undiagnosed) personality disorder traits. The settings may be very different, but our experiences of working outside Rampton suggest that the issues relating to patients and to staff described in this book will be recognizable across the whole range of forensic settings.

In developing the introduction to the book we have decided to look at what follows as representing an extended case study of our service. The chapters have been written by practitioners who have inhabited a distinct social context over the last decade and the themes they address represent their struggles as frontline practitioners trying to make sense of a complex and challenging clinical world. For those of us who inhabit the 'swampy lands' of practice it is often difficult to find sufficient reflective space to make sense of our experiences and communicate this to others. This book has therefore provided us with a unique opportunity to share our reflections with people who are interested in the way complex social institutions, and the practitioners within them, respond to the challenges of trauma-related personality difficulties in a therapeutically informed way. We believe the thinking and ideas evidenced in the following chapters will offer those outside our world an insight into what has motivated, challenged and informed this important work.

Practitioners appreciate case study approaches for their practical, down-to-earth and attention-holding properties. Furthermore, if we are to genuinely help our audience understand particular social systems and intervention programmes, we have to find a way of communicating with them that engages with their current understandings and areas of interest. We believe that the 10-year therapeutic project described in this book will be of interest to a diverse range of practitioners, service users and researchers, as it offers a detailed account of how a multi-professional group of clinicians responded with creativity to the needs of a marginalized client group.

Foreword

Kath Lovell

Most academic discourse exploring the complexities faced by workers within forensic or high secure settings has lacked any authentic inclusion of the patient's or offender's voice. Primarily due to the difficulty in viewing the patient without suspicion, the patient often loses their 'right' to be seen as a person, much less as a person with extreme traumatic aetiology. The preoccupation with risk, political and public pressures and the complex dilemma between punishment and treatment often reduces the patient to nothing more than something to constrain or restrict – the person's humanity further eroded, or lost completely, in the process or through the harsh brutalities of the system.

This book unites theory and experience in a truly authentic way, challenging the iatrogenic dynamics and unreflective working practices that have, at times, dominated these contexts. Through brave and thoughtful consideration of the patient voice by the authors, we see that there is an opportunity to create a helpful dialogue with all perspectives, a dialogue that offers a fertile soil for therapeutic growth. The co-authorship of chapter 9 with a current forensic patient is a poignant illustration that there is much to be learnt from the patient, his experience bringing theory to life in a way that can only stimulate the very thing that this setting has been so tragically devoid of – *hope*.

Acknowledgements

We must acknowledge all the people who have made this book possible. Eddie Kane, for recognizing the value of this project; everybody at Wiley, for their patience and help; Gopi Krishnan, John Wallace, Dick Phipps and Gerry Carton, for their leadership and support; and Sue Evershed, the unsung heroine of the Personality Disorder Service, without whose leadership and inspiration this would be a very slim volume. Also, Anne and Frances, for sharing their marriages with this book for the last year. Above all, the many colleagues and patients, past and present, who have each made their own mark on the PDS over the years and made it what it is today.

Introduction

Phil Willmot and Neil Gordon

History and context

Personality disorder has, until relatively recently, been seen as the 'Cinderella of Cinderella health services' (Howells, Krishnan & Daffern, 2007: 325), with mental health practitioners regarding people with a diagnosis of personality disorder as less deserving of care, and manipulative, annoying or attention-seeking (e.g., Lewis & Appleby, 1988; Markham & Trower, 2003). The so-called 'treatability clause' in the Mental Health Act 1983 legitimized and reinforced a widespread belief among clinicians and some patients that all or most people with the diagnosis were 'untreatable'.

Much has changed over the last decade to slowly bring personality disorder closer to the mainstream of mental health services. Clinically, a number of studies have shown that people with a diagnosis of personality disorder can benefit from psychological therapies (e.g., Duggan, Huband, Smailagic, Ferriter & Adams, 2006; Leichsenring & Leibing, 2003; Perry, Banon & Ianni, 1999), while evaluations of a number of new psychological therapies developed specifically for people with personality disorder have shown promising results (Bateman & Fonagy, 2001; Giesen-Bloo, van Dyck, Spinhoven, van Tilburg, Dirksen, van Asselt, Kremers, Nadort & Arntz, 2006; Linehan, Comtois, Murray *et al.*, 2006).

There was growing discomfort among clinicians and service managers about the ethics of stigmatizing and excluding from treatment a group of people with severe mental health and social problems. Unfortunately, and not for the first or

Working Positively with Personality Disorder in Secure Settings: A Practitioner's Perspective
Edited by Phil Willmot and Neil Gordon
© 2011 John Wiley & Sons, Ltd.

last time in the history of mental health services in the UK, it took a serious incident for change to take place. In 1998, Michael Stone was convicted of the murders of Lin and Megan Russell and the attempted murder of Josie Russell. During his trial, it was revealed that Stone had sought help from local forensic mental health services but, because he was diagnosed as suffering from an untreatable personality disorder, no treatment was provided.

The Stone case had a number of consequences for personality disorder services, particularly in forensic settings. Foremost among these has been the introduction of the concept of Dangerous and Severe Personality Disorder (DSPD), and the government has devoted considerable resources over the last decade to developing new DSPD services across the NHS and prison service. The concept of DSPD has been widely criticized as being, among other things, stigmatizing (Kingdon, 2007), contrary to human rights legislation (Corbett & Westwood, 2005), too expensive (Maden, 2007) and not cost-effective (Barrett, Byford, Seivewright, Cooper, Duggan & Tyrer, 2009). However, DSPD has also undoubtedly achieved some important successes. It has forced politicians, managers and clinicians at last to consider seriously the effective treatment of the most dangerous and needy offenders, and thereby moved the attention of decision-makers away from simply developing ever more draconian methods of incapacitating and punishing these individuals. It has also raised awareness throughout the criminal justice system of the needs of offenders with personality disorder traits, and it has attracted many high-profile researchers and clinicians, as well as large amounts of money to research and development in the field. Cinderella, at least in forensic services, has finally arrived at the ball!

The concept of DSPD has, however, been divisive for clinicians. Its very name creates an unhelpful and stigmatizing association between dangerousness and severe personality disorder, which has perhaps contributed to the estrangement between forensic and non-forensic personality disorder services just at the point, in recent years, when they have been expanding and collaborating more effectively. Also, while there is little clear evidence for a link between risk of offending and personality disorder, other than antisocial personality disorder which includes offending behaviour in its definition, the notion of a 'functional link' between personality disorder and risk is central to the definition of DSPD.

While DSPD services have attracted much publicity in recent years, it is important to remember that they provide a small fraction of the total number of beds for offenders with personality disorder, in both the health and prison systems. In the health sector, services for patients with a diagnosis of personality disorder have changed markedly in the last decade. The Fallon Inquiry into the Personality Disorder Unit at Ashworth proposed a new model for the management of personality disorder in forensic settings. Ten years on, the system has changed, though not quite as the authors of that report recommended. Their model proposed specialist services for personality disorder within the penal and hospital systems, the separation of patients with diagnoses of personality disorder and mental illness, and national standards for the assessment of personality disorder to end what they described as a 'lottery' of whether offenders with personality disorder were offered appropriate treatment. Ten years later, Rampton is the only one of the four high secure hospitals in the UK to have a specialist and separate personality disorder service. The picture in the medium secure sector has been somewhat more positive, with a significant increase in the number of beds and of services accepting patients with a diagnosis of personality disorder. However, even the recent publication of NICE guidelines on borderline and antisocial personality disorders (National Institute for Health & Clinical Excellence, 2009a, b) has not helped to standardize the assessment of personality disorder.

Meanwhile, elsewhere in the prison service, the state of services for people with personality disorder has changed little over the last decade. Despite evidence of high levels of personality disorder in prisons (Fazel & Danesh, 2002; Singleton, Meltzer, Gatward, Coid & Deasy, 1998), little has been done to directly assist this large proportion of the prison population other than in a small number of therapeutic community prisons. Mental Health In-Reach services have improved and expanded greatly over the last decade, but these were never designed or intended to provide long-term intensive therapy for prisoners with personality disorders. Indeed, taking responsibility for the mental health of prisoners away from the prison service and giving it to local NHS Trusts has arguably allowed the prison service to avoid responsibility for this issue and made it more difficult for the service to develop a national strategy for dealing with personality disorder.

The wider context

Outside forensic settings, progress has been slower, although there have been a number of recent encouraging developments. New Labour's focus on reducing social exclusion in society in general has also addressed social exclusion related to mental health problems. In 2003, following an extensive consultation process, the National Institute for Mental Health (NIMHE) published *Personality Disorder: No Longer a Diagnosis of Exclusion* (NLDE) (Department of Health, 2003), which was the first clearly articulated account of how existing mental heath services in England were failing to respond to the needs of people with personality disorder. It highlighted how only a few NHS Trusts had dedicated personality disorder services and how people with personality disorder often found themselves 'on the margins' in unsympathetic A&E services or equally unsuitable inpatient psychiatric wards. The guidance pointed out that the mental health workforce was ill prepared to respond positively to the needs of those with the diagnosis and unlikely to prioritize their needs. Within forensic services it was noted that a number of regional secure units actively excluded patients with a primary diagnosis of personality disorder because they did not consider this to be their core business. More worryingly, the report suggested that many clinicians and mental health practitioners were reluctant to work with people with personality disorder, in the belief that they did not have the skills, training or resources to provide an adequate service.

The best practice guidelines in NLDE advocated that service provision for personality disorder would be most appropriately provided by specialist multidisciplinary teams targeting those with significant distress and complex problems, supported by specialist day-patient services. It also suggested that forensic services needed to consider how to develop expertise in the identification and assessment of offenders with personality disorder, while improving their liaison with Multi-Agency Public Protection Panels and it committed the Department of Health (DoH) to supporting the development of a number of personality disorder centres financially within regional forensic services to improve the assessment, treatment and management of personality disordered offenders.

The other major developmental focus of the guidance was related to workforce development and this culminated in the publication of another document, *Breaking the Cycle of Rejection* (National Institute for Mental Health, 2003). This Capabilities Framework described a skills escalator to address the gap in the training curriculum of key mental health professions at pre-registration and post-qualification levels. The aspirations articulated in this document took nearly six years to come to fruition before the DoH and Ministry of Justice commissioned the development of the Knowledge and Understanding Framework (KUF) in 2007. This led to the creation of a national educational framework to support people to work more effectively with personality disorder. This educational development work built on the aspirations articulated within the two policy guidance documents discussed above. The key goal of the programmes is to improve service-user experiences by developing the capabilities, skills and knowledge of the multi-agency workforces in health social care and criminal justice. The multilevel educational package includes a working with personality disorder web-based awareness programme; an undergraduate degree programme (Developing Understanding and Effectiveness} and a Master's degree programme (Extending Expertise Enhancing Practice). The KUF was implemented in 2010 and it is intended to provide an educational career path for those working with the challenges of personality disorder and improve the knowledge and skills of frontline staff in a range of contexts.

Another development which will probably be positive for personality disorder services is the new Mental Health Act, which came into force in 2008, scrapping the treatability clause, removes the onus from the patient to prove their treatability and places it on the service provider to demonstrate that they are able to provide appropriate treatments. While the treatability clause was a significant contributory factor to the lottery of service provision, the early indications are that its removal has had little effect on referrals. The new Mental Health Act has also allowed professionals other than psychiatrists to fulfil the role of Responsible Clinician. Other professions have so far been slow to take up this role, though personality disorder services, where the role and usefulness of psychiatry has long been questioned, seems one of the areas most likely to see other professions move into the Responsible Clinician role – a development that is likely to foster the further demedicalization of personality disorder and the development of a greater diversity of clinical and management approaches.

The publication of NICE guidelines on borderline and antisocial personality disorder (National Institute for Health & Clinical Excellence, 2009a, b) will also help to raise the profile, standards and, more importantly, the funding of services for people with personality disorder. The guidelines on antisocial personality disorder in particular contain specific guidance for the assessment and management of people with antisocial personality disorder in prison and other criminal justice institutions. This is an important step, albeit a modest one, towards finally creating nationwide systems and standards for the care of people diagnosed with personality disorder in forensic settings.

Outline of this book

The book starts by setting out some of the context within which we work. The first chapter, by Jenny Marshall and Phil Willmot, describes how the patient population has increased in its level of dangerousness and mental disorder since the service began and outlines some of the factors that have contributed to these changes. The next chapter, by Amanda Tetley and Gopi Krishnan, explores some of the problems associated with moving patients on to less secure services.

Section 2 outlines our treatment process. Treatment of offenders with a diagnosis of personality disorder is informed by at least two areas of literature which have developed in almost complete isolation from each other. On the one hand, there is an extensive literature on the characteristics of effective psychological therapies stretching back to Rogers (1951), which has concentrated on the individual therapeutic relationship. On the other hand, there is the forensic literature (e.g., Andrews & Bonta, 2006; Andrews, Bonta & Hoge, 1990), which has concentrated on identifying the characteristics of effective correctional programmes and largely ignored the therapeutic relationship. This was partly in reaction to poorly targeted and poorly implemented (and hence ineffective or harmful) psychotherapy with offenders up to the 1970s, and partly because of the nature of many correctional programmes, with their large and rapid throughput. A subset of the correctional literature concerns the treatment of psychopathic individuals who present a particular set of problems to correctional treatment providers. The chapter by Phil Willmot and Amanda Tetley provides a review and integration of these literatures and provides the theoretical basis for the subsequent chapters.

The next two chapters, by Phil Willmot and Sue Evershed respectively, illustrate how these principles are applied in practice to the assessment and treatment processes. A key assumption in this service is that, for people with a diagnosis of personality disorder, serious violent or sexual offending cannot be understood or treated in isolation, but needs to be understood as one element in a lifetime of chaotic and dysfunctional coping and abusive interpersonal relationships. It is therefore important to address the patient's current dysfunctional and offence-paralleling behaviour first, before exploring the developmental roots of these behaviour patterns. Only then, as the final stage in the treatment pathway and usually several years into the treatment process, can the patient address their offending behaviour. Readers from a correctional background may therefore be surprised at the relatively little attention that is paid in these chapters to assessing or treating offending behaviour. However, we argue that this approach focuses on risk throughout and leads to much better levels of engagement in treatment, of understanding of the patient and their level of risk, of improved mental health and reduction of risk.

Section 3 is about the therapeutic relationship in forensic settings. A repeated theme in this book is the central importance of the therapeutic relationship. Hinshelwood (2002: S21) argues that a key characteristic of people described as suffering from severe personality disorder was that, because of their histories of abuse and alienation, they 'defeat help'. That phrase will doubtless ring true for any clinician who has experienced the frustrations of working with offenders with a diagnosis of personality disorder and the many and creative ways in which they undermine, sabotage or avoid treatment. The paradox with this client group is that, precisely because of their history of alienation and abuse, forming and maintaining a secure therapeutic relationship is essential to the success of treatment. To quote Linehan, describing dialectical behaviour therapy (DBT) for borderline personality disorder, 'The relationship is the vehicle through which the therapist can effect the therapy; it *is* also the therapy' (1993: 514; emphasis in the original). Working effectively with people with personality disorder requires a constant focus on the therapeutic relationship and the process of therapy and the need for flexibility within clear boundaries. The next three chapters address different aspects of this process. Louise Sainsbury provides a practical guide to using attachment theory to help to make sense of the dynamics within the therapeutic relationship and guide the therapist. Kerry Beckley, writing on adapting approaches to therapy, describes some practical examples of how clinicians need to be flexible and creative in their approach to patients, not only for the benefit of the patient, but also for their own mental health. Sue Evershed considers some of the boundary issues that clinicians, their supervisors and service managers need to consider.

Since this book stresses the need to focus on the patient and the therapeutic relationship, and to be sensitive to their needs, it was important to include a patient's account of being on the 'receiving end' of therapy. The final chapter in this section provides a powerful and insightful account by a former patient, James, describing his seven-year therapeutic journey through the service and includes a commentary by Louise Sainsbury, one of the psychologists who worked with him during that time. It also illustrates many of the principles discussed in sections 2 and 3.

Section 4 deals with workforce development and support issues in this setting. Not only are staff–patient relationships important, as discussed in section 3, strong staff–staff relationships are also essential to provide a safe environment for therapy to take place. The chapters in this section discuss the way staff have been supported and developed in meeting the challenges of working with personality disorder, while also examining the potential risks to teams and individuals if they do not create sufficient reflective space to manage the interpersonal impacts of the work. The chapter by Neil Gordon, Kerry Beckley and Graham Lowings provides an insight into the therapist experience of working with this patient group, while Kerry Beckley uses schema therapy, the service's core therapeutic model, to examine team dynamics and relationships. Andrea Daykin and Neil Gordon then discuss the essential role of supervision and support in this setting, emphasizing the usefulness of a range of individual and group methods to address the restorative, normative and educative needs of the frontline practitioner. Creating a healthy and challenging learning environment for all levels of the organization is an essential element of successful culture change (Senge, 1990). This is illustrated by Andrea Milligan and Neil Gordon, who describe the skills escalator that was created to focus on both multi-professional and discipline-specific training and development.

Section 5 is about outcomes. Monitoring of change is all the more important in this setting given the very real possibility that psychological treatments can lead to a deterioration in terms of risk (Hare, Clark, Grann & Thornton, 2000; Jones,

2007). At the same time, the small size and extreme and heterogeneous nature of this population make RCT outcome evaluations impractical and of limited use. Jason Davies provides a practical and understandable guide to the different approaches that can be used in the measurement of change with this patient group.

Phil Willmot illustrates a different approach to investigating outcomes, using qualitative methods to explore the patients' view of the therapeutic process and what they find helpful and unhelpful. The NHS Plan (Department of Health, 2001) included the principle that service users should have more say in their treatment and more influence over the way the NHS works, and there has been a growing use of qualitative methods to explore service users' perspectives in recent years. However, these methods have not been used so much with service users with a diagnosis of personality disorder or people in forensic services. This chapter shows that this group can nevertheless provide valuable insights into the therapeutic process.

The final chapter, by Neil Gordon and Phil Willmot, reviews the recurrent and emerging themes in the book, and highlights some of the issues that are likely to shape the development of forensic personality disorder services in the future.

A note about language

Although this is a book about personality disorder, the reader will find the term used relatively infrequently. Ironically, in the closed world of forensic mental health, there are many more stigmatizing labels: *murderer, rapist, psychopath, vulnerable prisoner*. To be labelled with personality disorder in this world of stigma can actually provide meaning and a sense of belonging for some patients. However, that does not mean we should promote the use of the term. The Mental Health Act requires a diagnosis of personality disorder before a patient can enter this service, but after a formal diagnosis has been made, it is seldom referred to again. We therefore regard the term as a 'convenient fiction', which enables people to access appropriate treatment.

We spent some time discussing how we should describe the people we work with since none of the commonly accepted terms adequately describes people who are detained under the Mental Health Act. 'Client' or 'service user' both imply that the person has a degree of choice and autonomy in 'using' a service. We have, therefore, chosen to refer to the people we work with as 'patients', not out of loyalty to a medical model of personality disorder, but as a more accurate reflection of the unequal power differential that exists between treatment provider and treatment recipient in forensic mental health settings and, more simply, because they are located in a hospital.

References

Andrews, D. A. & Bonta, J. (2006) *The psychology of criminal conduct*, 4th edition. Cincinnati: Anderson.

Andrews, D. A., Bonta, A. & Hoge, R.D. (1990) Classification for effective rehabilitation: Rediscovering psychology. *Criminal Justice & Behaviour*, 17, 19–52.

Barrett, B., Byford, S., Seivewright, H., Cooper, S., Duggan, C. & Tyrer, P. (2009) The assessment of dangerous and severe personality disorder: service use, cost, and consequences. *Journal of Forensic Psychiatry and Psychology*, **20**, 120–131.

Bateman, A. & Fonagy, P. (2001) Treatment of borderline personality disorder with psychoanalytically oriented partial hospitalization: An 18-month follow-up. *American Journal of Psychiatry*, **158**, 36–42.

Corbett, K. & Westwood, T. (2005) Dangerous and severe personality disorder: A psychiatric manifestation of the risk society. *Critical Public Health*, **15**, 121–133.

Department of Health (2001) *The NHS Plan*. Command Paper 4818 – 1. London: The Stationery Office.

Department of Health (2003) *Personality disorder: No longer a diagnosis of exclusion. Policy implementation guidance for the development of services for people with personality disorder*. London: DoH.

Duggan, C., Huband, N., Smailagic, N., Ferriter, M. & Adams, C. (2006) The use of psychological treatments for people with personality disorder: A systematic review of randomized controlled trials. *Personality and Mental Health*, **1**, 95–125.

Fazel, S. & Danesh, J. (2002) Serious mental disorder in 23,000 prisoners: A systematic review of 62 surveys. *The Lancet*, **359**, 545–550.

Giesen-Bloo, J., van Dyck, R., Spinhoven, P., van Tilburg, W., Dirksen, C., van Asselt, T., Kremers, I., Nadort, M. & Arntz, A. (2006) Outpatient psychotherapy for borderline personality disorder: randomized trial of schema-focused therapy vs. transference-focused psychotherapy. *Archives of General Psychiatry*, **63**, 649–658.

Hare, R. D., Clark, D., Grann, M. & Thornton, D. (2000) Psychopathy and the predictive validity of the PCL-R: An international perspective. *Behavioral Sciences and the Law*, **18**, 623–645.

Hinshelwood, R. (2002) Abusive help – helping abuse: The psychodynamic impact of severe personality disorder in caring institutions. *Criminal Behaviour and Mental Health*, **12**, S20–S30.

Howells, K., Krishnan, G. & Daffern, M. (2007) Challenges in the treatment of dangerous and severe personality disorder. *Advances in Psychiatric Treatment*, **13**, 325–332.

Jones, L. F. (2007) Iatrogenic interventions with personality disordered offenders. *Psychology, Crime and Law*, **13**, 69–79.

Kingdon, D. (2007) DSPD or 'Don't Stigmatise People in Distress'. *Advances in Psychiatric Treatment*, **13**, 333–335.

Leichsenring, F. & Leibing, E. (2003) The effectiveness of psychodynamic therapy and cognitive behaviour therapy in the treatment of personality disorders: A meta-analysis. *American Journal of Psychiatry*, **160**, 1223–1232.

Lewis, G. & Appleby, L. (1988) Personality disorder: the patients psychiatrists dislike. *British Journal of Psychiatry*, **153**, 44–49.

Linehan, M. M. (1993) *Cognitive-behavioural treatment of borderline personality disorder*. New York: Guilford Press.

Linehan, M., Comtois, K., Murray, A., *et al.* (2006) Two year randomized controlled trial and follow-up of dialectical behavior therapy vs. therapy by experts for suicidal behaviors and borderline personality disorder. *Archives of General Psychiatry*, **62**, 1–10.

Maden, A. (2007) Dangerous and severe personality disorder: antecedents and origins. *British Journal of Psychiatry*, **190**, S8–S11.

Markham, D. & Trower, P. (2003). The effects of the psychiatric label 'borderline personality disorder' on nursing staff's perceptions and causal attributions for challenging behaviours. *British Journal of Clinical Psychology*, **42**, 243–256.

National Institute for Health & Clinical Excellence (2009a) *Borderline personality disorder: treatment and management*. London: NICE.

National Institute for Health & Clinical Excellence (2009b) *Antisocial personality disorder: Treatment, management and prevention*. London: NICE.

National Institute for Mental Health (2003) *Personality disorder: No longer a diagnosis of exclusion*. London: DoH.

National Institute for Mental Health (2003) *Breaking the cycle of rejection: The personality disorder capabilities framework*. London: DoH.

Perry, J. C., Banon, E. & Ianni, F. (1999) Effectiveness of psychotherapy for personality disorders. *American Journal of Psychiatry*, **156**, 1312–1321.

Rogers, C. R. (1951). *Client-centered therapy*. Boston, MA: Houghton Mifflin.

Senge, P. (1990) *The fifth discipline: The art and practice of the learning organization*. London: Random House.

Singleton, N., Meltzer, H., Gatward, R., Coid, J. & Deasy, D. (1998) *Psychiatric morbidity among prisoners in England and Wales*. London: The Stationery Office.

Social Exclusion Unit, Office of the Deputy Prime Minister (2004) *Mental health and social exclusion: Social Exclusion Unit report*. London: Social Exclusion Unit.

Section One

Context

Chapter One

From 'Anxious and Sad' to 'Risky and Bad': Changing Patterns of Referrals to the Personality Disorder Service

Jenny Marshall and Phil Willmot

The Personality Disorder Service (PDS) at Rampton was created in 1997 and is now a 68-bed service comprising an admission and assessment ward, three treatment wards and a rehabilitation/pre-discharge ward. The service provides a specialist service for the treatment of male patients with a diagnosis of personality disorder who present a grave and immediate risk of harm to others (for a description of the treatment pathway, see this volume, Chapter 5) and is the longest established service of its type in the UK.

On the basis of observations and records, it appeared that the nature of patients being admitted to the PDS has changed since its creation. Krishnan (2005) found that levels of emotional dysregulation, self-harm, suicide attempts, hostage-taking, making threats and sexual and physical violence in this population had increased between 1997 and 2004. Patients also were shown to have been admitted with an increasing number of co-morbid mental health diagnoses after 2000, rising from two co-morbid diagnoses to four in 2004.

There has been a significant change since 1997 in mental health services in prison. The majority of referrals to the PDS have come from HM Prison Service. Poor mental health among prisoners is a major issue; for example, HM Chief Inspector of Prisons (2002) reported that 41% of inmates in high secure prisons should ideally be placed in secure hospitals or psychiatric wards due to the severity of their mental health problems. One particular aspect of mental health among prisoners that has caused much public concern was the high rate of suicide and self-harm. The suicide rate in prison more than doubled between 1982 and 1998

Working Positively with Personality Disorder in Secure Settings: A Practitioner's Perspective
Edited by Phil Willmot and Neil Gordon
© 2011 John Wiley & Sons, Ltd.

(Birmingham, 2003), from 54 to 128 per 100,000 of the average annual prison population. Liebling (1995) identified prisoners with mental problems as a group who were at particular risk of suicide or self-harm. Until the 1990s the prison service had relied on physical methods of suicide prevention, such as the use of 'strip (unfurnished) cells', despite the damaging effect that such approaches were likely to have on the mental health of vulnerable and distressed prisoners (Birmingham, 2003). However, over the last decade there has been greater emphasis on screening and risk assessment, staff awareness training and support through prisoner 'buddy' schemes and via improved mental health in-reach.

Until earlier this decade, responsibility for prisoners' healthcare lay with the Prison Medical Service, which had repeatedly resisted incorporation into the NHS, despite frequent criticism (Smith, 1999). During the 1990s the prison service came under increasing pressure to improve mental health services for prisoners. The new strategy, 'Changing the Outlook' (Department of Health & HM Prison Service, 2001), stated that prisoners should have access to the same range and quality of services as the general population had through the NHS. This strategy led to the introduction of specialist NHS mental health in-reach teams to support prisoners with the most serious mental health problems and to provide an equivalent function to community mental health teams. While the goal of matching standards of healthcare in prison to those in the community has probably not yet been achieved, standards of care for prisoners with mental health problems and those at risk of suicide have improved markedly in recent years.

Another significant change since 1997 has been the introduction of services for individuals with dangerous and severe personality disorders (DSPD). In 2004, the Peaks Unit opened at Rampton. This was one of four new DSPD units (Department of Health & Home Office, HM Prison Service, 2004). The PDS already treated patients who were dangerous and who had severe personality disorder, but the DSPD services had more stringent admission criteria in terms of level of risk, severity of personality disorder and the establishment of a functional link between patients' offending and their personality disorder.

On the basis of the previously reported changes in the characteristics of patients admitted to the PDS and the impact of the creation of a new service designed to accommodate the most dangerous and severely personality disordered patients, it was decided to investigate changes in the nature of patients admitted to the PDS since 1997. It might be expected that the trends reported by Krishnan (2005) of increasing seriousness of psychopathology and histories of violent behaviour among patients in the PDS between 1997 and 2004 would be reversed after 2004 as the patients with the most severe personality disorders, highest levels of psychopathy and greatest degree of risk were diverted into DSPD services. These hypotheses were explored by Marshall (2008), who reviewed changes in the levels of personality psychopathology in this population between 1997 and 2008.

Method

The study examined demographic, forensic and psychometric data on 145 male patients admitted to the PDS between 1997 and 2008. Patients ranged in age from 19 to 59 years at the time of admission. The majority (83.4%) were detained under the Mental Health Act classification of psychopathic disorder, 13.8% were dually classified as suffering from psychopathic disorder and mental illness, 2.1% were classified as having a mental impairment and psychopathic disorder and 1% classified with mental illness, mental impairment and psychopathic disorder.

All data used in the study were collected as part of patients' initial psychological assessment on first admission to the PDS. Measures of personality psychopathology and risk were chosen that had been consistently used during the period under investigation. Measures of personality psychopathology included clinical subscales measuring anxiety-related disorders, paranoia, borderline and antisocial features, and alcohol and drug problems from the Personality Assessment Inventory (PAI) (Morey, 1991), a self-report measure of Axis I and II mental health conditions, and the Personality Diagnostic Questionnaire-4 (PDQ-4) (Hyler *et al.*, 1994), which provides dimensional and categorical diagnostic measures of personality disorder traits. Standard measures of risk of recidivism changed between 1997 and 2008. Therefore, to allow for comparison of levels of risk of violence, a number of static indicators, which are included in standardized static measures of violence risk – e.g., Violence Risk Scale (VRS) (Wong and Gordon, 2000); Violence Risk Appraisal Guide (VRAG) (Harris, Rice & Quinsey, 1993); HCR-20 (Webster, Douglas, Eaves & Hart, 1997) – and which were available from the demographic and forensic information collected on all new admissions, were used. These static factors were patient's age at the time of admission, age at first violent conviction, number of young offender convictions, number of convictions after the age of 18, age at the time of index offence and level of psychopathy, as measured by the Psychopathy Checklist-Revised (PCL-R) (Hare, 1991).

Results

Of the 145 patients admitted to the PDS between 1997 and 2008, half (50.3%) had been first convicted between the ages of 13 and 16; 77 (53%) had committed an index offence of violence; 36 (25%) a sexual offence; 18 (12%) arson; and 14 (10%) other offences. The mean age at which index offences were committed was 25, with most index offences committed between the ages 18 and 25 (50.3%). Ninety-one (63%) had been sentenced to an indeterminate Hospital Order (section 37/41 of the Mental Health Act 1983), while the rest had originally been sentenced to imprisonment. Of these, 34 (23.5%) had been sentenced to an indeterminate or life sentence and the remaining 20 (14%) had been sentenced to a fixed term, but were now subject to indefinite detention in hospital (Mental Health Act 1983, section 4(5)).

The study used a retrospective between-groups design. Participants were divided into four groups according to their date of admission to Rampton and the PDS. Group 0 consisted of patients admitted to Rampton prior to 1997. While some of these patients had initially been admitted under the classification of psychopathic disorder before a separate PDS had been created, others had initially been admitted under the classifications of Mental Impairment or Mental Illness, and then subsequently reclassified. Group 1 consisted of patients admitted between 1997 and 2000, group 2 consisted of patients admitted between 2000 and 2004, and

Table 1.1   Key findings of differences between patients admitted to the Personality Disorder Service over time

Year of admission	Pre 1997	1997–2000	2000–2004	2004–2008
Antisocial traits measured by PAI (mean scores)	65.3	68.0	68.3	74.8
Drug-related problems measured by PAI (mean scores)	65.0	62.6	67.8	77.7
Aggressive traits measured by PAI (mean scores)	62.0	66.2	63.6	72.1
Number of convictions prior to age 18 (mean scores)	4.8	6.4	9.2	15.6
Total PCL-R Score (mean scores)	22.7	20.2	19.8	20.3

group 3 consisted of patients admitted between 2004 and 2008. The divide between groups 2 and 3 was set at 2004 because this was the point when the DSPD service opened, and it was hypothesized that the patient profile would change at this point.

An analysis of variance (ANOVA) was carried out to investigate differences between the groups (Table 1.1). This showed:

- A significant increase in the degree of antisocial personality traits between 1997 and 2008, as measured by the PAI. However, there was no significant difference in these features in patients admitted between 2004 and 2008.
- A significant increase in drug problems (as measured by the PAI) reported by patients admitted between 1997 and 2008.
- A significant increase in attitudinal and behavioural features associated with aggression (as measured by the PAI) reported by patients admitted in 1997 and 2008.
- A significant increase in the average number of personality disorder diagnostic categories (as measured by the PDQ-4) met by patients between 1997 and 2008; with the highest numbers of diagnostic categories among patients admitted between 2004 and 2008.
- A significant increase in the number of convictions prior to the age of 18 in patients admitted between 1997 and 2008 (from 4.77 to 15.6).
- No significant difference in psychopathy scores (as measured by the PCL-R) of patients admitted over time, including between 2004 and 2008, after the opening of the DSPD service. There were also no significant changes to average factor 1 or factor 2 scores over time.

Based on these results, the following profiles outline the difference between patients admitted to the PDS in 1997 and in 2007.

1997

Patients admitted to the PDS when it first opened in 1997 had an average of nine juvenile convictions before the age of 18 and a further 14 convictions after the age of 18. On average, the age of their first criminal conviction was 14. Assessments showed that they tended to be suffering from very high levels of anxiety and pre-sented predominantly borderline personality disorder traits. Their average age at the time of the offence for which they were admitted to hospital was 25. Their offences were predominantly of a non-sexual violent nature. Most were sentenced on conviction to be detained in hospital under the Mental Health Act, rather than being sentenced to imprisonment. As a result, their average age on admission to Rampton was also 25.

2007

Patients admitted to the PDS in 2007 had an average of 32 juvenile convictions before they were 18 and a further 13 convictions after the age of 18. On average the age of their first criminal conviction was 13. Assessments showed them to have predominantly antisocial personality traits, significant drug and alcohol problems and a history of aggression. Their average age at the time of the offence for which they were admitted to hospital was 23 and their offences were mostly of violence. However, patients in this cohort were equally likely to have been sentenced to detention in hospital or life imprisonment, and their average age on admission to Rampton was 35. The large difference between age of offence and age of admis-sion reflected the fact that a significant number of admissions to the service had been in the healthcare system for some time and had either been moved from other high secure hospitals or transferred from medium secure services because they were deemed to be 'unmanageable' in conditions of lower security.

These profiles illustrate some significant changes in the characteristics of patients admitted to the PDS between 1997 and 2008. There has been a significant increase in the number of juvenile convictions, a greater history of antisocial personality traits, aggression and problems associated with alcohol and drug use among patients admitted to the service. Although the average age at which patients com-mitted the offence for which they were currently detained had reduced slightly, from 25 to 23, the average age of patients on admission to the service had increased from 25 to 35 years of age. This reflects the fact that relatively few admissions now are admitted immediately after sentence and that an increasing number spend a significant period moving around the prison service or in less secure mental health facilities before being referred to the PDS as a 'last resort'.

In order to explore reasons for these changes in the types of patients admitted to the PDS, a thematic analysis of referral letters was carried out over the same period to identify why patients had been referred. Referrals were generally made by consultant forensic psychiatrists – either the patient's medium secure unit Responsible Clinician or a visiting psychiatrist from prison. Among referrals prior to 2000 a common theme was the prisoner's self-harm which had become unmanageable, particularly within the prison healthcare system. Referrals after 2000 also make frequent reference to the prisoner's self-injurious behaviour, however, this appeared to be dealt with more effectively within prison healthcare settings following the introduction of more specialist mental health in-reach care in prisons and changes to prison and procedure for managing prisoners at risk of suicide or self-harm. Instead, the primary reason for these more recent referrals was that they were judged to pose too great a risk to others within the institution where they were based. More specifically, there was increasing reference among referral letters to the subversion of institutional security, continuing use of illegal or prohibited substances and incidents of violence and aggression against patients/prisoners and staff to a level which the institution felt was unmanageable.

Another increasingly common reason for referrals from prison was that the prison service could not meet the individual's treatment requirements. This was particularly the case for prisoners serving life or other indeterminate sentences, for whom release by the parole board would be dependent on their demonstrating a reduction in their level of risk through engagement in accredited offending behaviour programmes. However, a significant number of prisoners with personality disorder traits will either be unable to engage in or complete such a programme because of their extreme emotional lability, behavioural impulsiveness or avoidance, or will be excluded from treatment on the grounds of their high levels of psychopathy or cognitive deficits. Such prisoners find themselves in a 'Catch-22' situation, unable to benefit from necessary treatment because of their personality disorder traits and unable to access treatment for those traits. For them a referral to a specialist personality disorder service is the only way out.

Changes in forensic mental health

There have been a number of changes to the profile of patients admitted to the PDS since it opened.

Reported levels of self-harming behaviour prior to admission remain high. However, self-harm is no longer the primary reason for referrals. Instead, patients tend to be referred because their violent or aggressive behaviour and risk to others are becoming increasingly difficult to manage, or because they present as 'stuck' in treatment and unable to make progress within the prison system. The fact that repeated self-harm and risk of suicide are no longer reasons for referral from the prison service ought to reflect the advances the service has made in the last decade in caring for prisoners at risk of self-harm. The inhumane and counterproductive policy of keeping suicidal prisoners in unfurnished cells has been replaced by a range of more caring and effective policies, which have seen a steady reduction in the number of suicides in prison since 2000. The greater involvement of mental health professionals in prison in-reach as part of this new policy may also have contributed to the prison service being better able to manage those extremely vulnerable prisoners who would previously have been referred to secure hospitals.

There has been a steady increase in the level of risk of violence presented by patients admitted to the PDS between 1997 and 2008, as indicated by the increase in incidents of threatening behaviour, physical and sexual assaults and hostage-taking, and patients' self-reports of aggression. It might have been expected that the creation of DSPD services for the most complex and high-risk cases would have led to a reduction in the degree of psychopathology and risk among patients admitted to the PDS since 2004, when DSPD services were opened. However, this has not been the case.

The Crime (Sentences) Act 1997 introduced automatic life imprisonment for offenders who were convicted for a second time for specific serious violence or sexual offences. The Criminal Justice Act 2003 replaced these with the Indeterminate Public Protection Sentence (IPP), which significantly lowered the threshold for passing an indeterminate sentence. IPP sentences can be imposed on any adult judged to pose a significant risk to the public who commits an offence warranting a two-year sentence or who has a previous conviction for specified violent or sexual offences. IPP sentences were introduced in 2005. In 2004, 489 indeterminate sentences were passed in England and Wales. In 2006, 1,738 indeterminate sentences were passed. In contrast, the number of indeterminate sentence prisoners released in 2008 was 138 (Ministry of Justice, 2009a). The proportion of the prison population serving indeterminate sentences has now passed 10% (Coyle, 2007), and it has been predicted that there could be as many as 25,000 people serving indeterminate sentences by 2012 (Solomon, 2007). The prison service, therefore, faces a crisis caused by the number of prisoners serving indeterminate sentences, many with very short tariffs. In particular, it seems likely that many individuals with personality disorder traits who would previously have passed through prison on determinate sentences and avoided or been judged unsuitable for treatment are now 'stuck' in prison on IPP sentences. Already overstretched offending behaviour programmes have struggled to cope with these individuals and a growing number of them are now being referred to secure hospitals for treatment.

While the overall prison population and the number of prisoners serving indeterminate sentences have risen sharply in recent years, the number of high secure psychiatric beds has been falling, from 1,115 in 2002 (Home Office, 2003) to 643 in 2007 (Ministry of Justice, 2009b). It is therefore likely that, with more prisoners 'competing' for fewer beds, admission criteria for high secure hospitals will have tightened, and the level of dangerousness and severity of mental disorder among patients admitted now will be greater than it was a decade ago.

Patients being admitted now tend to be older. This appears to reflect the length of time they have spent 'in the system' rather than the age at which they committed the offence that led to their admission. In part, this reflects the fact that, while the number of beds in high secure hospitals fell by 42% between 2002 and 2007, the number of restricted patients in low and medium secure services increased by 74% during the same period, from 1,874 (Home Office, 2003) to 3,263 (Ministry of Justice, 2009b). This has led to greater pressure on high secure services when patients could not be managed in medium secure services and were referred to more secure services. This is particularly ironic since the expansion in medium secure personality disorder services came about in part to reduce the 'log jam' of personality disorder patients waiting to move out of high secure services (Reed, 1997).

Patients now have higher levels of antisocial personality traits. They have more significant histories of violent behaviour and higher levels of substance abuse. Various studies (e.g., Coid, Kahtan, Gault, & Jarman, 1999; Tyrer, 2000) have found a strong association between drug dependence and a diagnosis of personality disorder, particularly antisocial personality disorder. The significant increase in the reporting of drug problems over time may reflect wider social trends in drug use, with increased use, particularly among younger people, and drug use now to be a more normalized part of some youth cultures (Booth, 2004).

Summary and conclusions

The changes outlined in this chapter reflect many of the important developments in the criminal justice and forensic mental health systems over the past decade; the inexorable rise in the prison population, prison healthcare reform and an increasing emphasis on risk management in both criminal justice and mental health. The changes also reflect important developments in the management and treatment of personality disorder. Berry, Duggan and Larkin (1999) reported that 44% of referrals to Rampton high secure hospital in 1994 with a diagnosis of personality disorder were deemed 'untreatable'. With the changes described in this chapter (the increase in risk of violence, antisocial personality traits and substance misuse history) it seems likely that many of the patients referred to high secure personality disorder services today would have been deemed 'untreatable' by the standards of 1994. In fact, the opposite is true; it is now extremely rare for a potential patient with a diagnosis of personality disorder to be turned down on the basis that the service cannot treat him. Advances in the understanding of personality disorder and in treatment technologies, together with the development of specialist personality disorder services, mean that many patients who would previously have been dismissed as 'untreatable' are now able to access treatment. The discredited notion of the 'untreatable' personality disorder has finally been consigned to where it belongs – the history books.

References

Berry, A. Duggan, C. & Larkin, E. (1999) The treatability of psychopathic disorder: How clinicians decide. *Journal of Forensic Psychiatry*, **10**, 710–719.

Birmingham, L. (2003) The mental health of prisoners. *Advances in Psychiatric Treatment*, **9**, 191–199.

Booth, L. (2004) *Statistics on young people and drug misuse: England 2003*, Department of Health Bulletin 2004/13.

Coid, J., Kahtan, N., Gault, S. & Jarman, B. (1999) Patients with personality disorder admitted to secure forensic psychiatry services. *British Journal of Psychiatry*, **175**, 528–536.

Coyle, A. (2007) Does custodial sentencing work? *Prison Service Journal*, **171**, 13–15.

Department of Health & HM Prison Service (2001) *Changing the outlook: A strategy for developing and modernising mental health services in prisons*. London: DoH.

Department of Health & Home Office, HM Prison Service (2004) *Dangerous and severe personality disorder (DSPD) high security services: Planning and delivery guide*. London: Home Office.

Hare, R. D. (1991) *The Hare psychopathy checklist – Revised (PCL-R)*, 2nd edition. Toronto: Multi-health Systems.

Harris, G. T., Rice, M. E. & Quinsey, V. L. (1993) Violent recidivism of mentally disordered offenders: The development of a statistical prediction instrument. *Criminal Justice and Behavior*, **20**, 315–335.

HM Chief Inspector of Prisons (HMCIP) (2002) *Annual report by HMCIP for England and Wales 2001–2002*. London: The Stationery Office.

Home Office (2003) *Statistics of mentally disordered offenders 2002 England and Wales*. London: Home Office Research Development and Statistics Directorate.

Hyler, S. E., Rieder, R. O., Williams, J. B. W. *et al.* (1994) *Personality diagnostic question-naire – PDQ-4.* Ottawa, Canada: Human Informatics Inc.

Krishnan, G. (2005) Evolution of a treatment services for high risk personality disordered patients. Paper presented at International Association of Mental Health, Melbourne.

Liebling, A. (1995) Vulnerability and prison suicide. *British Journal of Criminology*, **35**, 173–187.

Marshall, J. (2008) Psychopathology, complexity and change: The personality disorder directorate at Rampton hospital since 1997. Unpublished Master's dissertation, University of York.

Ministry of Justice (2009a) *Offender management caseload statistics 2008.* London: Ministry of Justice.

Ministry of Justice (2009b) *Statistics of mentally disordered offenders 2007 England and Wales.* London: Ministry of Justice.

Morey, L. C. (1991) *Personality assessment inventory, professional manual.* Tampa, FL: Psychological Assessment Resources, Inc.

Reed, J. (1997) The need for longer term psychiatric care in medium or low security. *Criminal Behaviour and Mental Health*, 7, 201–212.

Smith, R. (1999) Prisoners: An end to second class health care? *British Medical Journal*, **318**, 954–955.

Solomon, E. (2007) Dangerousness and society. *Prison Service Journal*, **175**, 28–33.

Tyrer, P. (2000) *Personality disorders, diagnosis, management and course*, 2nd edition. Oxford: Butterworth Heinemann.

Webster, C. D., Douglas, K. S., Eaves, D. & Hart, S. D. (1997) *HCR-20: Assessing risk for violence (Version 2).* Vancouver, Canada: Simon Fraser University.

Wong, S. & Gordon, A. (2000) *Violence risk scale.* Saskatoon, SK: Correctional Service of Canada.

Chapter Two

Trapped in the 'Special Hospital': The Problems Encountered in the Pathway to Medium Secure Units

Amanda Tetley and Gopi Krishnan

Introduction

For patients detained in high secure hospitals, the main route of discharge to the community is via medium secure services. However, there appear to be significant problems in moving patients with a diagnosis of personality disorder from high to medium secure services, with the result that they effectively become 'trapped' in the high secure service. The aim of this chapter is to explore the problems in the pathway from high to medium secure services for this group of patients. The chapter begins with an historical account of the growth of medium secure psychiatric services and their interface with high secure psychiatric hospitals. It then considers the specific difficulties in the pathway from high to medium secure services for patients with a diagnosis of personality disorder, in particular the limited accessibility of medium secure placements for these individuals and the problems that may occur during the transition to medium secure services. The final section considers future developments that may alleviate some of these problems.

Historical context

In the early 1960s, it was recognized that a subgroup of offenders detained in 'special hospitals' (i.e., high secure hospitals) required a lower level of security than that provided by these maximum secure institutions (Ministry of Health, 1961).

Working Positively with Personality Disorder in Secure Settings: A Practitioner's Perspective
Edited by Phil Willmot and Neil Gordon
© 2011 John Wiley & Sons, Ltd.

However, it was not until 1974 that the Committee on Mentally Disordered Offenders (Department of Health and Social Security, 1975) urged the provision of 2,000 beds for England and Wales offering security below that offered in 'special hospitals'. This provision was expected to meet the needs of three distinct groups: prisoners requiring treatment within secure mental healthcare facilities; patients within NHS mental health services who required greater levels of security than their current placement offered; and individuals detained in 'special hospitals' who did not require the procedural, relational and physical security imposed within these institutions (see Reed, 1997). Simultaneous to that report, the DHSS conducted a needs assessment within the NHS and recommended the provision of 1,000 beds regionally in conditions of medium security (Department of Health and Social Security, 1974; and see Reed, 1997).

Although medium secure units were developed regionally following the recommendations of these two reports, they did not produce the number of beds envisaged. Nelson (2003) estimated that, in 2003, there were only 602 medium secure beds in England. Perhaps not surprisingly, this limited provision has failed to meet the demands for such services. For example, Meltzer, Tom, Brugha, Fryers, Gatwald, Grounds, Johnson and Meltzer (2004) conducted a comprehensive study of referrals to medium secure units. They found that, of all the patients referred to 98% of the medium secure units in England and Wales in 1999, only 58% were admitted. Although a further 20% of the patients were considered appropriate for admission to conditions of medium security, they had to be placed on a waiting list due to the lack of beds.

One aim of medium secure provision was to provide a 'step-down' facility for patients from high secure services. However, patients from high secure services continued to be given the lowest priority for beds in medium secure services (Higgo & Shetty, 1991; Lelliott, Audini & Duffett, 2001; Murray, 1996). After surveying admissions to medium secure units, Murray (1996) concluded that the medium secure programme failed to provide for individuals no longer requiring high secure care. Not surprisingly, this inability to access medium secure units resulted in a significant number of patients being detained in high secure environments who would be manageable in conditions of medium security. Two studies (Harty, Shaw, Thomas, Dolan, Davies, Thornicroft, Carlisle, Moreno, Leese, Appleby & Jones, 2004; Maden, Curle, Meux, Burrow & Gunn, 1993) reported that clinical teams in high secure services considered approximately 40% of their patients to be suitable for conditions of medium security, yet these individuals remained within high secure services.

Perhaps not surprisingly, the difficulty encountered in accessing beds in medium secure units has caused a number of patients within high secure hospitals to wait for significant periods before transfer to medium secure units (Grounds, Meltzer, Fryers, & Brugha, 2004). A series of studies conducted between the late 1980s and early 1990s reported that, on average, patients could wait between 10 and 16 months from a referral being made to a medium secure unit until their eventual transfer (Brown, McKenna & Tomenson, 1996; Dolan & Shetty, 1995; Smith, Tomison, James & Donovan, 1995). These delays were mainly attributed to the limited availability of beds in medium secure units (Dolan & Shetty, 1995), the time taken to receive approval from the Home Office to transfer restricted patients (Dolan & Shetty, 1995; Smith *et al.*, 1995), and disagreement about which region was responsible for the patient's funding (Smith *et al.*, 1995). Understandably, excessive delays in the transfer to a medium secure unit can lead to intense frustration for patients. This is detrimental, given that this frustration is often transferred to the medium secure unit and can subsequently contribute to the patient's failure to cope within this new environment (Skelly, 1994a, b).

Securing a placement in medium security for personality disordered patients

Patients with a diagnosis of personality disorder appear to encounter difficulties accessing medium secure facilities regardless of the security status of their pre-referral placement. For example, the results of a number of studies have highlighted the relatively small number of these individuals *generally* admitted to medium secure services (Bullard & Bond, 1998; Coid & Kahtan, 2000; Coid, Kahtan, Gault, Cook & Jarman, 2001; Faulk & Taylor, 1986; Higgo & Shetty, 1991). It is therefore predictable that a significant proportion of this patient group within high secure hospitals are unable to access medium secure services, despite the fact that they are considered suitable for progression by their clinical team. Regional commissioners[1] have estimated that around a third of patients with a diagnosis of personality disorder in high secure hospitals could be appropriately detained in a less secure environment (Department of Health, 2003). Similarly, in a census of the three English high secure hospitals in 2001, Dolan, Thomas, Thomas and Thornicroft (2005) reported that 40% of patients detained under the Mental Health Act (1983) category of Psychopathic Disorder did not require high secure care according to their Responsible Medical Officers (RMOs). The majority of these patients were considered suitable for progression to medium secure units, while the rest were considered suitable for low secure services.

The difficulties in moving personality disordered patients from high to medium secure conditions could be due to a lack of available beds (Dolan *et al.*, 2005). Consistent with this, the Department of Health (2003) reported that only limited services were available for personality disordered patients in forensic settings outside of high secure hospitals. Many medium secure units reported that they would treat only one or two patients with personality disorder because they find it very difficult to manage this patient group on the same wards as mentally ill patients (Department of Health, 2003). It was also suggested that many mental health practitioners did not regard personality disordered patients to be their core business and were reluctant to work with this patient group because they believed that they had neither the skills nor the training to provide an adequate service (Department of Health, 2003).

Tetley, Evershed and Krishnan (2010) explored the difficulties encountered in the transfer to medium secure services among a sample of 68 male patients

---

[1] Regional commissioners are part of the NHS and commission specialized health services. These specialized services are commissioned on behalf of the relevant populations of the Primary Care Trust.

from a high secure personality disorder facility at Rampton Hospital who had been referred to a medium secure unit on at least one occasion between April 1997 and July 2007. The most notable finding was the limited success of referrals to medium secure units for this patient group. In the initial stage of the referral process, patients considered suitable for discharge to a medium secure service are referred to their 'gatekeeper' or catchment area regional NHS medium secure unit. The purpose of the 'gatekeeper assessment' is to assess the patient's suitability for transfer to conditions of medium security. Tetley *et al.* (2010) reported that 45% of referrals made to regional NHS medium secure units over the 10-year study period were not considered suitable for transfer to conditions of medium security. In the majority of cases this was either because the individual was considered to require further offence-related psychological treatment prior to step-down to a medium secure unit or because they were considered to present a greater than acceptable level of risk of reoffending. The latter finding could reflect a discrepancy between the level of treatment completion perceived by clinicians to be required prior to transfer to conditions of lower security. It might also reflect different perceptions of the reduction in risk that a patient should demonstrate prior to transfer to conditions of medium security (this is discussed in detail below). This finding suggests that greater communication is required between clinicians in these two types of services regarding the characteristics associated with 'readiness' for progression to medium secure services for these patients.

Patients considered to present an unacceptable level of risk for transfer to conditions of medium security were typically considered to present a high or very high risk of reoffending. It is important to note that medium secure units may typically be cautious about admitting patients with personality disorder because these individuals have been found to present an elevated risk of committing further serious offences on discharge to the community (see Jamieson & Taylor, 2004; Steels, Roney, Larkin, Jones, Croudace & Duggan, 1998). Duggan (2007) confirmed that medium secure units have to balance the satisfaction of moving a patient through the healthcare system against the likelihood of their committing further serious offences, and acknowledged that, if a transferred patient did reoffend, the receiving clinical team would be held responsible. This problem is exacerbated by the fact that specific criteria for the admission of personality disordered patients to medium secure units do not currently exist. As a result, Duggan (2007) acknowledged that decisions about transfers from high secure services tended to be based on the medium secure unit clinicians' perceptions of the risk posed by the individual. However, estimating a patient's level of risk is difficult in a context where the patient has limited exposure to the factors that were present at the time of his index offence, such as the disinhibiting effects of alcohol or drugs or humiliation by women (Duggan, 2007). This suggests that explicit 'entry' criteria for the admission of personality disordered patients stepping down to medium secure services would be beneficial.

Of patients surveyed by Tetley *et al.* (2010), 55% were considered suitable for transfer to medium secure units. However, almost a third of these patients were not accepted for transfer to their regional secure unit. In 60% of these cases this was because they had a diagnosis of personality disorder. This is consistent with previous reports, which suggested that many medium secure units excluded patients with this diagnosis (Department of Health, 2003; Grounds, Meltzer, Fryers & Brugha, 2004). Moreover, in interviews with clinicians from 36 medium secure units in England and Wales, Grounds, Gelsthorpe, Howes, Meltzer, Tom, Brugha, Fryers, Gatwald and Meltzer (2004) found that half the clinicians said that patients with a primary diagnosis of personality disorder would be considered unsuitable for medium secure care because it was assumed that they would block beds and be assaultive to staff.

Patients considered suitable for progression to conditions of medium security but not accepted by their regional secure unit can be referred to units in the independent sector if funding is available for such a placement. Medium secure units in the independent sector have been developed relatively recently and have been reported to exercise greater flexibility in their admission criteria, for example, being more willing to accept patients who pose management problems or who require longer-term care (Moss, 2000). However, Tetley *et al.* (2010) reported that almost 45% of referrals to medium secure units in the independent sector were rejected, despite these individuals being considered suitable for progression by their gatekeeper. Reasons provided by the independent units for not accepting patients were similar to those cited by NHS regional secure units. In some cases the patient was judged to pose an unacceptable level of risk to the public or to need further treatment. In other cases the patient was rejected because of their diagnosis of personality disorder or because the service could not provide the resources or facilities the patient required, most often where the patient needed specialist treatment related to their history of sexual offending.

Securing a placement in medium security for dangerous and severely personality disordered patients

The Dangerous and Severe Personality Disorder (DSPD) Programme was designed to deliver services for individuals who present a high risk of committing further serious sexual and violent offences as a result of their severe personality disorder (Department of Health & Ministry of Justice, 2008a). Individuals admitted to the DSPD Programme present a high risk of serious harm to others, have a severe personality disorder, and their level of risk and personality disorder must be functionally linked (Hogue, Jones, Talkes & Tennant, 2007; Howells, Krishnan & Daffern, 2007).

Although the DSPD Programme has explicit *admission* criteria, it does not have specific *exit* criteria (Duggan, 2007). Typically, the main route to discharge to the community for patients from the high secure hospital DSPD services is via medium secure units. Duggan (2007) argued that, in the absence of exit criteria from the high secure services, it is unclear what admission criteria medium secure units use for this patient group. However, he speculated that it would involve an assessment of risk of reoffending and the reduction in this risk brought about by treatment. He suggested that a balance would be sought between the risk of reoffending and satisfaction of moving a patient towards discharge. Duggan suggested that in these circumstances the transfer system would operate conservatively, with the 'transitional bar' being set so high that many patients would be unable to progress from high secure services to medium secure units.

Tetley *et al.* (2010) investigated the efficacy of the pathway from the DSPD Service at Rampton to medium secure units. This investigation involved 12 patients who had been referred to a medium secure unit on at least one occasion after their admission to the DSPD service. Similar to the findings from the evaluation of the Personality Disorder Service, this investigation highlighted the limited success of referrals to medium secure units. Of the 17 referrals to NHS regional secure units for the 12 patients, only 40% were considered suitable for transfer, and only a quarter of the referrals were accepted for admission to the regional secure unit. These findings suggest that regional secure units appear to be even less willing to accept patients from DSPD services than from non-DSPD personality disorder services. For patients considered suitable for progression to medium security but rejected by their regional secure unit, referrals to independent medium secure units met with greater success: 80% of these referrals were accepted for transfer.

The reasons patients from the DSPD service were considered unsuitable for transfer to conditions of medium security by their regional NHS secure unit were again for the most part due to their high risk of reoffending and a requirement for further psychological treatment, particularly surrounding their offending behaviour. The relatively low acceptance rate of DSPD patients by regional secure units appears to support Duggan's (2007) suggestions that the pathway between high and medium secure services for these patients is likely to operate conservatively. This will prevent some patients from progressing through the healthcare system, which could result in the high secure DSPD services 'silting up', as Duggan (2007) predicted. Commissioners of forensic psychiatric services should be aware of this potential problem and begin to consider the necessity of developing further medium secure units specializing in the assessment and treatment of patients with Dangerous and Severe Personality Disorder.

Negotiating the transition from high to medium secure services

When a patient is accepted for transfer from a high to a medium secure service, he is transferred on a 'trial leave' basis before being formally discharged from the high secure service. During the trial leave period, the patient is essentially 'tested out' and can be returned to the high secure service if deemed unsuitable for the medium secure unit. A significant number of patients are returned to a high secure service after their initial trial period. Skelly (1994b) reported that 43% of patients diagnosed with personality disorder or mental illness who had been transferred from Ashworth High Secure Hospital to a medium secure unit between 1988 and 1991 were returned after an unsuccessful period of trial leave. Tetley *et al.* (2010) found that almost 20% of patients with a personality disorder diagnosis who transferred from Rampton Hospital to a medium secure service were returned to the high secure service during the trial leave period. Exploration of the reasons provided by the units for these returns suggested that they occurred because the patient could not be managed in conditions of medium security or disengaged from treatment.

Skelly (1994a, b) investigated the reasons why patients failed on trial leave in a group who had been returned to Ashworth. Skelly (1994b) identified the following factors: the patient's faulty expectations about the transfer, having been given insufficient information; and frustration experienced by the delays encountered in the transfer process. Following transfer, perception of the transfer as a 'backward step' because of the removal of privileges, combined with the stigma associated with previous detention in a high secure unit, was believed to cause further stresses for patients. Skelly argued that the accumulation of these transfer stresses caused the patient to engage in inappropriate behaviour within the unit or disengage from treatment, which precipitated their return to the high secure service.

Although Skelly's (1994a, b) findings highlight some of the difficulties in the transition from high to medium secure services, they do not illuminate the more *specific* difficulties that may be encountered by patients with a diagnosis of personality disorder. In the light of this, research is currently underway to develop a greater understanding of the transition from high to medium secure services for personality disordered patients by exploring (i) these patients' experiences of the transition, and (ii) the experiences of medium secure clinicians receiving patients with a diagnosis of personality disorder from high secure services. This research is important because it is likely that personality disordered patients encounter different experiences negotiating the transition to medium secure services from those encountered by other psychiatric patients.

One reason why patients with a diagnosis of personality disorder could encounter different experiences negotiating the transition to medium secure units arises from the fact that treatment and management of this patient group require specific skills, resources and knowledge. The Department of Health (2003) reported that many clinicans in medium secure units believe that they have neither the necessary skills nor the resources to work with this patient group. This prompted recommendations for the development of forensic personality disorder service models, as well as relevant education and training for staff working with this patient group. These recommendations have allowed the development of resources and expertise relevant to personality disorder in some medium secure services. However, it is likely still to be the case that in many medium secure services practitioners have limited knowledge of this disorder, as was the case in 2003. This is problematic because patients with personality disorder typically require a different therapeutic approach from other patients and so the development of specific capabilities and skills among staff who provide care for these patients is important.

Recommendations for the development of the interface between high to medium secure services

Previously, services at different levels of security have been autonomous, with almost no clinical connection (Duggan, 2007). A greater integration of services at different levels of security would increase the efficiency of pathways from high to medium secure services (Duggan, 2007). This integration should include improved communication between clinicians and clinical teams about appropriate therapeutic approaches for patients and sharing effective techniques.

There should be agreed entry and exit criteria for each tier of secure care (Duggan, 2007). Collaborative working groups comprised of practitioners from both high and medium secure services could prove particularly useful in establishing these criteria. Such criteria would provide clinicians in high secure services with explicit guidelines for determining a patient's readiness for progression through the tiers of secure services.

A final innovation which may increase the efficiency of the pathway from high to medium secure services would be the creation of more medium secure units specifically designed for the treatment and rehabilitation of patients with a diagnosis of personality disorder. These services would benefit from a workforce with the capabilities, skills and knowledge base relevant to working with personality disordered patients. Recently, a small number of services specifically for patients with a diagnosis of personality disorder have been developed within medium secure units. Development of these services began with the publication of *Personality disorder: No longer a diagnosis of exclusion* (Department of Health, 2003), which acknowledged the failure of forensic and non-forensic mental health services to meet the needs of patients with this diagnosis. Following this publication, the Department of Health initiated the development of personality disorder services nationally to provide dedicated infrastructure for the assessment, management and treatment of patients with a diagnosis of personality disorder. It was recognized at this time that only one NHS medium secure unit in England had dedicated placements for this patient group and therefore pilot personality disorder services were developed at three medium secure units in England (the Oswin Unit; Millfields at John Howard; and Tony Hillis Unit at Lambeth Hospital). Entry to these pilot services was expected to be based on structured clinical assessment using an agreed set of psychiatric and psychological tools (Department of Health & Ministry of Justice, 2008b).

It is envisaged that, over time, the specialist provision for patients with a diagnosis of personality disorder will need to be expanded within forensic services. A clear pathway between high secure hospitals and these services will need to be created in order to provide a continuum of care. In addition, the workforce within these specialized medium secure units will need to be equipped with the appropriate skills to treat this specific patient group. In terms of positive progress, the implementation of the multi-level national personality disorder education programme (the Knowledge and Understanding Framework) in a range of medium secure settings offers a good foundation. However, there also needs to be a strategic development of skills-focused, evidenced-based interventions for those working in these settings. This will ensure that the care pathways created can offer a coherent and integrated treatment that builds on the therapeutic gains of those moving through the system. These improvements should help to alleviate the current problems in the transition from high to medium secure services for patients with a diagnosis of personality disorder.

References

Brown, P., McKenna, J. & Tomenson, B. (1996) Waiting for a bed at a regional secure unit. *The Journal of Forensic Psychiatry*, 7, 634–640.

Bullard, H. & Bond, M. (1998) Secure units: Why they are needed. *Medicine, Science and the Law*, **28**, 312–318.

Coid, J. & Kahtan, N. (2000) Are special hospitals needed? *The Journal of Forensic Psychiatry*, **11**, 17–35.

Coid, J., Kahtan, N., Gault, S., Cook, A. & Jarman, B. (2001) Medium secure forensic psychiatry: Comparison of seven English health regions. *The British Journal of Psychiatry*, **178**, 55–61.

Department of Health (2003) *Personality disorder: No longer a diagnosis of exclusion. Policy implementation guidance for the development of services for people with personality disorder.* London: DoH.

Department of Health and Ministry of Justice (2008a) Dangerous and Severe Personality Disorder (DSPD) high secure services for men. Retrieved from www.dspdprogramme .gov.uk/media/pdfs/High_Secure_Services_for_Men.pdf.

Department of Health & Ministry of Justice (2008b) *Forensic personality disorder medium secure and community pilot services: Planning and delivery guide.* London: DoH and Ministry of Justice.

Department of Health and Social Security (1974) *Revised report of the working party on security in NHS psychiatric hospitals.* London: DHSS.

Department of Health and Social Security (1975) *Better services for the mentally ill*, Cmnd 6233. London: HMSO.

Dolan, M. & Shetty, G. C. (1995) Transfer delays in a special hospital population. *Medicine, Science, and Law*, **35**, 237–244.

Dolan, M., Thomas, S.D., Thomas, S. L. & Thornicroft, G. (2005) The needs of males detained under the legal category of 'psychopathic disorder' in high security: Implications for policy and service development. *The Journal of Forensic Psychology and Psychiatry*, **16**, 523–537.

DSPD Programme (2005) Dangerous and Severe Personality Disorder (DSPD) High Secure Services for Men: Planning and delivery guide. DSPD Programme. http:// www.dspdprogramme.gov.uk/media/pdfs/High_Secure_Services_for_Men.pdf.

Duggan, C. (2007) To move or not to move – that is the question! Some reflections on the transfer of DSPD patients in the face of uncertainty. *Psychology, Crime & Law*, **13**, 113–121.

Faulk, M. & Taylor, J. (1986) Psychiatric interim regional secure unit: seven years' experience. *Medicine, Science and Law*, **26**, 17–22.

Grounds, A., Gelsthorpe, L., Howes, M., Meltzer, D., Tom, B. D. M., Brugha, T., Fryers, T., Gatwald, R. & Meltzer, H. (2004) Access to medium secure psychiatric care in England and Wales. 2: A qualitative study of admission decision-making. *The Journal of Forensic Psychiatry and Psychology*, **15**, 32–49.

Grounds, A., Meltzer, D., Fryers, T. & Brugha, T. (2004) What determines access to medium secure psychiatric provision? *The Journal of Forensic Psychiatry & Psychology*, **15**, 1–6.

Harty, M., Shaw, J., Thomas, S., Dolan, M., Davies, L., Thornicroft, G., Carlisle, J., Moreno, M., Leese, M., Appleby, L. & Jones, P. (2004) The security, clinical and social needs of patients in high security psychiatric hospitals in England. *The Journal of Forensic Psychiatry and Psychology*, **15**, 208–221.

Higgo, R. & Shetty, G. (1991) Four years' experience of a regional secure unit. *The Journal of Forensic Psychiatry*, **2**, 203–210.

Hogue, T. E., Jones, L., Talkes, K. & Tennant, A. (2007) The Peaks: A clinical service for those with dangerous and severe personality disorder. *Psychology, Crime & Law*, **13**, 57–68.

Howells, K., Krishnan, G. & Daffern, M. (2007) Challenges in the treatment of dangerous and severe personality disorder. *Advances in Psychiatric Treatment*, **13**, 325–332.

Jamieson, L. & Taylor, P. J. (2004) A reconviction study of special (high security) hospital patients. *British Journal of Criminology*, **44**, 783–802.

Lelliott, P., Audini, B. & Duffett, R. (2001) Survey of patients from an inner-London health authority in medium secure psychiatric care. *The British Journal of Psychiatry*, **178**, 62–66.

Maden, A., Curle, C., Meux, C., Burrow, S. & Gunn, J. (1993) The treatment and security needs of patients in hospital. *Criminal Behaviour and Mental Health*, **3**, 290–306.

Meltzer, D., Tom, B. D. M., Brugha, T., Fryers, T., Gatwald, R., Grounds, A., Johnson, T. & Meltzer, H. (2004) Access to medium secure psychiatric care in England and Wales. 3: The clinical needs of assessed patients. *The Journal of Forensic Psychiatry & Psychology*, **15**, 50–65.

Ministry of Health (1961) *Treatment of psychiatric patients under security conditions*, HM (61)69. London: Ministry of Health.

Moss, K. R. (2000) A comparative study of admissions to two public sector regional secure units and one independent medium-secure psychiatric hospital. *Medicine, Science & Law*, **40**, 216–222.

Murray, K. (1996) The use of beds in NHS medium secure units in England. *The Journal of Forensic Psychiatry*, 7, 504–524.

Nelson, D. (2003) Service innovations: The Orchard Clinic: Scotland's first medium secure unit. *Psychiatric Bulletin*, **27**, 105–107.

Reed, J. (1997) The need for longer term psychiatric care in medium or low security. *Criminal Behaviour and Mental Health*, 7, 201–212.

Skelly, C. (1994a) From special hospital to regional secure unit: a qualitative study of the problems experienced by patients. *Journal of Advanced Nursing*, **20**, 1056–1063.

Skelly, C. (1994b) The experience of special hospital patients in regional secure units. *Journal of Psychiatric and Mental Health Nursing*, **1**, 171–177.

Smith, J., Tomison, A., James, A. & Donovan, M. (1995). Maximum and medium security: The interface. *Medicine, Science and Law*, **35**, 249–254.

Steels, M., Roney, G., Larkin, E., Jones, P., Croudace, T. & Duggan, C. (1998) Discharged from special hospital under restrictions: a comparison of the fates of psychopaths and the mentally ill. *Criminal Behaviour and Mental Health*, **8**, 39–55.

Tetley, A. C., Evershed, S. & Krishnan, G. (2010) Difficulties in the pathway from high, to medium, secure services for personality disordered patients. *The Journal of Forensic Psychiatry and Psychology*, **21**, 189–201.

Section Two

The Treatment Process

Chapter Three

What Works with Forensic Patients with Personality Disorder? Integrating the Literature on Personality Disorder, Correctional Programmes and Psychopathy

Phil Willmot and Amanda Tetley

Introduction

Despite their multiple and complex needs and the difficulties associated with their management and treatment, there is very little literature on the treatment of forensic psychiatric patients with a diagnosis of personality disorder. As Howells, Langton and Hogue (2007) have pointed out, the evidence informing treatment issues with this population is at the intersection of three largely separate sets of literature. First, within the non-forensic psychotherapy literature there is a growing theoretical and empirical consensus about the characteristics of psychological therapies that are effective in the treatment of personality disorder. Secondly, there is an extensive literature on mainly prison-based treatment programmes designed to reduce offending among offenders. Finally, there is a literature on psychopathy, which has only relatively recently begun to consider the treatment of psychopathic individuals. Each literature has a different focus and draws different conclusions about the nature of effective interventions.

The starting point for this review is the assumption that effective treatment programmes for forensic patients with personality disorder, some of whom will be highly psychopathic, should be informed by to the principles of all three literatures.

Working Positively with Personality Disorder in Secure Settings: A Practitioner's Perspective
Edited by Phil Willmot and Neil Gordon
© 2011 John Wiley & Sons, Ltd.

What works in treating personality disorder?

Patients with personality disorder have been found to require more treatment resources (Bender, Dolan, Skodol, Sanislow, Dyck, McGlashan, Shea, Zanarini, Oldham & Gunderson, 2001) and to benefit less from treatments for Axis I disorders (Perry, Banon & Ianni, 1999). However, in recent years there has been a more optimistic approach to the treatment of individuals with personality disorder. There is a growing body of evidence that a range of psychological interventions are effective in the treatment of personality disorder (Duggan, Huband, Smailagic, Ferriter & Adams, 2007; Leichsenring & Leibing, 2003; Perry, Banon & Ianni, 1999), and a recognition that people with personality disorders have particular needs that require different forms of treatment. A number of authors have set out principles of treatment based on the limited empirical data that exist for this client group, together with what is known about effective treatments with other client groups and on theoretical models of personality and personality disorder.

Critchfield and Benjamin (2006) found that most of the principles of effective treatment for individuals with personality disorder are shared with effective treatments for Axis I disorders, albeit some appear to be more important in the treatment of personality disorder. In particular, their review identified two overarching themes that appear to distinguish psychological treatments for personality disorder. The first is the central importance of the therapeutic relationship. While the therapeutic relationship is important across a range of client groups (Martin, Garske & Davis, 2000), Critchfield and Benjamin argued that it is particularly important in the treatment of patients with personality disorder because of the specific problems of interpersonal functioning that this group experience. Thus, while the formation of an effective therapeutic relationship is more difficult where the client has a personality disorder, once an effective relationship is formed it provides an important means through which the client can learn effective interpersonal skills. Consistent with this, the most widely used therapies for personality disorder, including cognitive analytic therapy (Ryle, 1997), dialectical behaviour therapy (Linehan, 1993), mentalization-based therapy (Bateman & Fonagy, 1999) and schema focused therapy (Young, Klosko & Weishaar, 2003) all use the therapeutic relationship as a specific focus to address the client's interpersonal difficulties and underlying personality disorder. Safran, Muran, Samstag and Winston (2003) found that clients with personality disorder dropped out significantly less and showed better outcomes at the end of therapy and follow-up where the model of therapy specifically addressed ruptures in the therapeutic alliance.

The second theme Critchfield and Benjamin identified was that of therapist flexibility and the tailoring of treatment to the specific needs of the client over time. For clients with personality disorder these needs will be multiple and dynamic, requiring the therapist to alter and balance tasks and goals, even within individual sessions.

Critchfield and Benjamin's review also identified the therapist, relationship and technique factors that appeared to be common to effective therapies for a broad range of psychological disorders and those that appeared to be specific to the treatment of personality disorder.

Therapist-related factors

Fernandez-Alvarez, Clarkin, del Carmen Salguerio and Critchfield (2006) identified a number of therapist characteristics that appeared to be specific to working
with clients with personality disorder. These included being comfortable with
long-term, emotionally intense relationships, patience, adopting an open-minded,
flexible and creative approach and having training and experience in working with
personality disorder. These principles reflected the facts that treatments for personality disorder were usually long-term and emotionally intense, with slow or
uneven progress and significant risks including client injury or death. Critchfield
and Benjamin argued that these therapist characteristics were preconditions for
building a therapeutic alliance with a client group that struggled with feeling safe
in therapeutic encounters.

Relationship principles

Although there was relatively little evidence relating specifically to personality
disorder, Critchfield and Benjamin (2006) argued that most of the key elements
of effective therapeutic relationships in treatment of personality disorder were
shared with other disorders. These included: a strong working alliance or group
cohesion; shared goals; a collaborative approach; clear and consistent limit-setting
on unacceptable behaviour; and empathy, positive regard and genuineness on the
part of the therapist.

One factor identified by Smith, Barrett, Benjamin and Barber (2006) which
appeared to be unique to therapeutic relationships involving clients with borderline
personality disorder was that therapists were relatively active in terms of being able
to adapt their approach or style to reflect the shifting needs or presentation of
their client and attending to ruptures in the therapeutic relationship.

Technique principles

Critchfield and Benjamin (2006) outlined a number of broad themes and specific
techniques that were shared between effective treatments for personality disorder
and other disorders, including: focusing on presenting problems; early formulation
of patterns linked to the problem; transparency by the therapist about their limits
and about treatment; having a goal-oriented structure; and an emphasis on change.
However, they stressed that these principles were effective only if carried out in
the context of a good therapeutic relationship.

Linehan, Davison, Lynch and Sanderson (2006) identified a number of specific
technique factors which appeared to be specific to dialectical behaviour therapy
for borderline personality disorder. These included therapist availability during
crises, therapist transparency about their own limits, balancing a focus on change
with empathic support and validation, and the greater importance of effective
supervision and consultation for therapists with this client group.

Livesley's (2005, 2007) systematic framework for treating personality disorder
incorporates many of the principles outlined by Critchfield and Benjamin. Livesley

argued that since personality disorder generally involves multiple problems, comprehensive treatment should involve a combination of treatments which should be delivered in an integrated and coordinated way. Each aspect of treatment should involve general strategies to treat core self- and interpersonal pathology. These include a supportive, empathic, collaborative and validating therapist stance. General therapeutic strategies include:

- Building and maintaining a collaborative relationship.
- Maintaining structure and consistency in the treatment process.
- Maintaining a validating treatment process.
- Building and maintaining motivation to change.

Treatment should progress through a series of phases addressing different problems with specific interventions. Livesley identified five stages in the treatment process which reflect the stability and potential for change of different aspects of personality:

1. *Crisis management*: ensuring the safety of the client and others.
2. *Containment*: stabilizing emotions and impulses and restoring behavioural controls, mainly through general treatment strategies and the use of medication.
3. *Control and regulation*: reducing symptoms and learning self-regulation skills, involving both general and specific interventions.
4. *Exploration and change*: analysing maladaptive thoughts, behaviours and core beliefs, usually involving a combination of cognitive, interpersonal and psychodynamic approaches.
5. *Integration and synthesis*: developing a more adaptive self-system and lifestyle, involving more psychodynamic techniques.

Chapter 7 by Kerry Beckley on therapeutic style and Chapter 5 by Sue Evershed on the treatment pathway in a forensic personality disorder setting illustrate a number of these principles.

What works in treating offenders?

The literature on personality disorder has very little to say on interventions with offenders. In contrast, there is an extensive literature on correctional programmes aimed at reducing reoffending by offenders which has quite different professional and theoretical bases from the mainstream literature on psychological treatments. Offending behaviour is generally not seen as a mental health issue; for example, influential authors in the correctional field, such as Andrews and Bonta (2006), have taken a social learning theory rather than a psychopathology approach to crime and criminality. This may have been in reaction to the failure of correctional programmes targeting mental health problems in the 1960s and 1970s. Andrews and Bonta have identified a number of principles of effective correctional programmes. Their key principles are risk, need and responsivity.

- The risk principle states that treatment is most effective when it is applied to those who at the highest risk of offending.
- The need principle states that treatment should target 'criminogenic needs'; that is, those dynamic areas of need which are related to offending.
- The responsivity principle states that correctional programmes should use effective behaviour change techniques such as behavioural, social learning or cognitive behavioural strategies.

A number of meta-analytic studies have found that programmes incorporating all these principles were associated with the strongest reductions in recidivism, (e.g., Andrews, Zinger, Hoge, Bonta, Gendreau & Cullen, 1990; Dowden & Andrews, 2000).

The risk–needs–responsivity (RNR) literature has generated a number of large meta-analytic studies of correctional programmes which have supported these principles as well as others. For example:

- Successful programmes were more likely to be based on a sound conceptual model (Antonowicz & Ross, 1994).
- Successful programmes more often involved educational/vocational methods (Gottschalk, Davidson, Mayer & Gensheimer, 1987) or cognitive behavioral, skill-oriented and multi-modal methods (Antonowicz & Ross, 1994; Izzo & Ross, 1990; Lipsey, 1992).
- Community-based programmes that are institutional are more effective (Andrews, Zinger, Hoge, Bonta, Gendreau & Cullen, 1990; Izzo & Ross, 1990).
- Appropriate therapist practice and behaviour are associated with better outcomes (Dowden & Andrews, 2004).

The RNR literature has been subject to a number of criticisms which have focused on some of the values implicit in these principles which seem to run counter to more generally accepted principles of therapeutic practice.

- The authors of the RNR model were right not to conceptualize offending as primarily a mental health problem, since for the majority of offenders it is not. However, for a minority of offenders with significant mental health problems, it seems unlikely that these problems are totally unrelated to their offending.
- Thomas-Peter expressed disquiet at the implication of the RNR approach that 'individuals can be disaggregated into a series of unconnected problems' (2006: 34) rather than 'complex interconnected systems, in which changes in dynamic factors in one system influence those of another' (2006: 35). This conceptualization of the RNR model contrasts with current treatment models (discussed above), which conceptualize personality disorder as a complex and dynamic interaction of cognitive, affective, behavioural, interpersonal and self-concept systems (e.g., Livesley, 2003) and recommend eclectic and integrated treatment programmes to address the multiple problems of clients with personality disorders.

- Thomas-Peter (2006) has also criticized the rigid categorization of treatment needs as criminogenic or not criminogenic and cited the example of self-esteem, which has been described in the RNR literature as not a criminogenic factor (Dowden & Andrews, 1999; Hanson & Bussière, 1998). Thomas-Peter cited evidence that aspects of self-esteem are important determinants of anger arousal and violent behaviour and argued that self-esteem is a complex and dynamic construct and that global measures of self-esteem may not identify key dimensions that are related to risk. This illustrates a broader criticism of the need principle – that needs which are criminogenic for a minority of offenders will not be identified through the meta-analytic studies on which much of the RNR literature is based.
- Ward, Mann and Gannon (2007) argued that RNR programmes have tended to focus on avoidance goals (e.g., avoiding offending) rather than approach goals (e.g., leading a safe, law-abiding life). A focus on avoidance is difficult to reconcile with Livesley's (2005) goal of treatment for personality disorder – developing a more adaptive lifestyle. However, Ward *et al.* (2007) argued that a focus on approach goals and offenders' strengths was not fundamentally at odds with the RNR model and Mann, Webster, Schofield and Marshall (2004) have described how programmes can be modified to remedy this weakness.
- The focus of RNR programmes on criminogenic needs contradicts some of principles of effective work with personality disorder. Such a prescriptive approach is hard to reconcile with the principle that the focus of treatment for personality disorder should be on current presenting problems, at least in the early stages of treatment. The focus of the RNR model on a prescribed range of criminogenic needs is also hard to reconcile with the principle that treatment goals should be agreed collaboratively.

An over-reliance on the RNR literature risks ignoring other areas of psychological research, particularly from non-forensic fields, which can also inform what constitutes effective therapy. For example, the RNR literature has paid relatively little attention to the importance of the therapeutic relationship. Dowden and Andrews (2004) conducted a meta-analytic study of the impact of staff practice and behaviour on the outcome of programmes. They largely concentrated on social learning principles, such as the modelling and reinforcing of pro-social attitudes and what they describe as a 'firm but fair' use of authority, although they did mention relationship factors and therapeutic alliance as 'arguably the most important' (2004: 205) element of staff behaviour. Unfortunately, few of the studies in their meta-analysis had described therapeutic process issues, and only 5% mentioned therapeutic relationship factors. Nevertheless, Dowden and Andrews reported that staff practice and behaviour appeared to be important determinants of treatment outcome. Unfortunately, it appears that the criticism by authors such as Andrews and Bonta (2006) of the poorly applied use of psychotherapy with offenders has led clinicians in the field to disregard the entire body of psychotherapy research.

Despite these criticisms, even the RNR model's critics agree that the model has delivered demonstrably effective programmes (e.g., Thomas-Peter, 2006; Ward, Mann & Gannon, 2007). On the whole, the RNR principles do not appear to be incompatible with the principles of effective interventions for personality disorder and programmes addressing offending behaviour ought to adhere to these principles as well as to the principles of effective therapy in general. The main area where the two literatures might clash is on the RNR 'need' principle, but this need not be the case if the scope and limits of the RNR are considered. The RNR principles are based on and apply to the provision of services to groups of offenders as a whole, based on correlational and meta-analytic studies. As Andrews himself said, 'systematic quantitative surveys of risk/need are best supplemented by individualized assessments that uncover particular patterns of high risk situations applicable to an individual case' (1995: 55–56). Forensic patients with personality disorder have needs at different levels, as described by Livesley (2005). The relationship between personality disorder and forensic risk appears to be a complex one, which is, as yet, poorly understood. Within the five-stage model of treatment for personality disorder described by Livesley (2005), treatments that reduce risk of offending are more likely to occur in the later stages, as is the case with the Personality Disorder Service (PDS) treatment pathway (see this volume, Chapter 5 on the treatment pathway).

Within this treatment model some criminogenic factors, such as criminal peers, pro-criminal attitudes or deviant sexual interests, do not appear to be related to personality or personality disorder, at least to the extent that they are not diagnostic criteria for personality disorder. Other criminogenic factors are personality disorder traits such as interpersonal exploitativeness or grandiosity. These factors are all likely to be addressed in the fourth and fifth stages described by Livesley, and it would be during these later stages of treatment that the greatest reductions in risk of reoffending would be likely to occur. However, other factors which may also be criminogenic may begin to be addressed during the earlier stages of treatment (e.g., emotional lability, impulsivity and feelings of paranoia).

What works in treating psychopathy?

As with personality disorder, the literature on psychopathy has generally concluded that psychopathic individuals engage less well in treatment and are more likely to drop out of treatment (Hobson, Shine & Roberts, 2000; Ogloff, Wong & Greenwood, 1990; Olver & Wong, 2009). They are also more likely to reoffend than non-psychopathic individuals (e.g., Looman, Abracen, Serin & Marquis, 2005; Olver & Wong, 2006; Seto & Barbaree, 1999). Moreover, a number of studies have suggested that institutional infractions and reoffending actually increase following treatment among psychopathic individuals (Hare, Clark, Grann & Thornton, 2000; Richards, Casey & Lucente, 2003; Seto & Barbaree, 1999). As Thornton and Blud (2007) have argued, a number of psychopathic traits are likely to adversely affect the outcomes of psychological treatments. For example, affective traits, such as shallow affect and lack of empathy, and interpersonal traits, such as a tendency towards lying and duplicity, grandiosity, conning and dominance, tend to be disruptive to the therapeutic alliance in individual therapy and damaging to group processes and cohesion. Lifestyle traits, such as impulsivity and proneness to boredom, and antisocial traits, such as disregard for rules, are also inconsistent with long-term structured therapeutic activity.

There have been no published studies of programmes designed for psychopathic individuals or to treat psychopathic traits. Instead, psychopathy has been approached as a responsivity issue, rather than a disorder to be treated in its own right. Comparisons of treatment outcomes for psychopathic and non-psychopathic individuals have been carried out for several different therapeutic approaches.

Correctional programmes

Wong and Hare (2005) have argued that psychopathic traits, such as irresponsibility, aggressiveness, impulsivity and criminal attitudes, are extremely common among offenders in general and that treatment programmes for psychopathic individuals should adhere to the principles of effective correctional programmes. Nevertheless, psychopathic individuals are generally more disruptive and respond less well in correctional programmes. There is also evidence that inappropriate treatments can lead to an increase in risk. Hare *et al.* (2000) reported that brief prison treatment programmes, such as anger management and social skills training, were ineffective for offenders with medium or low scores on the PCL-R, but that they led to increased recidivism among those who scored high on factor 1.

Looman *et al.* (2005) concluded that well-run correctional programmes can lead to a reduction in risk for some psychopathic individuals and that where psychopathic individuals are appropriately motivated, correctional programmes can lead to a decrease in their risk.

Therapeutic communities

Studies of psychopathic individuals in therapeutic communities have generally found that their behaviour in the community is often disruptive and unmotivated (Ogloff *et al.*, 1990; Hobson *et al.*, 2000) and they make less progress than non-psychopathic community members (Ogloff *et al.*, 1990). Most famously, Rice, Harris and Cormier (1992), comparing psychopathic and non-psychopathic patients at the Oak Ridge forensic psychiatric unit, concluded that psychopathic individuals who had been through the unit were more likely to reoffend violently than matched untreated psychopathic individuals. Although both the treatment and the experimental design have been criticized (e.g., D'Silva, Duggan & McCarthy, 2004; Looman *et al.*, 2005), when considered with other studies of psychopathic individuals in therapeutic communities, it appears that unstructured programmes which give patients a high degree of autonomy are not suitable for a patient group characterized by manipulative and irresponsible behaviour.

One apparent exception to the generally poor response of psychopathic individuals to therapeutic communities was the Barlinnie Special Unit, described by Cooke (1997). Cooke reported high levels of psychopathy among most prisoners in this unit, but a significant reduction in the number of assaults and other serious incidents committed by them following their admission to the unit. Cooke attributed these results not to the therapeutic community but to other aspects of the regime, such as the highly skilled and experienced staff group, the high levels of purposeful activity and the relatively low levels of control and coercion used by staff. Unfortunately, these confounding variables make it difficult to draw any conclusions about the specific effectiveness of the therapeutic community aspects of the Barlinnie regime.

Psychodynamic approaches

Salekin's (2002) meta-analysis of treatments for psychopathic individuals found that psychotherapeutic approaches were more effective than cognitive behavioural or therapeutic community approaches. While Salekin's is the most positive review of treatments for psychopathy, a number of methodological weaknesses have been pointed out (e.g., Harris & Rice, 2006; Looman *et al.*, 2005). For example, most of the studies did not include recidivism as an outcome measure, and most used therapist ratings which, as discussed previously, are likely to be unreliable and even negatively correlated with recidivism.

Other approaches

Hare *et al.* (2000) reported that while prison education programmes reduced reoffending among offenders for whom poor education had been identified as a criminogenic need, among prisoners with high PCL-R factor 1 scores prison education led to an increase in reoffending. This result suggests that the apparent counterproductive effects of treatment for psychopathic individuals may apply not just to 'therapy', but to a wider range of training programmes.

Opinion about the treatment of psychopathic individuals appears to be shifting from a position of therapeutic nihilism to the view that at least some individuals can benefit from certain treatments (e.g., Looman *et al.*, 2005). Recent reviews of treatment approaches with psychopathic individuals have drawn conclusions that would apply equally to other individuals with personality disorder. These include:

- Establishing a positive therapeutic alliance (Hemphill & Hart, 2002; Wong & Hare, 2005).
- Making therapy-interfering behaviours a specific focus of treatment (Thornton & Blud, 2007; Wong & Hare, 2005).
- Structuring treatment and paying close attention to boundaries (Wong & Hare, 2005).
- Avoiding the use of assessment and treatment techniques that are vulnerable to therapy-interfering behaviours (Thornton & Blud, 2007).
- Using enhanced staff training, supervision and procedures to maintain clear boundaries (Thornton & Blud, 2007; Wong & Hare, 2005).
- Using motivators that are relevant for psychopathic individuals (Hemphill & Hart, 2002; Thornton & Blud, 2007).
- Using intensive, long-term and multi-modal treatments (Salekin, 2002; Wong & Hare, 2005).
- Having robust evaluation and measurement systems in place that do not rely solely on patient self-report or therapist ratings (Harris & Rice, 2006; Thornton & Blud, 2007; Wong & Hare, 2005).
- Having management structures and practices that support treatment (Wong & Hare, 2005).

These commonalities are perhaps not surprising given the overlap between psychopathic and DSM-IV cluster B personality disorder traits. However, it is striking that these reviews reached these conclusions without any reference to the literature on the treatment of personality disorder.

A number of other themes emerge from the literature on psychopathy:

- Behaviour in treatment when viewed in isolation is a poor indicator of treatment effectiveness (e.g., Looman *et al.*, 2005; Seto & Barbaree, 1999). However, overall institutional behaviour does appear to be related to later recidivism (Looman *et al.*, 2005).
- Treatment programmes for high psychopathy individuals should adhere to the risk, needs and responsivity principles of effective correctional programmes (Wong & Hare, 2005).
- Despite its methodological flaws, Salekin's (2002) review provides some suggestion that therapies that pay particular attention to the therapeutic relationship, as in psychodynamic psychotherapy, may be effective.
- A number of studies (e.g., Hare *et al.*, 2000; Hobson *et al.*, 2000; Olver & Wong, 2006; Richards *et al.*, 2003) have identified that factor 1 psychopathic traits are particularly related to poor treatment outcomes. One possible explanation for this is that factor 1 traits, such as shallow affect, lack of empathy and superficiality in relationships, are particularly likely to hamper the development of securely attached therapeutic relationships. Wong and Hare (2005) recommended that the number of individuals with high factor 1 scores on the same treatment group should be limited.
- Cooke (1997) points to the systemic nature of psychopathic behaviour in institutions. Regimes with high degrees of overt security and control can paradoxically lead to more violence and greater subversion because of a desire to 'save face' in the face of a rigid and authoritarian regime. Wong and Burt (2007) argued that psychopathic individuals tended to be stigmatized and rejected by staff because of their label, or charmed and exploited staff, both of which were likely to be detrimental to treatment outcome.

Principles for the treatment of this client group

Treatments should be informed by all the relevant literatures

In the absence of any significant evidence base specific to this group, it seems reasonable to apply the evidence bases from the partially overlapping literatures relating to the treatment of personality disorder, offenders and psychopathic individuals, at least where these sources do not contradict each other. In fact, from this review, there do not appear to be any serious contradictions. Different literatures have had different foci. The psychotherapy literature has mainly focused on client–therapist interactions within sessions and at the psychological processes of therapeutic change, whereas the literature on the treatment of offenders and psychopathic individuals has focused more on the characteristics of the programme and the organization that promote change. There has been relatively little crossover between the two.

Individualized case formulations should identify the responsivity, core personality disorder and criminogenic needs of the individual and should be clear about which category each need falls into

Some needs, including many psychopathic traits, will fall into all three categories. For example, impulsivity, lack of empathy, deceitfulness, irresponsibility, superficiality and shallow affective responses could all potentially impede a patient's response to treatment, affect their mental health and ability to form and maintain secure attachments and healthy relationships, and increase their risk of reoffending. However, which of these categories each treatment need falls into will differ from case to case.

In the case of psychopathy, a simplistic focus on PCL-R scores ignores the fact that psychopathy is an extremely heterogeneous construct. If the most widespread definition of psychopathy – a score of 30 or more on the 20-item Psychopathy Checklist-Revised (Hare, 1991) – is used, there are over 14 million[1] combinations of traits that would be defined as psychopathic, so a treatment approach based on a single score is woefully simplistic. Management and treatment approaches for psychopathic individuals should be tailored to their individual pattern of psychopathic traits.

Responsivity needs should be addressed first, followed by core personality disorder needs and criminogenic needs

The RNR need principle states that treatments should specifically target criminogenic needs. However, not all treatment targets for forensic clients with personality disorder will be criminogenic; as Andrews and Bonta (2006) themselves argue, treatment decisions should consider, among other things, ethical and humanitarian considerations in recognition that a narrow focus on purely criminogenic factors would be unrealistic where a client is unable to engage in treatment or is in distress. Secondly, within mental health as opposed to criminal justice settings, the treatment of core personality disorder needs should be a legitimate and necessary goal in itself. However, where that is the case and clinicians decide to address the core personality disorder needs of a client, they should be clear to themselves, the patient and other stakeholders that this intervention will not necessarily, of itself, reduce the risk of reoffending for that patient.

The integrated approach proposed by Livesley (2005, 2007), and the treatment pathway described in Chapter 5 both describe multimodal and integrated pathways

---

[1] Given that the PCL-R consists of 20 items, each with three possible values, there is one combination of scores that would yield a score of 40, 20 ways of scoring 39, 210 ways of scoring 38, 1520 ways of scoring 37, 8455 ways of scoring 36, 38304 ways of scoring 35, 146490 ways of scoring 34, 484500 ways of scoring 33, 1409895 ways of scoring 32, 3656360 ways of scoring 31 and 8533660 ways of scoring 30, making a total of 14279415 ways of scoring 30 or more.

of treatment for this patient group which address responsivity needs first, then core personality disorder needs and finally criminogenic needs, and in which it is necessary to address responsivity and core personality disorder needs first in order to maximize responsivity and treatment gain from offence-focused treatments.

Conclusions

This brief review of the literature has identified a number of similar patterns from the three areas of literature despite their developing almost completely separately. Each literature also appears to have a similar 'narrative', with earlier themes of therapeutic nihilism about the treatability of people with personality disorder, offenders and psychopathic individuals giving way to a more measured and balanced set of conclusions about the challenges presented by that client group and about what constitutes effective treatment. Unfortunately, the forensic and psychotherapy literatures have developed in largely separate but parallel directions. However, clinical practice with this patient group needs to be informed by all the relevant literature if it is to be maximally effective.

References

Andrews, D. A. (1995) The psychology of criminal conduct and effective treatment. In J. McGuire (Ed.) *What works: Reducing reoffending – Guidelines from research and practice* (pp. 35–62). Chichester: Wiley.

Andrews, D. A. & Bonta, J. (2006) *The psychology of criminal conduct*, 4th edition. Cincinnati: Anderson.

Andrews, D. A., Zinger, I., Hoge, R. D., Bonta, J, Gendreau, P. & Cullen, F. T. (1990) Does correctional treatment work? A clinically relevant and psychologically informed meta-analysis, *Criminology*, **28**, 369–404.

Antonowicz, D. & Ross, R. R. (1994) Essential components of successful rehabilitation programs for offenders. *International Journal of Offender Therapy and Comparative Criminology*, **38**, 97–104.

Bateman, A. & Fonagy, P. (1999) Effectiveness of partial hospitalisation in the treatment of borderline personality disorder: A randomised controlled trial. *American Journal of Psychiatry*, **156**, 1563–1569.

Bender, D. S., Dolan, R. T., Skodol, A. E., Sanislow, C. A., Dyck, I. R., McGlashan, T. H., Shea, M. T., Zanarini, M. C., Oldham, J. M. & Gunderson, J. G. (2001) Treatment utilization by patients with personality disorder. *American Journal of Psychiatry*, **158**, 295–302.

Cooke, D. J. (1997) The Barlinnie Special Unit: The rise and fall of a therapeutic experiment. In E. Cullen, L. Jones & R. Woodward (Eds.) *Therapeutic communities for offenders* (pp. 101–120). Chichester: Wiley

Critchfield, K. L. & Benjamin, L. S. (2006) Integration of therapeutic factors in treating personality disorders. In L. G. Castonguay & L. E. Beutler (Eds.) *Principles of therapeutic change that work* (pp. 253–271). New York: Oxford University Press.

Dowden, C. & Andrews, D. A. (1999) What works in young offender treatment: A meta-analysis. *Forum on Corrections Research*, **11**, 21–24.

Dowden, C. & Andrews, D. A. (2000) Effective correctional treatment and violent reoffending: A meta-analysis. *Canadian Journal of Criminology*, **42**, 449–467.

Dowden, C. & Andrews, D. A. (2004) The importance of staff practice in delivering effective correctional treatment: A meta-analytic review of core correctional practice. *International Journal of Offender Therapy and Comparative Criminology*, **48**, 203–214.

D'Silva, K., Duggan, C. & McCarthy, L. (2004) Does treatment really make psychopaths worse? A review of the evidence. *Journal of Personality Disorders*, **18**, 163–177.

Duggan, C., Huband, N., Smailagic, N., Ferriter, M. & Adams, C. (2007) The use of psychological treatments for people with personality disorder: A systematic review of randomised controlled trials. *Personality and Mental Health*, **1**, 95–125.

Fernandez-Alvarez, H. Clarkin, J. F., del Carmen Salguerio, M. & Critchfield, K. L. (2006) Participant factors in treating personality disorders. In L. G. Castonguay & L. E. Beutler (Eds.) *Principles of therapeutic change that work* (pp. 203–218). New York: Oxford University Press.

Gottschalk, R., Davidson II, W. S., Mayer, J. & Gensheimer, L. K. (1987) Behavioral approaches with juvenile offenders. A meta-analysis of long-term treatment efficacy. In E. K. Morris & C. J. Braukman (Eds.) *Behavioral approaches to crime and delinquency* (pp. 399–423). New York: Plenum Press.

Hanson, K. & Bussière, M. T. (1998) Predicting relapse: A meta-analysis of sexual offender recidivism studies. *Journal of Consulting and Clinical Psychology*, **66**, 348–362.

Hare, R. D. (1991) *The Hare psychopathy checklist – revised.* Toronto, ON: Multi-Health Systems.

Hare, R. D., Clark, D., Grann, M. & Thornton, D. (2000) Psychopathy and the predictive validity of the PCL-R: An international perspective. *Behavioral Sciences and the Law*, **18**, 623–645.

Harris, G. T. & Rice, M. E. (2006) Treatment of psychopathy: A review of empirical findings. In C. J. Patrick (Ed.) *Handbook of psychopathy* (pp. 555–572). New York: Guilford Press.

Hemphill, J. F. & Hart, S. D. (2002) Motivating the unmotivated: Psychopathy, treatment and change. In M. McMurran (Ed.) *Motivating offenders to change: A guide to enhancing engagement in therapy* (pp. 193–219). Chichester: Wiley.

Hobson, J., Shine, J. & Roberts, R. (2000) How do psychopaths behave in a prison therapeutic community? *Psychology, Crime & Law*, **6**, 139–154.

Howells, K., Langton, C. & Hogue, T. (2007) Introductory comments to the special issue, high risk offenders with personality disorders: conceptual and scientific bases. *Psychology, Crime & Law*, **13**, 3–5.

Izzo, R. L. & Ross, R. R. (1990) Meta-analysis of rehabilitation programs for juvenile delinquents. A brief report. *Criminal Justice and Behavior*, **17**, 134–142.

Leichsenring, F. & Leibing, E. (2003) The effectiveness of psychodynamic therapy and cognitive behaviour therapy in the treatment of personality disorders: A meta-analysis. *American Journal of Psychiatry*, **160**, 1223–1232.

Linehan, M. M. (1993) *Cognitive-behavioural treatment of borderline personality disorder.* New York: Guilford Press.

Linehan, M. M., Davison, G. C., Lynch, T. R. & Sanderson, C. (2006) Technique factors in treating personality disorders. In L. G. Castonguay & L. E. Beutler (Eds.) *Principles of therapeutic change that work* (pp. 239–252). New York: Oxford University Press.

Lipsey, M. W. (1992) The effect of treatment on juvenile delinquents: Results from meta-analysis. In F. Lösel, D. Bender & T. Bleisener (Eds.) *Psychology and Law: International perspectives* (pp. 131–143). Berlin and New York: de Gruyter.

Livesley, W. J. (2003). *Practical management of personality disorder.* New York: Guilford Press.

Livesley, W.J. (2005) Principles and strategies for treating personality disorder. *Canadian Journal of Psychiatry*, **50**, 442–450.

Livesley, W. J. (2007) The relevance of an integrated approach to the treatment of personality disordered offenders. *Psychology, Crime & Law*, **13**, 27–46.

Looman, J., Abracen, J., Serin, R. & Marquis, P. (2005) Psychopathy, treatment change, and recidivism in high-risk, high-need sexual offenders. *Journal of Interpersonal Violence*, **20**, 549–568.

Mann, R. E., Webster, S. D., Schofield, C. & Marshall, W. L. (2004) Approach versus avoidance goals in relapse prevention with sexual offenders. *Sexual Abuse: A Journal of Research and Treatment*, **16**, 65–75.

Martin, D. J., Garske, J. P. & Davis, M. K. (2000) Relation of the therapeutic alliance with outcome and other variables: A meta-analytic review. *Journal of Consulting and Clinical Psychology*, **68**, 438–450.

Ogloff, J., Wong, S. & Greenwood, A. (1990) Treating criminal psychopaths in a therapeutic community program. *Behavioral Sciences and the Law*, **8**, 181–190.

Olver, M. E. & Wong, S. C. P. (2006) Psychopathy, sexual deviance, and recidivism among sex offenders. *Sexual Abuse: A Journal of Research and Treatment*, **18**, 65–82.

Olver, M. E. & Wong, S. C. P. (2009) Therapeutic responses of psychopathic sexual offenders: treatment attrition, therapeutic change, and long-term recidivism. *Journal of Consulting & Clinical Psychology*, **77**, 328–336.

Perry, J. C., Banon, E. & Ianni, F. (1999) Effectiveness of psychotherapy for personality disorders. *American Journal of Psychiatry*, **156**, 1312–1321.

Rice, M. E., Harris, G. T. & Cormier, C. A. (1992) An evaluation of a maximum security therapeutic community for psychopaths and other mentally disordered offenders. *Law and Human Behavior*, **16**, 399–412.

Richards, H. J., Casey, J. O. & Lucente, S. W. (2003) Psychopathy and treatment response in incarcerated female substance abusers. *Criminal Justice and Behavior*, **30**, 251–276.

Ryle, A. (1997) *Cognitive analytic therapy and borderline personality disorder: The model and the method*. Chichester: Wiley

Safran, J. D., Muran, J. C., Samstag, L. W. & Winston, A. (2003) Evaluating an alliance-focused treatment for personality disorders. *Psychotherapy: Theory, Research, Practice, Training*, **42**, 532–545.

Salekin, R. T. (2002) Psychopathy and therapeutic pessimism: Clinical lore or clinical reality? *Clinical Psychology Review*, **22**, 79–112.

Seto, M. C. & Barbaree, H. E. (1999) Psychopathy, treatment behaviour and sex offender recidivism. *Journal of Interpersonal Violence*, **14**, 1235.

Smith, T. L., Barrett, M. S., Benjamin, L. S. & Barber, J. P. (2006) Relationship factors in treating personality disorders. In L. G. Castonguay & L. E. Beutler (Eds.) *Principles of therapeutic change that work* (pp. 219–238). New York: Oxford University Press.

Thomas-Peter, B. A. (2006) The modern context of psychology in corrections: Influences, limitations and values of 'what works'. In G. J. Towl (Ed.) *Psychological Research in Prisons* (pp. 24–39). Oxford: BPS Blackwell.

Thornton, D. & Blud, L. (2007) The influence of psychopathic traits on response to treatment. In H. Hervé & J. C. Yuille (Eds.) *The psychopath: Theory, research & practice* (pp. 505–539). Mahwah, NJ: Lawrence Erlbaum Associates.

Ward, T., Mann, R. E. & Gannon, T. A. (2007) The good lives model of offender rehabilitation: Clinical implications. *Aggression and Violent Behavior*, **12**, 87–107.

Wong, S. C. P. & Burt, G. (2007) The heterogeneity of incarcerated psychopaths: Differences in risk, needs, recidivism and management approaches. In H. Hervé & J. Yuille (Eds.) *The psychopath: Theory, research, and practice* (pp. 461–484). Mahwah, NJ: Lawrence Erlbaum and Associates.

Wong, S. & Hare, R. D. (2005) *Guidelines for a psychopathy treatment program*. North Tonawanda, NY: Multi-Health Systems.

Young, J. E., Klosko, J. S. & Weishaar, M. E. (2003) *Schema therapy: A practitioner's guide*. New York: Guilford Press.

Chapter Four

Assessing Personality Disorder in Forensic Settings

Phil Willmot

Introduction

It is always essential to begin assessment with a clear understanding of what is being assessed. In the case of assessing personality this is no simple task. Personality is a complex and dynamic system and its boundaries are ill-defined. There are overlapping literatures in the social and clinical psychology fields and from psychiatry.

This chapter begins by describing some of the drawbacks of existing methods for assessing personality disorder in forensic settings. Next, it sets out some key principles for clinicians to adopt in order to maintain a positive, patient-centred focus and counteract some of the unhelpful and counter-therapeutic assumptions that clinicians sometimes hold about patients with personality disorder, either explicitly or implicitly. Finally, it outlines the assessment process. To illustrate these main points, the chapter is based around a hypothetical case: Alex. Although this is not a real case, the issues raised are all based on clinical experience.

Case example: Alex

Alex is 39 years old and has been in prison or hospital since the age of 17, when he was convicted of attempted rape. He had two previous convictions for sexual assaults, as well as a number of convictions for burglary and criminal

---

Working Positively with Personality Disorder in Secure Settings: A Practitioner's Perspective
Edited by Phil Willmot and Neil Gordon
© 2011 John Wiley & Sons, Ltd.

damage. All of his sexual offences were apparently impulsive attacks on previously unknown adults or children he met in the street. He was initially given a life sentence with a four year tariff, but has now been incarcerated for over 20 years.

Reports from prison often described Alex as 'subversive' and 'manipulative'. He made frequent use of the complaints system, often for apparently trivial grievances that could have been resolved in other ways, and tended to become agitated and verbally abusive when he felt that staff members were infringing his rights or not following appropriate procedures. On several occasions, when these complaints were not resolved to his satisfaction, Alex had demanded a transfer to another prison and engaged in covert 'targeting' of the staff members he saw as responsible for his problems, for example by spreading rumours about them and inciting other prisoners to assault them. He had been suspected of inciting serious assaults on two prison officers and in his last prison had made allegations of sexually inappropriate behaviour by a psychologist, which had resulted in her suspension until the allegations were found to be groundless.

There had also been several reported instances of his being flirtatious or otherwise sexually inappropriate with female members of staff, though on most occasions he had stopped once the staff member concerned had reminded him of appropriate boundaries. There had also been several unproven allegations of his sexually exploiting more vulnerable prisoners.

Alex had completed several sex offender treatment programmes in prison but with limited impact on his behaviour or his reported level of risk. Previous reports had described his extremely rigid and concrete cognitive style and his lack of insight into his offending. Alex would maintain that his offences were committed a long time ago when he had been a sexually naïve teenager and that he could not remember what he was thinking or feeling so long ago, though he felt that the main reason he had offended was that he had been sexually abused himself. He was adamant that he would not reoffend sexually because he now knew that sexual offending was wrong and he had matured, though he could not explain what had changed to make him so confident. The contrast between Alex's positive assessment of his progress and the negative evaluations of the programme facilitators led Alex to complain about the facilitators, accusing them of lying about him and victimizing him. Following his last programme he had made allegations about the female psychologist on the programme which had resulted in her suspension. He had also refused to have anything further to do with prison psychologists or treatment programmes.

Alex remained adamant he would not engage in any more treatment in prison for several years after these events and was eventually referred to hospital and assessed as meeting the criteria for a diagnosis of antisocial personality disorder with paranoid and passive–aggressive traits.

On admission Alex's behaviour was very different from what had been previously reported. He was generally warm and engaging with nursing staff and would often seek advice and support from them. Although he could at times be demanding and verbally abusive if they did not make themselves available as quickly as he would have liked, he was usually apologetic once the reason for the delay was explained. He was often very critical of the prison service and the fact that he had felt forced to repeat treatments that he believed he had completed satisfactorily. He

> *was pleased to be referred to hospital, mainly because he was out of the prison system. While he agreed to engage in the initial psychological assessment process, Alex refused to discuss many issues around his previous offending and prison behaviour, telling the psychologist that he found it distressing and had discussed it numerous times before in prison, and that he would find all the information he needed in his previous psychological assessment reports.*

Some drawbacks of existing methods for assessing personality disorder in forensic settings

Alex's case illustrates some of the drawbacks of traditional methods of assessment with this patient group. The first of these is that formal diagnoses of personality disorder give clinicians very little information about the patient's treatment needs or level of risk. In order to be detained under the Mental Health Act, clinicians must demonstrate that the patient suffers from a mental disorder. In Alex's case, the only definite diagnosis that could be applied was one of antisocial personality disorder, a diagnosis shared with approximately 47% of the male prison population (Fazel & Danesh, 2002). However, it was not his antisocial behaviour or traits that had prompted his referral, but rather his pattern of passive aggressive behaviour and disengagement from treatment, neither of which would be captured by any formal diagnosis.

Whichever diagnostic categories were applied, they would tell us nothing about Alex's underlying personality problems, his level of risk, treatment needs or specific responsivity issues. Even at the level of individual traits, knowing that Alex's diagnosis of antisocial personality disorder was based on the facts that he had repeatedly committed criminal offences, that he showed high levels of irritability and aggression and appeared to lack remorse would not be not particularly helpful in formulating a treatment plan for him.

A corollary of this opacity of personality disorder diagnoses is that they provide no means of measuring change. The *Diagnostic and Statistical Manual of Mental Disorders* (DSM-IV-TR), for example, defines personality disorder as '[a]n enduring pattern of inner experience and behaviour' (American Psychiatric Association, 2000: 685) and contains no guidelines on how much or for how long such an enduring pattern has to change before it can be concluded the patient no longer has a personality disorder. So, once an enduring pattern of behaviour amounting to a personality disorder has been established for an individual, there are no standards for agreeing when the individual no longer has a personality disorder. Similarly, in the forensic field, the Psychopathy Checklist – Revised (PCL-R) (Hare, 2003) involves rating lifetime history of psychopathic traits and offers no guidance on how change can be recorded or measured.

Another problem with traditional diagnostic measures in this case is that assessment is hampered by the dynamic nature of personality disorder. Zimmerman, Rothschild and Chelminski (2005) reported that assessments of personality disorder traits are affected by the presence of Axis I disorders, and patients' presentations are likely to be affected by their levels of anxiety, paranoia, depression, hostility and other emotions, which in turn are likely to be affected by their interpersonal environment. In Alex's case, his behaviour changed dramatically as soon as he arrived in hospital. Whereas in prison he was generally hostile, distant and disengaged, on admission to hospital he was much more approachable and responsive.

There are several potential explanations why patients' behaviour improves, or deteriorates, on moving from prison to hospital. Secure hospital environments are very different from prison; wards are generally a fraction of the size of prison wings with much higher staff/patient ratios and so can feel safer for the patient. On the other hand, the greater level of staff–patient interaction that this allows can feel very threatening to patients who generally avoid interacting with staff members. Criminal attitudes and prison culture are generally less prevalent and less tolerated in hospital than in prison, which can be either a liberating or a disorienting and frightening experience for men who have spent a long time in prison. The presence of other patients with obvious and dramatic mental health problems can also be a frightening experience, or, for the more criminally minded, an opportunity to exploit potentially vulnerable individuals. Finally, as discussed in Chapter 15 on patients' experiences of therapy, a change of environment can sometimes offer patients an opportunity to break out of dysfunctional cycles of interpersonal behaviour and make a 'fresh start' in a new environment.

Whatever the reason, such changes are both a threat and an opportunity for the assessment process. Traditional diagnostic systems treat personality disorder as an enduring and stable condition and have no way of recognizing changes in presentation due to changes in the environment. On the other hand, such dramatic changes in presentation provide an opportunity to generate and test hypotheses about the underlying causes of the individual's personality disorder.

A final problem illustrated by Alex's case is that forensic psychological assessments can often be experienced by the patient as repetitive, aversive and shaming experiences which largely focus on the most negative aspects of their lives, such as their offending, substance misuse, failed relationships and antisocial behaviour, and pay little attention to their positive achievements or to their experiences of victimization and trauma. Patients like Alex who have been detained for many years will probably have been asked about all these issues many times before. Repeating the same questions can risk reinforcing the patient's negative beliefs about themselves as bad and defective, and about professionals, that they regard the patient in the same way. To begin a therapeutic relationship with a patient by focusing solely on the patient's negative aspects can risk causing serious harm to the therapeutic relationship between psychologist and patient, not just for that psychologist, but also for their successors.

Some principles of assessing personality disorder in forensic settings

To understand and treat forensic patients with personality disorder, it is essential to understand the patient's core beliefs and self-concept

All the major psychological approaches to personality disorder assume that cognitive structures relating to the self and the world are core components of personality and personality disorder, and that modifying these cognitive structures is the goal of treatment. Our service has found Young's schema-focused approach (Young, Klosko & Weishaar, 2003) to be easily grasped and applied by this patient group. Schema theory provides a simple model that links basic childhood needs (e.g., for nurturance, protection, safety, love), a developmental history that failed to provide one or more of these basic needs, and ways of coping and patterns of thinking and behaviour that relate to schemas, in an adaptable form which is readily understood by most patients and which provides a framework for understanding themselves and their behaviour in simple, non-judgemental language. It also, often for the first time, provides patients with a vocabulary with which to describe painful and distressing aspects of their lives and their personality that they have previously been unable to express, and to do so in a way that allows them to externalize their thoughts, emotions and behaviours and make them easier to reflect upon.

Previous formal assessments with Alex had described his antisocial, paranoid and passive–aggressive personality traits and rigid cognitive style, but his offending was little understood. Following his admission, the initial assessment with Alex took the form of an extended life history-taking and schema assessment.

Case example: Alex

Alex was the third of four children. He had twin elder sisters and a younger brother who had cerebral palsy. Alex's father left shortly after his younger brother was born and his mother was the children's only carer for much of Alex's childhood. In fact, much of her time and energy was taken up with caring for Alex's brother and, because his elder sisters tended to play together, Alex was often left by himself. During the assessment he spoke of wanting to be noticed by his mother and of her always being too busy for him. He found the most effective way of getting her attention was to misbehave or have a temper tantrum, and though these behaviours were effective, they resulted in him being punished by being sent to his room or sent outside to play in the street.

Alex had few friends of his own age and disliked school, where he struggled academically and was bullied because of his brother's disability. He wanted friends but was too shy to make friendships and was particularly awkward with girls. When his mother sent him outside he would wander the streets by himself and, as he grew older, increasingly engaged in petty crime, such as vandalism and shoplifting.

One summer holiday at the seaside, when he was 12, Alex was befriended by a 15-year-old boy who was staying in the same place. They would play together and the other boy also began sexually abusing Alex by getting him to engage in mutual masturbation. Alex found this distressing and confusing but did not want to lose the boy's friendship and so acquiesced. This abuse carried on for the duration of the holiday and ended when they both went home. Alex never spoke about this abuse until he engaged in a sex offender treatment programme several years later in prison.

Alex's first sexual offence occurred some weeks after his return from this holiday. He spent much of his free time wandering the local streets on his own. One morning he approached a 10-year-old boy and was seen to try to masturbate this boy before a neighbour saw him and stopped him.

On the basis of this developmental history, a preliminary formulation emerged. Alex's experiences of his absent father, unavailable mother and distant elder sisters generated a schema of other people as being distant, rejecting and unwilling to meet his needs to be loved or cared for, and a schema of himself that he was fundamentally unlovable and flawed and so responsible for other people's rejection of him. In the language of Young *et al.* (2003), his core schemas were of defectiveness, abandonment/ rejection and emotional deprivation.

Although Alex was initially reluctant to discuss his family history yet again, he found the process different from previous assessment experiences in that he found his childhood feelings of being ignored and rejected validated by the empathic and non-directive style of his psychologist. Moreover, the framework provided by the schema assessment helped him for the first time to make sense of his beliefs and emotions and to reframe his childhood experiences as resulting from his dysfunctional family dynamics rather than from his own defectiveness.

It should be assumed that dysfunctional and extreme behaviours were at some stage functional and had survival value for the patient

There can often be an implicit assumption about this patient group, particularly those with antisocial or psychopathic traits, that they have fundamentally different goals from other people, for example that they only value interpersonal relationships for what they can get out of them, or that their motives are always malevolent. There is, however, no empirical evidence for this. The good lives model (e.g., Ward, Mann & Gannon 2007; Ward & Stewart 2003) suggests that all meaningful human behaviour reflects attempts to achieve specific goals – experiences, characteristics and states of mind that are intrinsically beneficial – and that these goals are universal. According to the good lives model, criminal behaviour occurs not because the offender's goals are inappropriate, but because he or she uses inappropriate means to achieve them, has a limited range of goals or because goals conflict with each other.

In Alex's case, his institutional behaviour had variously been described as 'manipulative', 'obsessed with power and control', 'psychopathic' and 'sadistic' by those working with him, and these pejorative labels had led to prison staff becoming more and more suspicious and distant with him, which had the effect of reinforcing his sense of defectiveness and rejection. A more helpful understanding of his behaviour came from the recognition that these behaviours paralleled his attempts as a child to obtain nurturance and support when he felt ignored or rejected.

Bowers (2003a) has pointed out that 'manipulative' behaviour in prisons or hospitals can be seen as a normal response to incarceration, protecting against institutionalization and generating status, respect and self-esteem. In Alex's case, his litigiousness was a clumsy but effective way of ensuring that people that he saw as rejecting or abandoning him could not simply leave him but had to stay around.

Stereotyping and stigmatizing labels that are applied to personality disordered patients, such as being 'manipulative', 'splitting teams' or 'psychopathic', tend to locate the problem entirely in the patient. In contrast, effective case formulation is likely to involve a more systemic understanding of the problem behaviour which recognizes the role of the patient, other people and the environment in triggering, maintaining and managing the behaviour. In Alex's case, his behaviour change following admission to hospital could be understood as an interaction between Alex and his schema-driven behaviours, staff in his care team and the new environment, and different expectations that Alex and others had about his relationships.

Developing a formulation of the patient's core schemas and personality disorder will assist in understanding their offending

Alex's experience of sexual abuse had been an almost unique occasion during his childhood when he had felt connected to somebody else, accepted and loved. The apparent similarity between Alex's first offence and his own experience of abuse suggested that this might be the key to understanding the developmental ante-cedents to his offending. Nearly 30 years after he was sexually abused, he was still ambivalent about the experience, expressing anger about it but still describing his abuser as 'caring' and a 'friend'. Although he could not explain the link, he said repeatedly that he believed that if he had not been abused, he would not have gone on to abuse others.

Within this preliminary formulation, Alex's first and subsequent sexual offences could be understood as attempts to overcompensate for his feelings of rejection and emotional deprivation and create a sense of feeling loved and cared for. This formulation was supported by the observation that feeling lonely or rejected appeared to be a significant antecedent in all of Alex's subsequent sexual offences.

According to this formulation, Alex's subsequent flirtatious behaviour and engagement in sexual relationships with other prisoners paralleled his earlier need to feel accepted and loved, while his passive–aggressive reactions to feeling lonely or rejected paralleled his over-compensatory reaction to these feelings, which resulted in his sexual offending. Both were examples of offence paralleling behav-iours, which could be addressed not just in offence-focused therapies with Alex, but throughout his treatment pathway.

As with his family history, Alex was initially reluctant to discuss his offending again. However, the fresh perspective provided by the understanding of his core schemas allowed him to start to understand his offending in terms of lifelong pat-terns of thinking, emotion and interpersonal relationships rather than, as previ-ously, events that had happened 'out of the blue'.

In previous discussion of his sexual offending, Alex had talked about how he had offended because he had been sexually abused himself and this had often been met with a dismissive response that he was 'making excuses'. This response had generally triggered Alex's sense of emotional deprivation and he had responded angrily, often by disengaging from the assessment or treatment process. Using a schema framework, Alex was able to understand and articulate more clearly his conflicting emotions surrounding his abuse, and to explore the parallels between the emotions triggered by his abuse and the emotional states he hoped to achieve through his own offending.

A formulation of the patient's core schemas will help to understand institutional and current behaviours

In prison Alex managed his core schemas of defectiveness, rejection and emotional deprivation in various ways; most of the time he would avoid the risk of being rejected by avoiding close contact with others, but this was not always possible. At times when he had to engage with staff, such as when he was working with psychologists or asking for help from his personal officer, he would be hyper-vigilant for signs of rejection or failure to meet his emotional needs and would protest at any hint of these on the part of the staff member. Even when no sign of rejection was apparent, Alex would set 'tests' for the staff member by making increasingly extreme demands until the staff member failed to meet them, at which point his suspicion would be confirmed that the staff member did not care, or had been pretending to care in order to hurt him even more. As soon as he felt rejected, Alex felt angry and betrayed by the staff member. Rather than express this anger directly, which he perceived as risking an outright rejection, Alex would 'punish' the staff member indirectly by passive–aggressive behaviours, such as spreading rumours or making complaints.

Ironically, as in childhood, Alex's behaviour tended to prompt exactly the behaviour that he feared. Staff would be more distant and suspicious of him and his needs would be met even less, leading to an escalation in his demanding and passive–aggressive behaviours. This had culminated in his making false allegations against his psychologist, which had led to staff being extremely wary of any contact with him, which had further exacerbated his mistrust of them. Alex's move to hospital provided him with an opportunity for a 'fresh start' with a new set of staff who had no connection with prison, so his behaviour immediately improved, his relationships with staff were more mutually trusting, allowing them to establish realistic boundaries with him from the outset, whereas previously when he had been more anxious and hyper-vigilant, any attempt by staff to impose boundaries had been experienced as a rejection. Such self-perpetuating cycles of interpersonal behaviour are extremely common among people with personality disorder. The mechanism by which core dysfunctional schemas are maintained and reinforced by patient's interpersonal behaviour and the reactions of others is illustrated in Figure 4.1.

In Alex's case, formulating his behaviour through a simple diagram like Figure 4.1 allowed Alex and members of his clinical team to understand his behaviour and to make sense of his emotional reaction when he felt he was being ignored or rejected. He was also able to recognize the dysfunctional cycle of behaviour that he had previously got into and to develop some simple skills to avoid getting into this cycle, such as simple distraction techniques to use when he felt rejected, and being able to express how he was feeling in an appropriate and assertive manner.

Use multiple perspectives in assessing this patient group, not forgetting the patient's own view

Disagreement within clinical teams is probably inevitable when assessing this patient group. People with personality disorder tend to behave in different and

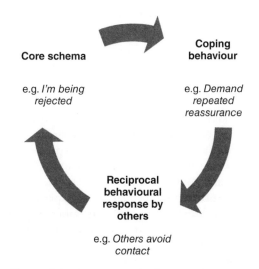

Core schema   **Coping**
                                    behaviour

e.g. *I'm being*   e.g. *Demand*
rejected   *repeated*
                                    reassurance

Reciprocal
behavioural
response by
others

e.g. *Others avoid*
contact

Figure 4.1   Interpersonal schema maintenance

sometimes extreme ways with teams, particularly where different team members adopt different roles with the patient. Within forensic mental health settings, life-long patterns of insecure attachment, abusive and transient relationships and trauma are the norm for patients (Paris, 2001). It should be no surprise that this patient group should experience intense anxiety, discomfort and negative transference reactions when faced with new relationships with people in authority, people who want to get close to them, health professionals or other groups that may have previously been associated with trauma. Nor should it be a surprise that people who are perceived as caring, nurturing or protecting should trigger equally intense positive transference reactions. In Alex's case, he tended to be most likely to engage in demanding and boundary-violating behaviour with his named nurse and psychologist, those members of his team who were most likely to trigger his feelings of rejection, whereas he was generally polite and appropriate with members of his team with whom he had a more superficial relationship.

This tendency of people with personality disorder to present very differently in different environments and with different people is often construed negatively by the team as the patient deliberately trying to 'split the team'. However, such behaviours can be seen as reflecting how the patient sees the world and key relationships. Also, as Bowers (2003b) has pointed out, most people are manipulative of others, but what distinguishes people with personality disorder is their use of more coercive techniques and lack of concern for others. 'Manipulative' behaviours can therefore provide an important source of assessment information about the patient and their likely treatment needs.

Differences of opinion will inevitably occur within the team when faced with such different behaviours. Such disagreements should be seen as a natural manifestation of personality disorder and healthy clinical teams should be able to discuss such differences of opinion and synthesize them into a formulation that is shared by the whole team and the patient. The inevitability of such disagreements among teams working with patients with personality disorders highlights the need for regular and protected forums for team formulation and supervision. (See this volume, Chapter 13 on supervision.)

Assessment of patients with personality disorder is always a two-way process

As the clinician is assessing the patient, he or she is also being assessed. In any institution or service, the time spent in initial assessment will be the time when patients form impressions and expectations about psychologists and other professionals, about relationships, about their environment and about their own ability to engage in a process and to affect their own behaviour. For patients with personality disorder in forensic settings, their prior experiences of institutions are often overwhelmingly negative, so it is all the more important that their first impressions of staff and relationships in a new institution are positive.

For Alex, his experiences during the assessment process helped to undermine a number of beliefs that were therapy-interfering for him. Previously, he saw assessment and therapy as processes in which things were 'done to him' and he was a passive 'subject'. His view of psychologists and other mental health professionals was that they were critical, their approval of him was conditional on his making progress in treatment and that they would ultimately reject him when he inevitably let them down. His view of himself was as defective, incapable of change and doomed to fail. Even an extended assessment process lasting several months will not dispel such beliefs as they have built up and been reinforced over the patient's lifetime. However, it can start to provide an alternative perspective, one that is more conducive to therapeutic change. In Alex's case, when he left the assessment ward after completing his six-month assessment, he was more optimistic about his chances of making progress and was eager to start engaging in therapy to address his interpersonal difficulties and dysfunctional core schemas. While he was still reluctant to re-engage in offence-specific work, he accepted that he would benefit from it once he had completed schema therapy.

Assessment of this patient group should address criminogenic, responsivity and mental health needs

Criminogenic needs. As with other forensic populations, treatment should address criminogenic needs (Andrews & Bonta, 2006). However, as is argued elsewhere in this volume (see Chapter 3), the literature on criminogenic needs should be applied to patients in a mental health setting with caution as they are not necessarily typical of the offender populations on which many of the meta-analytic and correlational studies of correctional research are based. In practice this means taking an individual, formulation-based approach to assessment that is informed by the risk–needs–responsivity literature, but not constrained by it. For Alex, a major criminogenic need appeared to be his ability to manage feelings of rejection effectively. While there is no empirical evidence that rejection is a criminogenic need, as Andrews has argued, 'risk factors may be highly individualistic and thus individualized reviews of high risk personal states, thought processes, thought content, circumstances and situations are indicated' (1995: 56).

Responsivity needs.   People with personality disorder have difficulties in interpersonal relationships, and in general the closer the relationship the more problems will be encountered. Moreover, other common characteristics of personality disorder including emotional lability or avoidance, impulsivity and unstable self-concept, can also significantly impede engagement and therapeutic change. Identified responsivity factors for Alex included his sensitivity to feeling rejected or feeling that his emotional needs were not being met, his avoidance of expressing thoughts or feelings that might trigger rejection by others, poor emotional control, rigid cognitive style and low sense of self-efficacy about his ability to change.

It is essential that any assessment and formulation of a forensic personality disordered patient includes an assessment and formulation of responsivity and potential therapy interfering behaviours. The concept of therapy interfering behaviours was first used by Linehan (1993) in developing dialectical behaviour therapy for borderline personality disorder, but is equally applicable with any patient with a personality disorder. In DBT's hierarchy of treatment goals, therapy interfering behaviours come only second in importance to life-threatening behaviours since they have the potential, if not addressed, to terminate the therapy process.

Mental health needs.   Rates of Axis I disorders are high among people with personality disorders (Oldham, Skodol, Kellman, Hyler, Doidge, Rosnick & Gallaher, 1995; Zimmerman *et al.*, 2005). Ward's Good Lives model suggests that it is important and legitimate to address issues which help patients to lead lifestyles that are intrinsically healthy, rewarding and positive, and addressing mental health needs is likely to improve patients' abilities to achieve other important life goals.

Needs may fall into all three of these categories; for example, factors such as impulsivity or irritability could be a criminogenic need, a responsivity need and a mental health need for some offenders.

The assessment process

Assessment of forensic patients with personality disorder should always be tailored to the needs and responsivity factors of the individual, so this section is not intended to be prescriptive or exhaustive. However, it describes the issues which are most commonly encountered.

History-taking

Even when personal history information is already available, it is useful to start the assessment process with an extended history-taking, since the narrative process is itself an invaluable source of information about how the patient sees himself and others, recurring themes in their life and the interpersonal dynamics between patient and assessor. Taking a life history also demonstrates to the patient the developmental basis of personality disorder and helps the assessor and patient to start to develop a collaborative personality formulation.

Key topics to discuss during the history-taking include:

- Relationships with family and key attachment figures.
- Key developmental events and transitions, and the patient's reaction to them.
- Important episodes of loss, separation, trauma and abuse.
- Key interpersonal relationships.
- Forensic history.
- Offence paralleling behaviours.

Assessment of symptoms and traits

In selecting assessments of personality traits the assessor should be clear about whether they require a formal diagnosis of personality disorder. In mental health settings where a formal diagnosis is required for a patient to be detained or to receive treatment, interview-based measures are considered the gold standard for diagnosing personality disorders (Clark & Harrison, 2001: 300). Suitable interview-based measures include the International Personality Disorder Examination (IPDE) (Loranger, 1999) and Structured Clinical Interview for DSM-IV Axis II Personality Disorders (SCID-II) (First, Gibbons, Spitzer, Williams & Benjamin, 1997). In settings where a diagnosis is not required, the assessor should consider the implications of generating a formal diagnosis of personality disorder if such a diagnosis will not help the patient to access appropriate services, and may indeed have a stigmatizing effect which hinders their access to treatment. In these circumstances, self-report measures, such as the Millon Clinical Multiaxial Inventory-III (MCMI-III) (Millon, Davis & Millon, 1994) or Personality Diagnostic Questionnaire (PDQ-4+) (Hyler, 1994), may be more appropriate means of eliciting similar information. Self-report measures such as the MCMI-III and Personality Assessment Inventory (PAI) (Morey, 1991) also include measures of commonly occurring Axis I disorders, as well as measures of personality. These measures also include validity scales to detect biased or random responding. As an alterative to these scales, measures such as the Brief Symptom Inventory (BSI) (Derogatis, 1993) provide a simple and comprehensive screening of common mental health symptoms.

Assessment of psychopathy

The Psychopathy Checklist- Revised (PCL-R) (Hare, 2003) and the shorter Screening Version (PCL:SV) (Hart, Cox & Hare, 1995) remain the standard assessments for psychopathy in most services and are useful not only in identifying traits as significant treatment targets or responsivity needs, but also in risk assessment. The PCL-R has been subject to a number of criticisms (e.g., Thomas-Peter & Jones, 2006), but two in particular limit its usefulness as an assessment tool: (i) it is a static measure based on lifetime history and so cannot be used to measure change; and (ii) the PCL-R is purely descriptive and does not help the clinician to formulate psychopathic traits or to decide how to manage or treat them. As an alternative or adjunct to the PCL-R, clinicians may therefore wish to use the Comprehensive Assessment of Psychopathic Personality (CAPP) (Cooke, Hart, Logan & Kreis, 2009), which addresses many of the shortcomings of the PCL-R.

Assessment of risk

The varied and sometimes unusual range of criminogenic needs and risk factors displayed by this population can cause problems for risk assessment using standard risk assessment measures. Since risk will be an important treatment outcome measure, it is important to use risk measures which are sensitive to change resulting from treatment, and which can be re-administered at regular intervals through the treatment process. The Violence Risk Scale (VRS) (Wong & Gordon, 2001) and Violence Risk Scale – Sex Offender Version (VRS-SO) (Wong, Olver, Nicholaichuk & Gordon, 2006) both assess risk of reoffending and use dynamic variables to identify treatment targets and to measure changes in risk as a result of treatment or other factors. Both scales incorporate a range of static and dynamic risk factors and measure change using a modified version of the trans-theoretical model of change (Prochaska, DiClemente & Norcross, 1992). Both have both been validated on samples of forensic mental health patients (Olver, Wong, Nicholaichuk & Gordon, 2007; Wong & Gordon, 2006). They are therefore both appropriate measures not only of initial risk of sexual or violent recidivism, but also of treatment outcomes.

Assessment of core beliefs

Since changing the maladaptive core beliefs or schemas and associated interpersonal behaviour is a long-term goal in treating people with personality disorder, an assessment of these core beliefs is important. The Young Schema Questionnaire (YSQ) (Young & Brown, 2001) measures 18 maladaptive core schemas. Although devised for use within a Schema Focused Therapy setting (SFT) (Young *et al.*, 2003), the YSQ is just as useful with other theoretical approaches. Given that any assessment of core beliefs is likely to involve triggering those core beliefs, it is best left until the end of the assessment process when the therapeutic relationship is strongest. Nevertheless, some schemas, in particular defectiveness and emotional deprivation, can still be too distressing and anxiety-provoking for patients to acknowledge, even to themselves. The schema assessment may therefore not be completely accurate at this stage.

Assessment of comorbid conditions

During the history-taking and other assessments, the assessor should be aware of other comorbid conditions and, if necessary, conduct additional assessments as necessary. Common conditions among forensic personality disorder populations include:

- *Neuropsychological impairment:* Lumsden, Chesterman and Hill (1998) reported high rates of neuropsychological impairment among admissions to a UK high secure hospital;: 26% had a history of obstetric complications and 31% had a history of head injury resulting in loss of consciousness and requiring hospitalization; 59% showed clear signs of neuropsychological abnormalities and in 25% these were regarded as moderate or severe. Neuropsychological impairments may affect not only a patient's treatment needs but also their ability to engage in and respond to treatment. It is therefore important to screen during the history-taking for possible indicators of neuropsychological impairments such as birth complications, head injuries or delays in developmental or educational achievement and to conduct further assessments as necessary.

- *Substance misuse*: Singleton, Farrell and Meltzer (1999) reported high rates of hazardous drinking and substance misuse among prisoners with a diagnosis of personality disorder, while Marshall (2008) reported increasing levels of drug dependence over recent years among forensic personality disorder patients. Substance misuse may be both a criminogenic treatment need and a mental health treatment need.
- *Attention deficit hyperactivity disorder (ADHD)*: There is evidence of a high rates of adult ADHD among forensic populations (Young, 2007), and of a correlation between a diagnosis of ADHD during childhood and later diagnosis of borderline personality disorder (Fossati, Novella, Donati, Donini & Maffei, 2002). Adult ADHD may be a criminogenic treatment need if it involves significant impulsivity, as well as a mental health treatment need and a factor affecting treatment responsivity.
- *Trauma symptoms and post-traumatic stress disorder (PTSD)*: There is evidence of higher rates of PTSD among people with a diagnosis of personality disorder (Zanarini, Frankenburg, Dubo, Sickel, Trikha, Levin & Reynolds, 1998) and among prisoners (Goff, Rose, Rose & Purves, 2007). While this is likely to reflect the increased rates of early trauma and abuse suffered by these groups, there is also evidence that sexual and violent offenders can suffer PTSD as a result of their offending (e.g., Gray, Carman, Rogers, MacCulloch, Hayward & Snowden, 2003). Trauma symptoms will be a mental health treatment need and may also affect treatment responsivity.

Assessment of therapy interfering behaviours

Many aspects of personality disorder will affect the patient's ability to engage in a therapeutic relationship and to consistently engage in therapy, including dysfunctional core beliefs about the self and others, insecure patterns of attachment, impulsivity and affective instability. Many patients in forensic personality disorder services already have an extensive history of avoiding or disengaging from previous treatments. At the same time, most patients will have had some positive experiences of therapy or therapeutic relationships, and it is useful to review the patient's treatment history, collaboratively identify the interpersonal and situational factors associated with both positive and negative experiences of treatment and incorporate these into the patient's treatment plan. The assessment process itself may trigger episodes of disengagement which can be analysed to identify their causes and solutions, a process which can be useful in demonstrating to the patient that relationship ruptures can be resolved. It is also helpful, once other aspects of the assessment are complete, to identify with the patient the traits, symptoms and core beliefs that are likely to interfere with future treatment and to develop a set of plans and coping strategies that the patient and future therapists can use to minimize the risk of disengagement from treatment.

Assessment of offence paralleling behaviours

Jones (2004) has pointed out that for many offenders in the criminal justice and mental health systems, interventions which directly address offending behaviour can happen several years after the most recent offence. In contrast, a key focus for most personality disorder interventions is on current behaviours. A simple approach to this dilemma, proposed by Jones, is to make offence paralleling behaviours a focus of treatment. Jones defined offence paralleling behaviour as 'any form of offence related behavioural (or fantasized behaviour) pattern that emerges at any point before or after an offence' (2004: 38). Offence paralleling behaviours do not have to result in an offence; they simply need to resemble, in some significant respect, the sequence of behaviours leading up to the offence.

Conclusions

As with any target of psychological therapy, a sound and thorough assessment is an essential foundation for subsequent treatment success. However, this is arguably even more true when assessing forensic patients with personality disorder because the assessment not only provides important information to the clinical team, it should also provide the patient with experiences of a safe, boundaried and secure relationship, of being able to manage ruptures in that relationship and of engaging collaboratively in a task. For some patients these will be completely new experiences, but even when they are not, they will help to provide important disconfirming evidence of previously held beliefs about treatment and about people in authority, and a template for future therapeutic encounters. Assessment should therefore be seen not just as assessment, but as the first stage in the treatment process.

References

American Psychiatric Association (2000) *Diagnostic and Statistical Manual of Mental Disorders*, 4th edition, text revision. Washington, DC: Author.

Andrews, D. A. (1995) The psychology of criminal conduct and effective treatment. In J. McGuire (Ed.) *What works: Reducing reoffending – guidelines from research and practice* (pp. 35–62). Chichester: Wiley.

Andrews, D. A. & Bonta, J. (2006) *The psychology of criminal conduct*, 4th edition. Cincinnati, OH: Anderson.

Bowers, L. (2003a) Manipulation: searching for an understanding. *Journal of Psychiatric and Mental Health Nursing*, 10, 329–334.

Bowers, L. (2003b) Manipulation: description, interpretation and ambiguity. *Journal of Psychiatric and Mental Health Nursing*, 10, 323–328.

Clark, L. A. & Harrison, J. A. (2001) Assessment instruments. In W. J. Livesley (Ed.) *Handbook of personality disorders* (pp. 277–306). New York: Guilford Press.

Cooke, D. J., Hart, S. D., Logan, C. & Kreis, M. K. F. (2009) Recent developments in the use of the comprehensive assessment of psychopathic personality (CAPP). Symposium conducted at the Ninth International Association of Forensic Mental Health Services (IAFMHS) annual conference, Edinburgh.

Derogatis, L. R. (1993) *BSI: Brief symptom inventory. Administration, scoring, and procedures manual*, 4th edition. Minneapolis, MN: National Computer Systems.

Fazel, S. & Danesh, J. (2002) Serious mental disorder in 23,000 prisoners: A systematic review of 62 surveys. *The Lancet*, **359**, 545–550.

First, M., Gibbons, M., Spitzer, R.L. Williams, J. B. W. & Benjamin, L. S. (1997) *User's guide for the structured clinical interview for the DSM-IV Axis II personality disorder*. Washington, DC: American Psychiatric Press.

Fossati, A., Novella, L., Donati, D., Donini, M. & Maffei, C. (2002) History of childhood attention deficit/hyperactivity disorder symptoms and borderline personality disorder: A controlled study. *Comprehensive Psychiatry*, **43**, 369–377.

Goff, A., Rose, E., Rose, S. & Purves, D. (2007) Does PTSD occur in sentenced prison populations? A systematic literature review. *Criminal Behaviour and Mental Health*, **17**, 152–162.

Gray, N., Carman, N., Rogers, P., MacCulloch, M., Hayward, P. & Snowden, R. (2003) Post-traumatic stress disorder caused in mentally disordered offenders by the committing of a serious violent or sexual offence. *Journal of Forensic Psychiatry & Psychology*, **14**, 27–43.

Hare, R. D. (2003) *Manual for the revised psychopathy checklist*, 2nd edition. Toronto: Multi-Health Systems.

Hart, S. D., Cox, D. N. & Hare, R. D. (1995) *Manual for the psychopathy checklist: Screening version (PCL: SV)*. Toronto: Multi-Health Systems.

Hyler, S. E. (1994) *Personality diagnostic questionnaire-IV (PDQ-IV)*. New York: New York State Psychiatric Institute.

Jones, L. (2004) Offence paralleling behaviour (OPB) as a framework for assessment and interventions with offenders. In A. Needs & G. Towl (Eds.) *Applying psychology to forensic practice* (pp. 34–63). Oxford: BPS Blackwell.

Linehan, M. M. (1993) *Cognitive-behavioral treatment of borderline personality disorder*. New York: Guilford Press.

Loranger, A. W. (1999) *IPDE: International personality disorder examination: DSM-IV and ICD-10 modules*. Washington, DC: American Psychiatric Press.

Lumsden, J., Chesterman, L.P. & Hill, G.M. (1998) Neuropsychiatric indices in a high security admission sample I: Estimating the prevalence. *Criminal Behaviour and Mental Health*, **8**, 285–310.

Marshall, J. (2008) Psychopathology, complexity and change: The personality disorder directorate at Rampton Hospital since 1997. Unpublished Master's dissertation.

Millon, T., Davis, R. & Millon, C. (1994) *Manual for the Millon Clinical Multiaxial Inventory-III (MCMI-III)*. Minneapolis, MN: National Computer Systems.

Morey, L. C. (1991) *Personality assessment inventory*. Odessa, FL: Psychological Assessment Resources Inc.

Oldham, J. M., Skodol, A. E., Kellman, H. D., Hyler, S. E., Doidge, N., Rosnick, L. & Gallaher, P. E. (1995) Comorbidity of Axis I and Axis II disorders, *American Journal of Psychiatry*, **152**, 571–578.

Olver, M., Wong, S., Nicholaichuk, T. & Gordon, A. (2007) The validity and reliability of the Violence risk scale: sexual offender version: Assessing sex offender risk and evaluating therapeutic change. *Psychological Assessment*, **19**, 318–329.

Paris, J. (2001) Psychosocial adversity. In W. J. Livesley (Ed.) *Handbook of personality disorders: Theory research and treatment* (pp. 231–241). New York: Guilford Press.

Prochaska, J. O., DiClemente, C. C. & Norcross, J. C. (1992) In search of how people change: Applications to the addictive behaviors. *American Psychologist*, **47**, 1102–1114.

Singleton, N., Farrell, M. & Meltzer, H. (1999) *Substance misuse among prisoners in England and Wales*. London: Office of National Statistics.

Thomas-Peter, B. & Jones, J. (2006) High-risk inferences in assessing high risk: Outstanding concerns in the clinical use of the PCL-R. *British Journal of Forensic Practice*, **8**(4), 3–18.

Ward, T., Mann, R. & Gannon, T. (2007) The good lives model of offender rehabilitation: Clinical implications. *Aggression and Violent Behaviour*, **12**, 87–107.

Ward, T. & Stewart, C. A. (2003) Good lives and the rehabilitation of sexual offenders. In T. Ward, D. R. Laws & S. M. Hudson (Eds.) *Sexual deviance: Issues and controversies* (pp. 21–44). Thousand Oaks, CA: Sage.

Wong, S. & Gordon, A. (2001) *The violence risk scale*. Saskatoon: University of Saskatchewan.

Wong, S. & Gordon, A. (2006) The validity and reliability of the violence Risk scale: A treatment-friendly violence risk assessment tool. *Psychology, Public Policy, and Law.* **12**, 279–309.

Wong, S., Olver, M., Nicholaichuk, T., & Gordon, A. (2006) *Violence risk scale: Sexual offender version*. Saskatoon: University of Saskatchewan.

Young, J. E. & Brown, G. (2001) *Young schema questionnaire: Special edition*. New York: Schema Therapy Institute.

Young, J. E., Klosko, J. S. & Weishaar, M. E. (2003) *Schema therapy: A practitioner's guide*. New York: Guilford Press.

Young, S. (2007) Forensic aspects of ADHD. In M. Fitzgerald, M. Bellgrove & M. Gill (Eds.) *Handbook of attention deficit hyperactivity disorder* (pp. 91–108). Chichester: Wiley.

Zanarini, M., Frankenburg, F., Dubo, E., Sickel, A., Trikha, A., Levin, A. & Reynolds, V. (1998) Axis I Comorbidity of Borderline Personality Disorder. *American Journal of Psychiatry*, **155**, 1733–1739.

Zimmerman, M., Rothschild, L. & Chelminski, I. (2005) The prevalence of DSM-IV personality disorders in psychiatric outpatients. *American journal of Psychiatry*, **162**, 1911–1918.

Chapter Five

A Treatment Pathway for High Security Offenders with a Personality Disorder

Sue Evershed

About the Service

The specialist personality disorder treatment service at Rampton was set up in 1994 in the belief that patients with a personality disorder have different treatment and management issues from other patient groups and would benefit from a dedicated service geared to their specific needs. From its inception as the Psychological Treatment Unit (PTU) there has been an explicit recognition that the unit would have a psychological orientation as the key means of helping patients address their personality disorder and offending needs.

Originally, the PTU comprised a single, 16-bed ward. A standardized assessment package specifically tailored to meet the needs of this patient group was designed, but the treatment offered was largely individual therapy because the patient treatment needs were heterogeneous. Nevertheless, treatment and management protocols and a specific service ethos were developed. This stemmed from the view that consistency of approach was crucial to success with this patient group, and this led to the need for multidisciplinary working to underpin all aspects of the service, with patient involvement being paramount at all stages of assessment and treatment.

In 1997 two more wards were integrated with the PTU to form the Personality Disorder Service. The PDS now comprised an eight-bed admission ward, a 16-bed treatment ward and a pre-discharge ward with 20 beds. The patients were at different stages of their treatment, and many had completed treatment programmes elsewhere. Patient needs were disparate and the treatment programmes reflected this: they addressed assessed need but, as in many services at the time, were not organized into a coherent pathway.

The service continued to grow over the following two years. The service currently consists of five wards: an eight-bed admission ward, three treatment wards of 15 beds each and a step-down ward, also with 15 beds. Our current treatment pathway, developed in 2000, has been based on observations of our patients' responses to therapy and published developments in the design of treatment for forensic and personality disordered patients.

Our patients

The patient group reflects the service's admission criteria: male patients who constitute a 'grave and immediate danger to the public' and who are detainable under the Mental Health Act due to a personality disorder. Our patients present as complex cases where personality disorder is related to the patients' high risk of offending. There is limited learning disability in the population, to the extent that it might severely limit understanding (although some patients are in the mild-to-borderline range). There is also rarely any active mental illness, although most do have comorbid Axis I disorders – mostly mood disorders. Most arrive with a willingness to make therapeutic change, although for many this motivation will fluctuate, and a few patients are reluctant to participate in treatment when they are admitted. The majority of patients arrive with poor expectations and negative experiences of treatment, having been refused or having dropped out of treatment in the past.

Our patients have committed very serious offences against the person, and many are still engaged in risk-related behaviour, cognitions or emotions on admission. Many have been offending from an early age and have diverse, and sometimes bizarre, offending histories. Most have poor or abusive developmental histories and ongoing disturbed relationships, with little familial support. They have had problems for many years, across many areas of functioning, with dysfunctional thinking styles, emotions and social behaviour. Our patient population is characterized by high levels of impulsivity, poor interpersonal or pro-social skills, anti-authority attitudes and antisocial behaviour. Many present with several psychopathic traits (Hare, 2003) and about 25% are rated as clinical psychopaths (Scoring ≥30 on the Psychopathy Checklist Revised; PCL-R, Hare, 2003).

Our patients also have differing sets of personality disorder symptoms, averaging three or more 'types' of personality disorder (Coid, 1992). Thus they do not constitute a homogeneous group, but present different constellations of impairment. Each patient's treatment needs are different; each responds to treatment in a different way; and the problems they present which interfere with effective therapy are diverse. Thus an individualized, detailed formulation of offending, personality and related issues is necessary to prescribe the pathway through therapy for each patient, and the service has to provide a range of different psychological approaches to meet individual responsivity needs.

Treatment, personality disorder and high secure population needs

The treatment of high risk patients with a personality disorder remains an area where there is little theoretical agreement and a relative paucity of comprehensive research (Duggan, Huband, Smailagic, Ferriter & Adams, 2008; Perry, Banon & Ianni, 1999). Discussion documents on the management of 'dangerous and severe personality disorders' (Home Office & Department of Health, 1999) reveal a concern about the treatability of this population.

Research has shown that personality disordered patients are difficult to engage; they attend therapy sporadically, and their self-damaging and challenging behaviours interrupt treatment (Chiesa & Fonagy, 2000; Diguer, Barber & Luborsky, 1993; Reich & Vasile, 1993). Many patients fail to improve with standard mental health interventions (Livesley, 2007), and this can lead to therapist burnout (Gunderson, 1984). In forensic settings, also, treatment has been considered less effective with high risk personality disordered patients (Blackburn, 2000; Dolan, 1998; Goldstein, Powers, McCusker, Lewis, Bigelow & Mundt, 1998; Lipsey, 1995). In particular, patients with high levels of psychopathy (Hare, 2003) do not seem to do well in therapy (Harris, Rice & Cormier, 1994). Patients present with behaviours such as self-harm and offence paralleling behaviours that are not conducive to therapy (Bender, Dolan, Skodol, Sanislow, Dyck, McGlashan, Shea, Zanarini, Oldham & Gunderson, 2001). Some writers have suggested that patients' problems are amplified by treatment because of the fundamental characteristics of their personality disorder (Harris *et al.*, 1994; Rice, 1997). Others have noted the potential for treatment to produce adverse effects in patients suffering from personality disorder (Jones, 2009). Personality disordered patients thus came to be seen as treatment 'abusers' (Warren & Dolan, 1996) and personality disorder became a 'diagnosis of exclusion' from services (Department of Health, 2003).

However, over the last 15 years several new treatments have been designed to address personality disorder itself. Accordingly, there is a growing body of evidence suggesting that personality disordered patients can respond to therapy, although outcome studies provide little guidance on the optimal approach (Bateman & Tyrer, 2004; Davidson, 2008; Duggan *et al.*, 2008; Leichsenring & Leibing, 2003; Perry *et al.*, 1999; Shea, 1993). Typically, patients with personality disorder exhibit multiple problems, including symptoms, situational problems, emotion and impulse dysregulation, maladaptive traits, maladaptive interpersonal patterns and a poorly developed self or identity (Livesley, 2005).

Patients with personality disorder who have offended have additional needs. Not only do they require treatment for their personality disorder, but they also need interventions to address their risk of reoffending. The therapeutic needs of mentally disordered offenders have been assessed in a number of research studies. Assessed needs include offence-related needs, safety with regard to self, dangerous behaviour, substance misuse and psychological distress. As expected, high secure patients, especially those with personality disorder, report significantly more needs than other patients (Harty, Shaw, Thomas, Dolan, Davies, Thornicroft, Carlisle, Moreno, Leese, Appleby & Jones, 2004; Leese, Thornicroft, Shaw, Thomas,

Mohan, Harty & Dolan, 2006; Thomas, Leese, Dolan, Harty, Shaw, Middleton, Carlisle, Davies, Thornicroft & Appleby, 2004).

Livesley (2005) proposed a systematic framework for treating personality disorder which can be applied to high risk forensic patients. He recommended an eclectic approach which combined interventions from different therapeutic models and delivered them in an integrated and systematic manner. He suggested that the approach should be multidimensional, incorporating treatment interventions from various models, that the treatments should be coordinated and integrated in terms of their delivery, and that an emphasis should be placed on facilitating the development of more integrated and coherent personality functioning. Since the needs of high secure personality disordered patients are relatively disparate, Piper and Joyce (2001), reviewing the literature on treatment outcome, concluded that the best results occurred when treatment was individually tailored.

Treatment assumptions

A key treatment assumption is that patients with a personality disorder, including those with high levels of psychopathy traits, are treatable. However, our patients will have multiple difficulties and deficits, which means that programmes with a single focus (risk or clinical) are unlikely to meet all of the identified needs (Livesley, 2007). Thus a menu of integrated treatments is required to address different areas of difficulty.

The core features of personality disorder involve a poorly developed self-system or identity and chronic interpersonal problems. Thus the generic pathway must include interventions to address these issues. However, this patient group presents with a disparate set of clinical needs according to the 'type' of personality disorder, expressed through dysfunctional relating, behaving, feeling and thinking. Thus the treatment offered should be based on individual formulation incorporating all the patient's assessed needs. This approach lends itself very well to structured psychological interventions. Cognitive behavioural therapy, in its broadest definition, has provided some of the strongest evidence so far, in terms of treatment effects on personality disorder (Davidson, 2008; Duggan *et al.*, 2008; Shea, 1993). Consequently, a clinical strategy providing a blend of cognitive behavioural interventions was developed.

The role of the Special Hospital is to reduce risk to the public. The treatment pathway, therefore, focuses on the reduction of future offence-related risk and those aspects of patients' personality structure related to the maintenance of risk. It is generally recognized that cognitive behavioural approaches to offending are effective, and a number of well-respected programmes are now available. Research has demonstrated that successful programmes are those that target criminogenic needs and offence paralleling behaviours, teach pro-social skills, match treatment dosage and methods to participants' needs and attend to responsivity issues (Andrews & Bonta, 1998; Hollin, 1995; McGuire & Priestley, 1995).

However, research and clinical practice demonstrate that appropriate programmes also require appropriate delivery (Porporini & Fabiano, 2007; Van Voorhis, Spruance, Ritchey, Listwan & Seabrook, 2004). It is crucial to create an effective practice framework that is sensitive to the individual responsivity needs of the patient. Programmes, therefore, need to be flexible enough to encourage change to start, to notice it when it begins, to reinforce and support it when it occurs and to intervene when it does not.

Since evidence suggests our patients do not do well in traditional therapies (Blackburn, 2000; Dolan, 1998; Goldstein *et al.*, 1998; Lipsey, 1995), they are also unlikely to do well in standard programmes targeting criminogenic needs (Livesley, 2007; Ward & Stewart, 2003). Jones (2009) goes further, suggesting that this treatment can have adverse effects. Discussing the details of offending within a group can increase offending or detection evasion repertoires, retraumatize patients with abuse histories or heighten arousal in those with deviant interests. Confrontation in a group setting can reinforce paranoid thinking or enhance defectiveness and failure schemas, and so engender shame and hopelessness. Thus the standard programmes have been adapted to minimize possible adverse effects and manage pervasive personality difficulties which impact on 'treatment resistance'.

Linehan (1993a) coined the phrase 'therapy interfering behaviours' to describe the challenging or avoidant behaviours in which patients engage during therapy. She (and other writers, e.g., Safran & Muran, 2003) took the view that these behaviours are simply maladaptive coping strategies which should be targeted as part of therapy. The treatment pathway, and the adaptations to the programmes within the pathway, reflect this approach: a focus on building a collaborative relationship by building and maintaining the alliance, maintaining consistency, promoting validation and building motivation and a commitment to change (Livesley, 2003).

The provision of individual sessions alongside group work for most of our core programmes is also central to the treatment ethos. This offers a number of advantages. First, it allows for the therapeutic advances made in group work to be personalized to the individual and generalized across different situations in individual sessions. Secondly, a strong therapeutic alliance is likely to produce improved outcomes for the patient and can be used as a means of keeping him engaged in the treatment. More importantly perhaps, the therapeutic alliance can offer a vehicle for the patient to improve general relationship skills (Horvath & Bedi, 2002; Linehan, 1993a; Safran & Muran, 2003).

Key concerns with our patient group centre on failure to engage and fluctuating motivation. Thus a strong motivational context and a consistent approach is required to persuade patients to go into therapy and to maintain them within it. The therapeutic milieu is seen as crucial and is promoted through an overt philosophy of care and a clear multidisciplinary ethos. The PDS treatment pathway is founded on the principle that evidence-based psychological interventions should be provided within a framework of individualized, needs-led and consistent multidisciplinary care.

Patients are encouraged to attempt the group-based programmes; additional support is offered to assist in this if necessary. However, if it becomes clear that the group process is detrimental to their (or others') well-being, the programme is offered on an individual basis. Despite the common view in forensic circles that group-based programmes produce better outcomes, there is no evidence for this (DiFazio, Abracen & Looman, 2001; Tucker & Oei, 2007). Patients undertaking

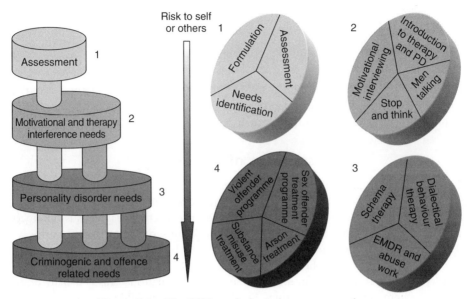

Figure 5.1 The PDS psychological treatment pathway

programmes individually work to the same treatment manuals/guidelines and complete the same pre- and post-treatment outcome measures.

A final significant issue from the research literature, and central to our offence-related treatments, is the notion of helping patients to 'build better lives' by focusing on the achievement of a good quality of life through pro-social means (Ward & Maruna, 2006).

The psychological treatment pathway offered in the PDS falls into four stages: (i) assessment; (ii) motivational treatments; (iii) personality disorder treatments; and (iv) criminogenic need treatments. The pathway is set within a strong motivational context and a treatment milieu that is based on the use of community meetings, a behavioural philosophy of care and a focus on current offence paralleling and therapy interfering behaviour. The need to build an evidence base for offence-related and personality-focused interventions requires that the service is underpinned by continuous clinical evaluation of the effectiveness of the interventions in instituting clinical change.

The service's aim is for all patients to be involved in therapy, and a range of evidence-based interventions is offered to ensure a 'best fit' between treatment and the patient's need or preferred treatment style. Progress through the treatment pathway is reflected in Figure 5.1, with the stages building on each other. However, it is also possible for patients to access therapies from all the stages at any time, should their ongoing assessment indicate a need.

Stage 1: Assessment

On admission to the PDS, patients spend approximately six months on the admission ward undergoing initial assessment. The assessment stage comprises a rigorous clinical assessment focusing on personality, other mental health needs, offending behaviour, and risk and responsivity issues. Because patients often come to the service with histories of poor motivation and disengagement from therapy, the assessment phase is seen as an important first step in the treatment pathway and has a strong emphasis on motivation. It is also important that the assessment process is responsive to the needs and abilities of the patient; that the patient is involved in setting the pace and order of assessment; that assessments reflect the concerns of the patient; and that regular feedback is provided.

Assessment of personality

Because the Mental Health Act requires that patients have a formal diagnosis of mental disorder in order to be legally detained, an assessment of personality disorders is part of the assessment process. However, once that diagnosis is obtained it is of little importance in planning the patient's subsequent treatment pathway. The assessment of personality, therefore, involves building a detailed picture of the patient's family, attachment and interpersonal, emotional and behavioural history in order to develop an initial personality formulation. This is usually done using a schema framework (Young, Klosko & Weishaar, 2003), which has been found to be easily understood by most patients and able to provide them with a clear model and framework for understanding themselves. It is this formulation which principally informs the patient's treatment pathway.

Assessment of other mental health needs

The assessment process is flexible and able to incorporate assessments not only of commonly co-occurring Axis I disorders, such as anxiety and depression, but also of other mental health conditions that are found relatively frequently in this population, including neurological impairment, attention deficit hyperactivity disorder (ADHD) or trauma symptoms. These conditions may not only be significant treatment needs, they may also have a significant impact on patients' ability to engage in and benefit from other treatments.

Assessment of offending behaviour needs and risk

The assessment and formulation of personality include a formulation of offending behaviour which generally links offending behaviour to personality and core schemas. The initial assessment also includes a baseline assessment of risk, involving a range of static and dynamic measures of risk including the Risk Matrix (RM2000 & RM2000-S) (Hanson & Thornton, 2000), Psychopathy Checklist-Revised (PCL-R) (Hare, 2003) and Violence Risk Scales (VRS & VRS-SO) (Wong & Gordon, 2001; Wong, Olver, Nicholaichuk & Gordon, 2006).

Assessment of responsivity needs

Numerous factors affect the ability of patients with personality disorder to respond effectively to treatment. These include emotional dysregulation, attachment problems, high levels of impulsivity, other psychopathic traits, neurological impairments, ADHD, trauma symptoms and past histories of failure in treatment. An important element of the initial assessment is to identify and anticipate problems that the patient may experience in engaging with treatment, many of which will be apparent during the assessment process, and developing strategies that the patient, together with staff involved in his future treatment, can use to maximize engagement.

Although the initial assessment process generally lasts approximately six months, assessment in the PDS is iterative, with the shared formulation being refined and updated as the patient progresses through the subsequent stages of treatment and their level of insight improves or they become better able to reflect on distressing or shaming developmental or offending experiences and to make sense of them.

Certain parts of the assessment process are repeated at regular intervals throughout the treatment pathway in order to evaluate the effectiveness of specific elements within that pathway. In addition, patients are subject to reviews of key measures of personality and psychological functioning and of risk of offending at the end of each stage of the treatment pathway and at three-yearly intervals throughout their time in the PDS. (Further details of the assessment stage of the treatment pathway can be found in this volume, Chapter 4.)

Stage 2: Motivation and therapy interference needs

Personality disordered patients are known to present particular problems in therapeutic processes. Key issues are problems in engaging consistently, fluctuating motivation and therapy interfering behaviours (Linehan, 1993a). Most of our patients have attempted to engage in psychological interventions prior to arriving in the service, but have dropped out or failed to benefit. Others have been excluded from services because they are seen as untreatable. Despite wanting to change at a basic level, many have limited confidence in their psychological processes or in their ability to change.

Studies examining therapy drop-out have indicated several causal factors, including poor interpersonal skills, an inability to form alliances with others, 'feedback overload', breaches of norms (e.g., confidentiality) and unrealistic expectations of therapy (Dishion, McCord & Poulin, 1999; Lieberman, 1994; Roback & Smith, 1987). Roback (2000) made a number of recommendations to reduce attrition rates, many of which are addressed within these programmes.

A review of motivational interviewing with offenders to improve motivation for change and engagement in treatment (McMurran, 2009) indicated that it can lead to improved retention in treatment, enhanced motivation to change and reduced offending. The trans-theoretical model of change (Prochaska & DiClemente, 1984) has been applied to a number of relevant patient populations, including violent offenders (Williamson, Day, Howells, Bubner & Jauncey, 2003), mentally disordered offenders (McMurran, Tyler, Hogue, Cooper, Dunseath & McDaid, 1998) and sex offenders (Tierney & McCabe, 2001). All three studies demonstrated that the model has some validity with these populations.

Most research on psycho-educational approaches has come from work with psychotic illness and there has been a relative lack of interest in the needs of personality disordered patients, although Schultz, Schultz, Hamer & Resnick (1985) demonstrated that patients with borderline and schizotypal symptoms know relatively little about their disorders. Despite the lack of research evidence, many clinicians advocate psycho-educational input to promote awareness and motivation for treatment. Lesquene & Hersh (2004) outlined the arguments for and against, and concluded in favour of education for patients with personality disorder. Colom, Vieta, Sánchez-Moreno, Martínez-Arán, Torrent, Reinares, Goikolea, Benabarre & Comes (2004) found that psycho-education increased the time to relapse and decreased the number of hospitalized days in patients with comorbid personality disorder and bipolar disorder.

Poor social problem-solving skills appear to be linked to criminal behaviours in mentally disordered offenders (McMurran, Egan, Blair & Richardson, 2001). Social problem-solving skills programmes have been employed in correctional settings where they were aimed at and have been successful in reducing offending (Landenburger & Lipsey, 2005; Tong & Farrington, 2006; Wilson *et al.*, 2005). The Stop and Think Programme (McMurran, Egan & Duggan, 2005) is one such programme and has been shown to be effective in increasing and maintaining social problem-solving skills with male forensic personality disordered patients (McMurran, Fyffe, McCarthy, Duggan & Latham, 2006).

A key feature of these initial treatment programmes is that they allow patients to feel safe and contained. The programmes are all highly structured so that patients know in advance what format and style the sessions will take. They tend to be didactic in nature, primarily comprising the teaching of new skills or the facilitation of thinking about experiences in a new way, and they demand a low but slowly increasing level of personal disclosure. A problem-solving approach is taken to the difficulties experienced by patients participating in the programmes and high levels of support are available to patients if required.

Details of the treatment programmes in the motivation and therapy interference needs stage of the treatment pathway can be found in appendix 5.1.

Stage 3: Personality disorder needs

Evidence for the efficacy of treatments to address personality disorder by modifying dysfunctional cognitions, behaviours and emotions is increasing. Whilst this research has mostly been undertaken with borderline personality disorder patients in community settings, adaptations can be made to suit male forensic inpatients (Bateman & Tyrer, 2004; Davidson 2008; Duggan *et al.*, 2008; Leichsenring & Leibling, 2003; Perry *et al.*, 1999; Roth & Fonagy, 2004; Shea, 1993). Several treatments show promise in this area, but it is not yet possible to determine which are the most efficacious. The PDS treatment pathway includes two such therapies: dialectical behaviour therapy (DBT) and schema therapy (ST).

These programmes focus on behavioural, affective and cognitive patterns linked to the personality structure, targeting specific areas of need and work to implement new skills, modify cognitive structures and validate existing strengths. Much of the work is undertaken through the management of therapy interfering behaviour and the development of a strong therapeutic alliance.

Two randomized controlled trials have indicated that DBT is more effective than treatment-as-usual and these benefits were maintained over a 12-month period. DBT seemed to have positive effects on therapy engagement, parasuicidal acts, length of hospitalization, anger and psychiatric symptoms (Linehan, Armstrong, Suarez, Allmon & Heard, 1991; Linehan, Heard & Armstrong, 1993; Linehan, Tutek, Heard & Armstrong, 1994).

Various adaptations have been made to DBT to treat different patient populations, including inpatients, British patients, substance-dependent women, and male and female forensic patients (Barley, Buie, Peterson, Hollingsworth, Griva, Hickerson, Lawson & Bailey, 1993; Evershed, Tennant, Boomer, Rees, Barkham & Watson, 2003; Linehan, Schmidt, Dimeff, Kanter, Craft, Comtois & Recknor, 1999; Low, Jones, Duggan, Power & McLeod, 2001; Springer, Lohr, Burchel & Silk, 1996). Generally, results have been encouraging and support the value of DBT in treating patients with borderline personality disorder.

A recent multi-centre trial in the Netherlands found that ST led to recovery from borderline personality disorder in about half the sample, with two-thirds experiencing a clinically significant improvement (Giesen-Bloo, van Dyck, Spinhoven, Tilburg, van, Dirksen, van Asselt, Kremers, Nadort & Arntz, 2006). Group-based ST has also been found to be an effective treatment for borderline personality disorder compared to treatment-as-usual (Farrell, Shaw & Webber, 2009). Within forensic populations, two trials are being conducted at Ashworth Hospital (Dolan, Doyle, Cooper & Povey, 2005) and secure forensic services across the Netherlands (Bernstein, 2008).

The pathway also includes treatment for trauma in the form of eye movement desensitization reprogramming (EMDR) for trauma. There is evidence to link adverse life-events to later personality disorder, in particular, family dysfunction, trauma, emotional, physical and sexual abuse (Paris, 1997). Livesley (2003) presents a model of how these adverse experiences affect the different components of personality. He proposes three factors which appear important in the development of dysfunctional personality traits: (i) traumatic memories affect the way the survivor feels about himself and lead to conflicting future relationships; (ii) the experience of trauma leads to chronic symptoms, including re-experiencing and intrusive symptoms, rumination, hyper-vigilance, anger, anxiety and avoidant behaviours; (iii) repeated exposure to adversity affects the patient's core schemas, which in turn impact on interpersonal behaviour and the way they are expressed, and emotion regulation.

EMDR was developed by Shapiro (1989). It is based on a theoretical model which hypothesizes that dysfunctional intrusions, emotions and physical sensations experienced by trauma patients are due to the faulty storage of the traumatic event in the memory. EMDR stimulates information-processing systems which help to assimilate the memory in an adaptive way (Shapiro, 2001). Various meta-analyses have been conducted to examine the effectiveness of EMDR and all support its efficacy (Foa, Keane & Friedman, 2000; National Collaborating Centre for Mental Health, 2005; Van Etten & Taylor, 1998).

Details of the treatment programmes in the personality disorder needs stage of the treatment pathway can be found in appendix 5.2.

Stage 4: Criminogenic and offence-related needs

Our patient group clearly requires offence-based treatments to reduce risk, but standard criminogenic treatments generally target a narrow range of targets, focusing on the cognitive, emotional and behavioural patterns that precede offending without any understanding of how and where those patterns developed. Generally, they do not work as well with high risk patients (Mann, 2006). However, if offending is seen as a manifestation of personality disorder, a broader range of treatment targets is implied – a spectrum of maladaptive personality traits that influence many different areas of cognitive, affective and interpersonal functioning.

Our offending programmes have a broader focus, addressing a wider range of targets which may be related to risk. This is consistent with the 'good lives' approach to treatment (Ward & Brown, 2004). This approach also allows the reframing of 'treatment resistance', such as denial, poor motivation or offence paralleling behaviours. Normally these might simply be seen as responsivity issues. With a broader, personality-focused approach, they are treated as expressions of the underlying personality disorder and therefore as important targets for treatment.

The programmes also integrate work from previous programmes in the pathway using schema formulations of offending and including a focus on DBT skills to help patients manage their dysfunctional cognitive, emotional and behavioural patterns. All the programmes provide individual therapy alongside the group programme, and all have a motivational focus.

Much of the evidence for the effectiveness of criminogenic treatments comes from prison services populations. With regard to sex offender treatment, one of a series of evaluation studies carried out by the STEP team (Beckett, Beech, Fisher & Fordham, 1994) revealed that more than half of the total sample showed a treatment effect. The programmes also significantly reduced the extent to which offenders justified their offending and reduced distorted thinking about children and sexuality. Generally, studies have revealed positive, although not always remarkable, effects for treatment (e.g., Alexander, 1999; Hall, 1995; Hanson & Bussière, 1998; Marshall, 1999), including evidence to allow cautious optimism that treatment has been effective, even for the highest risk offenders (Hanson, Gordon, Harris, Marques, Mercy, Quinsey & Seto, 2002; Looman, Abracen & Nicholaichuk, 2000).

With regard to violent offender rehabilitation, over the last 10 years a number of meta-analytical outcome studies suggest that treatment can have a small but significant effect and be cost-effective in terms of reducing recidivism, although much of the data are taken from correctional settings (Hollin, 2002). This and other similar meta-analytic studies also highlighted those components of treatment for violent offending that were most associated with successful programmes: a focus on criminogenic needs; the use of cognitive-behavioural and psycho-educational models of treatment; a focus on skills and multimodal approaches; the importance of the therapeutic alliance; and the use of motivational interviewing techniques. Evidence for the effectiveness of the Violence Reduction Programme (Gordon & Wong, 2000) is based on recidivism rates for a sample of high risk offenders. A treated group had a significantly lower violent reoffending rate when compared to a matched control group (Di Placido, Simon, Witte, Deqiang & Wong, 2006).

A locally developed programme to address substance misuse has been developed. The programme uses motivational interviewing techniques which have been demonstrated to be of particular use with substance users who are less motivated and more oppositional (Miller & Rollnick, 2002). McMurran and Hollin (2003) advocate the use of motivational interviewing in working with mentally disordered offenders, suggesting that motivation for change is the most important determinant of treatment outcome in offender populations. By incorporating motivational interviewing strategies with the Stages of Change model (Prochaska & DiClemente, 1984), an effective treatment model emerges that enables patients to be better matched to their treatment needs. The integration of these two paradigms has a good evidence base across a number of addictive type behaviours and has been demonstrated to be effective in engaging individuals with dual diagnosis and preventing the high attrition rates associated with this population (Pearson, Lipton, Cleland & Yee, 2002).

The programme has cognitive behavioural therapy as its foundation and incorporates a module on relapse prevention. This approach has been shown to be effective in the treatment of those with a mental disorder and comorbid substance misuse (Gossop, Marsden & Stewart, 1999). Overall, there is a paucity of evidence in relation to effective treatment for substance misuse in the mentally disordered offender population and there are no published UK outcome studies to date (Ley & Jeffrey, 2003). However, the evidence does indicate the need for treatment interventions specifically tailored to the needs of people with mental health problems and with a history of substance misuse.

The Arson Treatment Programme is based on a functional analysis and 'adaptive response' model of arson (Jackson, Glass & Hope, 1987). There is substantial evidence that fire-setting, similar to other offending, is determined by multiple interacting variables (Canter & Fritzon, 1998) and that arson offenders constitute a markedly heterogeneous group (Prins, 1995). Canter & Fritzon (1998) demonstrated four distinct themes to arson in terms of offence behaviour and arsonist characteristics, with a significant relationship between the two. It is on these principles that the current programme is based. The research literature on the efficacy of the Arson Treatment Programme is very limited indeed (Canter & Almond, 2002). A small number of studies have found positive outcomes for programmes for juveniles (Franklin, Pucci, Arbabi, Brandt, Wahl & Taheri, 2002).

Details of the treatment programmes in the criminogenic and offence-related needs stage of the treatment pathway can be found in appendix 5.3.

Challenges

Even though most programmes in the pathway are based on cognitive behavioural therapy, they use a variety of concepts and language. In order to integrate the programmes and allow the building of one programme or stage of treatment on those preceding it, staff must fully understand the different concepts and how they relate to each other. In other words, programme facilitators must be expert in all of the treatment programmes. Lead facilitators have therefore been trained in all treatment programmes, and awareness training (including how the programmes relate to each other) is offered to all programme facilitators and core staff. It is also important that patients understand all treatment concepts and how they relate to treatment targets in all stages of the pathway. It is not unusual, therefore, to hear DBT terminology used within schema therapy or schema concepts applied to offending patterns. This is encouraged in the patient group. Nevertheless, the integration of the different concepts and language remains a challenge.

The PDS treatment pathway is based on research and theory regarding the treatment of offenders (McGuire, 1995) and of patients with personality disorder (Duggan *et al.*, 2008). Unfortunately, the research base is inadequate at best. Although the literature is clear that personality disorder can be treated, it is too limited to determine which treatments are most helpful or to allow the development of a comprehensive, empirically-based treatment (Livesley, 2007). Whilst the 'what works' literature for the treatment of offenders is widely accepted, how it applies to the treatment of high risk forensic patients with personality disorder is less clear since there are almost no evaluative studies of this population. Consequently, the validity of the treatment pathway can be challenged. The adaptations to accepted and accredited treatment programmes used within the pathway are also vulnerable to criticism. Although they have been developed from guidance on clinical practice with offender and personality disorder populations, the changes to standard programmes could be seen as undermining treatment integrity. Accordingly, it is crucial that all the programmes within the pathway, and the pathway in its entirety, are subject to rigorous review and evaluation. At present the PDS subjects every programme to an internal annual review of proscribed treatment standards. In addition, every programme participant completes pre- and post-treatment evaluation measures with a view to determining outcome on an individual and a group basis. Even so, it is not always easy to persuade the Ministry of Justice and the parole board (who are more familiar with standard, 'accredited' programmes) that our patients have engaged in valid and effective treatment which can help to reduce their risk.

The pathway was designed to address the core problems exhibited by our patient population, but inevitably it cannot address all their treatment needs. Some can be met through DBT or schema therapy (e.g., generalized anxiety, anger management or depression) or through the offending programmes (e.g., institutional violence, domestic violence or stalking behaviours) if they are related to the treatment targets identified within these programmes. However, where this is not the case, or where the difficulties cannot be addressed through the pathway, patients work individually with a member of the psychology team. Treatment needs addressed in this way have included mental health awareness and coping with Axis I disorders, gambling problems and social phobia. This individualized approach has also been taken to accommodate the treatment needs of patients in the service who have Asperger's syndrome or organic brain damage.

Over the last 10 years there is evidence that the profile of our patient group has changed (see this volume, Chapter 1). It is important, therefore, that the treatment pathway is flexible enough to incorporate the changing needs of the population. Increases in the evidence base surrounding the treatment of risk and personality disorder also need to be incorporated to ensure that the service provides the optimal treatment for patients. Lead facilitators are tasked with amending their programmes in the light of research developments through the annual standards review process. The service also maintains a clinical database, allowing the scores from admission psychometrics to be examined regularly. Nevertheless, it is important for clinicians to remain alert to changes in the research base and in the patient group. This means, however, that the treatment pathway is dynamic and changes over time.

References

Alexander, M. (1999) Sexual offender treatment efficacy revisited. *Sexual Abuse: A Journal of Research and Treatment*, **11**, 101–116.

Andrews, D. A. & Bonta, J. (1998) *The psychology of criminal conduct*, 2nd edition. Cincinnati OH: Anderson Publishing.

Barley, W. D., Buie, S. E., Peterson, E. W., Hollingsworoth, A. S., Griva, M., Hickerson, S. C., Lawson, E. & Bailey, B. J. (1993) Development of an inpatient cognitive-behavioural treatment programme for borderline personality disorder. *Journal of Personality Disorders*, 7, 232–240.

Bateman, A. W. & Tyrer, P. (2004) Psychological treatments for personality disorders. *Advances in Psychiatric Treatment*, **10**, 378–388.

Beckett, R. C., Beech, A. R., Fisher, D. & Fordham, A. S. (1994) *Community based treatment for sex offenders: An evaluation of seven treatment programmes*. London: Home Office.

Beckley, K. A. & Gordon, N. S. (2010) Schema therapy within a high secure setting. In A. Tennant & K Howells (Eds.) *Using time, not doing time: Practitioner perspectives on personality disorder and risk* (pp. 95–110). Chichester: Wiley Blackwell.

Bender, D. S., Dolan, R. T., Skodol, A. E., Sanislow, C. A., Dyck, I. R., McGlashan, T. H., Shea, M. T., Zanarini, M. C., Oldham, J. M. & Gunderson, J. G. (2001) Treatment utilization by patients with personality disorders. *American Journal of Psychiatry*, **158**, 295–302.

Bernstein, D. P. (2008) *RCT of forensic schema therapy in TBS clinics*. Annual fall congress of the Vereniging voor Gedrags en Cognitieve Therapie [Association of Behavior and Cognitive Therapy]. Eindhoven, the Netherlands, November.

Bernstein, D. P., Arntz, A. & de Vos, M. (2007) Schema focused therapy in forensic settings: Theoretical model and recommendations for best clinical practice. *International Journal of Forensic Mental Health*, 6, 169–183.

Blackburn, R. (2000) Treatment or incapacitation? Implications of research on personality disorders for the management of dangerous offenders. *Legal and Criminological Psychology*, **5**, 1–21.

Canter, D. & Almond, A. (2002) The burning issue: research and strategies for reducing arson. Arson Control Forum, August. London: Office of the Deputy Prime Minister.

Canter, D. & Fritzon, K. (1998) Differentiating arsonists: a model of firesetting actions and characteristics. *Legal & Criminological Psychology*, 3, 73–96.

Chapman, T. & Maitland, A. (1995) *Stop think and change: An integrated and progressive programme of change for high risk offenders*. Belfast: Probation Board for Northern Ireland.

Chiesa, M. & Fonagy, P. (2000) Cassel personality disorder study: Methodology and treatment effects. *British Journal of Psychiatry*, **176**, 485–491.

Coid J. W. (1992) DSM III diagnosis in criminal psychopaths: A way forward. *Criminal Behaviour and Mental Health*, **2**, 78–94.

Colom, F., Vieta, E., Sánchez-Moreno, J., Martínez-Arán, A., Torrent, C., Reinares, M., Goikolea, J. M., Benabarre, A. & Comes, M. (2004) Psychoeducation in bipolar patients with comorbid personality disorders. *Bipolar Disorder*, **6**, 294–298.

Davidson, K. (2008) Cognitive-behavioural therapy for personality disorders. *Psychiatry*, 7, 117–120.

Department of Health (2003) *Personality disorder: No longer a diagnosis of exclusion – policy implementation guidance for the development of services for people with personality disorder*. London: Department of Health.

DiFazio, R., Abracen, J. & Looman, J. (2001) Group versus individual treatment of sex offenders: a comparison. *Forum of Corrections Research*, 13, 56–59.

Diguer, L., Barber J. P. & Luborsky, L. (1993) Three concomitants: Personality disorders, psychiatric severity, and outcome of dynamic psychotherapy of major depression. *American Journal of Psychiatry*, 150, 1246–1248.

Di Placido, C., Simon, T., Witte, T., Deqiang, G. & Wong, S. (2006) Treatment of gang members can reduce recidivism and institutional misconduct. *Law and Human Behavior*, 30, 93–114.

Dishion, T., McCord, J. & Poulin, F. (1999) When interventions harm: Peer groups and problem behavior. *American Psychologist*, 54, 755–764.

Dolan, B. (1998) Therapeutic community treatment for severe personality disorders. In T. Millon, E. Simonsen, M. Birket-Smith and R. D. Davis (Eds.) *Psychopathy: Antisocial, criminal and violent behaviour* (pp. 407–430). New York: Guilford Press.

Dolan, M., Doyle, M., Cooper, K. & Povey, A. (2005) Evaluation of schema therapy in a high secure personality disorder service. Paper presented at the International Association of Forensic Mental Health, Melbourne, April.

Duggan, C., Huband, N., Smailagic , N., Ferriter , M. & Adams, C. (2008) The use of psychological treatments for people with personality disorder: A systematic review of randomized controlled trials. *Personality and Mental Health*, 1, 95–125.

Evershed, S., Tennant, A., Boomer, D., Rees, A., Barkham, M. & Watson, A. (2003) Practice-based outcomes of dialectical behaviour therapy (DBT) targeting anger and violence, with male forensic patients: A pragmatic and non-contemporaneous comparison. *Criminal Behaviour & Mental Health*, 13, 198–213.

Farrell, J. M., Shaw, I. A. & Webber, M. A. (2009) A schema-focused approach to group psychotherapy for outpatients with borderline personality disorder: A randomized controlled trial. *Journal of Behaviour Therapy and Experimental Psychiatry*, 40, 317–328.

Foa, E. B., Keane, T. & Friedman, M. (2000) *Effective treatments for PTSD: Practice guidelines from the International Society for Traumatic Stress Studies*. New York: Guilford Press.

Franklin, G. A., Pucci, P. S., Arbabi, S., Brandt, M. M., Wahl, W. L. & Taheri, P. A. (2002) Decreased juvenile arson and firesetting recidivism after implementation of a multidisciplinary prevention program. *Journal of Trauma-Injury Infection & Critical Care*, 53(2), 260–266.

Giesen-Bloo, J., van Dyck, R., Spinhoven, P., van Tilburg, W., Dirksen, C., van Asselt, T., Kremers, I., Nadort, M. & Arntz, A. (2006) Outpatient psychotherapy for borderline personality disorder, randomized trial of schema-focused therapy vs. transference-focused psychotherapy. *Archives of General Psychiatry*, 63, 649–658.

Goldstein, R. B., Powers, S. I., McCusker, J., Lewis, B. F., Bigelow, C. & Mundt, K. A. (1998) Antisocial behavioral syndromes among residential drug abuse treatment clients. *Drug and Alcohol Dependence*, 49, 202–216.

Gordon, A. & Wong, S. (2000) The violence reduction program. Unpublished programme manual.

Gossop, G., Marsden, S. & Stewart, T. W. (1999) Methadone treatment practices and outcome for opiate addicts treated in drug clinics and in general practice: results from the National treatment Outcome Research Study. *British Journal of General Practice*, 49, 31–34.

Gunderson, J. G. (1984) *Borderline personality disorder.* Washington, DC: APA.

Hall, G. C. N. (1995) Sexual offender recidivism revisited: A meta-analysis of recent treatment studies. *Journal of Consulting and Clinical Psychology*, **63**, 802–809.

Hanson, R. K. & Bussière, M. T. (1998) Predicting relapse: A meta-analysis of sexual offender recidivism studies. *Journal of Consulting and Clinical Psychology*, **66**, 348–362.

Hanson, R. K., Gordon, A., Harris, A. J. R., Marques, J. K., Mercy, W., Quinsey, V. L. & Seto, M. C. (2002) First report of the collaborative outcome data project on the effectiveness of psychological treatment for sex offenders. *Sexual Abuse: A Journal of Research and Treatment*, **14**, 169–194.

Hanson, R. K. & Thornton, D. (2000) Improving risk assessment for sexual offenders: A comparison of three actuarial scales. *Law and Human Behaviour*, **24**, 119–136.

Hare, R. D. (2003) *Manual for the revised psychopathy checklist*, 2nd edition. Toronto: Multi-Health Systems.

Harris, G., Rice, M. & Cormier, C. (1994) Psychopaths: Is a therapeutic community therapeutic? *International Journal of Therapeutic Communities*, **15**, 283–299.

Harty, M., Shaw, J., Thomas, S., Dolan, M., Davies, L., Thornicroft, G., Carlisle, J., Moreno, M., Leese, M., Appleby, L. & Jones, P. (2004) The security, clinical and social needs of patients in high security psychiatric hospitals in England. *Journal of Forensic Psychiatry and Psychology*, **15**, 208–221.

Hollin, C. (1995) The meaning and implications of 'programme integrity'. In J. McGuire (Ed.) *What works: Reducing reoffending – Guidelines from research and practice.* (pp. 195–208). Chichester: Wiley.

Hollin, C. (2002) An overview of offender rehabilitation: Something old, something borrowed, something new. *Australian Psychologist*, **37**, 159–164.

Home Office & Department of Health (1999) *Managing dangerous people with severe personality disorder: proposals for policy development.* London: DoH.

Horvath, A. O. & Bedi, R. P. (2002) The therapeutic alliance. In J. C. Norcross (Ed.) *Psychotherapy relationships that work: Therapist relational contributions to effective psychotherapy* (pp. 37–70). New York: Oxford University Press.

Jackson, H. F., Glass, C. & Hope, S. (1987) A functional analysis of recidivist arson. *British Journal of Clinical Psychology*, **26**, 175–185.

Jones, L. (2009) Working with sex offenders with personality disorder diagnoses. In A. R. Beech, L. A. Craig & K. D. Browne (Eds.) *Assessment and treatment of sex offenders: A handbook* (pp. 409–430). Chichester: Wiley.

Landenburger, N. A. & Lipsey, M. W. (2005) The positive effects of cognitive-behavioral treatment programs for offenders: a meta-analysis of factors associated with effective treatment. *Journal of Experimental Criminology*, **1**, 451–476.

Leese, M., Thornicroft, G., Shaw, J., Thomas, S., Mohan, R., Harty, M. & Dolan, M. (2006) Ethnic differences among patients in high-security psychiatric hospitals in England. *British Journal of Psychiatry*, **188**, 380–385.

Leichsenring, F. & Leibing, E. (2003) The effectiveness of psychodynamic therapy and cognitive behavior therapy in the treatment of personality disorders: A meta-analysis. *American Journal of Psychiatry*, **160**, 1223–1232.

Lequesne, E. R. & Hersh, R. G. (2004) Disclosure of a diagnosis of borderline personality disorder. *Journal of Psychiatric Practice*, **10**, 170–176.

Ley, A. & Jeffery, D. (2003) Cochrane review of treatment outcome studies and its implications for future developments. In H. Graham, A. Copello, M. J. Birchwood & K. T. Mueser (Eds.) *Substance misuse in psychosis: Approaches in treatment and service delivery* (pp. 349–365). Chichester: Wiley.

Ley, A., Jeffrey, D., McLaren, S. & Siegfried, N. (2001) Treatment programmes for people with both severe mental illness and substance misuse. *Cochrane Database of Systematic Reviews*, No. 3.

Lieberman, M. (1994) Growth groups in the 1980s. In A. Fuhriman & G. Burlingame (Eds.) *Handbook of group psychotherapy: an empirical and clinical synthesis.* (pp. 527–558). New York: Wiley.

Linehan, M. M. (1993a) *Cognitive-behavioural treatment of borderline personality disorder.* New York: Guilford Press.

Linehan, M. M. (1993b) *Skills training manual for treating borderline personality disorder.* New York: Guilford Press.

Linehan, M. M., Armstrong, H. E., Suarez, A., Allmon, D. & Heard, H. L. (1991) Cognitive-behavioural treatment of chronically parasuicidal borderline patients. *Archives of General Psychiatry*, **48**, 1060–1064.

Linehan, M. M., Heard, H. L. & Armstrong, H. E. (1993) Naturalistic follow-up of a behavioural treatment of chronically parasuicidal borderline patients. *Archives of General Psychiatry*, **50**, 971–974.

Linehan, M. M., Schmidt, H., Dimeff, L. A., Kanter, J. W., Craft, J. C., Comtois, K. A. & Recknor, K. L. (1999) Dialectical behavior therapy for patients with borderline personality disorder and drug-dependence. *American Journal on Addiction*, **8**, 279–292.

Linehan, M. M., Tutek, D. A., Heard, H. L. & Armstrong, H. E. (1994) Interpersonal outcome of cognitive-behavioural treatment for chronically suicidal borderline patients. *American Journal of Psychiatry*, **151**, 1771–1776.

Lipsey, M. W. (1995) What do we learn from 400 research studies on the effectiveness of treatment with juvenile delinquents? In J. McGuire (Ed.) *What works: Reducing offending – Guidelines from research and practice* (pp. 63–78). Chichester: Wiley.

Livesley, W. J. (2003) *Practical management of personality disorder.* New York: Guilford Press.

Livesley, W. J. (2005) Principles and strategies for treating personality disorder. *Canadian Journal of Psychiatry*, **50**, 442–450.

Livesley, W. J. (2007) The relevance of an integrated approach to the treatment of personality disordered offenders. *Psychology, Crime & Law*, **13**, 27–46.

Looman, J., Abracen, J. & Nicholaichuk, T. P. (2000) Recidivism among high risk treated sex offenders and matched controls. *Journal of Interpersonal Violence*, **15**, 279–290.

Low, G., Jones, D., Duggan, C., Power, M. & McLeod, A. (2001) The treatment of deliberate self-harm in borderline personality disorder using dialectical behaviour therapy: A pilot study in a high security hospital. *Behaviour & Cognitive Psychotherapy*, **29**, 85–92.

Mann, R. (2006) Sex offender therapy in the correctional setting. Presentation given at International Association for the Treatment of Sex Offenders (IATSO), Hamburg, September.

Marshall, W. L. (1999) Current status of North American assessment and treatment programs for sexual offenders. *Journal of Interpersonal Violence*, **14**, 221–239.

McGuire, J. (1995) What works: Reducing reoffending: Guidelines from research and practice. *Criminal Behaviour and Mental Health*, 7, 427–428.

McGuire, J. & Priestley, P. (1995) Reviewing what works past, present and future. In J. McGuire (Ed.) *What works: Reducing reoffending – Guidelines from Research and Practice* (pp. 3–34). Chichester: Wiley.

McMurran, M. (2009) Motivational interviewing with offenders: A systematic review. *Legal and Criminological Psychology*, **14**, 83–100.

McMurran, M., Egan, V., Blair, M. & Richardson, C. (2001) The relationship between social problem-solving and personality in mentally disordered offenders. *Personality and Individual Differences*, **30**, 517–524.

McMurran, M., Egan, V. & Duggan, C. (2005) Stop & think! social problem-solving therapy with personality-disordered offenders. In M. McMurran & J. McGuire (Eds.) *Social problem solving and offending* (pp. 207–220). Chichester: Wiley.

McMurran, M., Fyffe, S., McCarthy, L., Duggan, C. & Latham, A. (2006) Stop & think! Social problem-solving therapy with personality disordered offenders. *Criminal Behaviour and Mental Health*, **11**, 273–285.

McMurran, M. & Hollin, C. (2003) Social problem solving in mentally disordered offenders: a brief report. *Criminal Behaviour and Mental Health*, **2**, 205–207.

McMurran, M., Tyler, P., Hogue, T., Cooper, K., Dunseath, W. & McDaid, D. (1998) Measuring motivation to change in offenders. *Psychology, Crime and Law*, **4**, 43–50.

Miller, W. R. & Rollnick, S. (2002) *Motivational interviewing: Preparing people to change*, 2nd edition. New York: Guilford Press.

National Collaborating Centre for Mental Health (2005) *Post-traumatic stress disorder: The management of PTSD in adults and children in primary and secondary care*. National Clinical Practice Guideline 26. Commissioned by the National Institute for Clinical Excellence. London: Royal College of Psychiatrists & British Psychological Society.

Paris, J. (1997) Childhood trauma as an etiological factor in the personality disorders. *Journal of Personality Disorders*, **11**, 34–49.

Pearson, F. S., Lipton, D. S., Cleland, C. M. & Yee, D. S. (2002) The effects of behavioural/cognitive-behavioural programs on recidivism. *Crime and Delinquency*, **48**, 476–496.

Perry, J. C., Banon, E. & Ianni, F. (1999) Effectiveness of psychotherapy for personality disorders. *American Journal of Psychiatry*, **156**, 1312–1321.

Piper, W. E. & Joyce, A. S. (2001) Psychosocial treatment outcome. In W. J. Livesley (Ed.) *Handbook of personality disorders* (pp. 323–343). New York: Guilford Press.

Porporino, F. & Fabiano, E. (2007) Case managing offenders within a motivational framework. In G. McIvor & P. Raynor (Eds.) *Developments in social work with offenders* (pp. 184–211). London: Jessica Kingsley.

Prins, H. (1995) Classification of fire-setters. *British Journal of Psychiatry*. **166**, 821.

Prochaska, J. O. & DiClemente, C. C. (1984) *The transtheoretical approach: Crossing traditional boundaries of therapy*. Homewood, IL: Dow Jones-Irwin.

Reich, J. H. & Vasile, R. G. (1993). Effect of personality disorder on the treatment outcome of Axis I conditions: An update. *Journal of Nervous and Mental Disease*, **181**, 475–484.

Rice, D. (1997) Psychopaths in special hospitals: treatment and outcome. *British Journal of Psychiatry*, **168**, 99–105.

Roback, H. B. (2000) Adverse outcomes in group psychotherapy: Risk factors, prevention, and research directions. *Journal of Psychotherapy Practice Research*, **9**, 113–122.

Roback, H. B. & Smith, M. (1987) Patient attrition in dynamically oriented treatment groups. *American Journal of Psychiatry*, **144**, 426–431.

Rollnick, S. & Miller, W. R. (1995) What is motivational interviewing? *Behavioural and Cognitive Psychotherapy*, **23**, 325–334.

Roth, A. & Fonagy, P. (2004) *What works for whom?* New York: Guilford Press.

Safran, J. D. & Muran, J. C. (2003). *Negotiating the therapeutic alliance: A relational treatment guide*. New York: Guilford Press.

Schultz, P. M., Schultz, S. C .H., Hamer, R. & Resnick, R. (1985) The impact of borderline and schizotypal personality disorders on patients and their families. *Hospital Community Psychiatry*, **36**, 879–881.

Shapiro, F. (1989) Eye movement desensitization: a new treatment for post-traumatic stress disorder. *Journal of Behavior Therapy and Experimental Psychiatry*, **20**, 211–217.

Shapiro, F. (2001) *Eye movement desensitization and reprocessing: Basic principles, protocols, and procedures*, 2nd edition. New York: Guilford Press.

Shea, M T (1993) Psychosocial treatment of personality disorders. *Journal of Personality Disorders*, Suppl. 1, 167–180.

Springer, T., Lohr, N. E., Burchel, H. A. & Silk, K. R. (1996) A preliminary report of short-term cognitive-behavioural group therapy for inpatients with personality disorders. *Journal of Psychotherapy Practice and Research*, **5**, 57–71.

Swaffer, T., Haggett, M. & Oxley, T. (2001) Mentally disordered firesetters: A structured intervention programme. *Clinical Psychology and Psychotherapy*, **8**, 468–475.

Thomas, G. & O'Rourke, S. (2002) *Mental disorder and substance misuse treatment manual*. Nottingham: Nottinghamshire Healthcare Trust.

Thomas, S., Leese, M., Dolan, M., Harty, M., Shaw, J., Middleton, H., Carlisle, J., Davies, L., Thornicroft, G. & Appleby, L. (2004) The individual needs of patients in high secure psychiatric hospitals in England. *Journal of Forensic Psychiatry & Psychology*, **15**, 222–243.

Tierney, D. W. & McCabe, M. P. (2001) The validity of the transtheoretical model of behaviour change to investigate motivation to change among child molesters. *Clinical Psychology and Psychotherapy*, **8**, 176–190.

Tong, L. S. J. & Farrington, D. P. (2006) How effective is the 'Reasoning and Rehabilitation' programme in reducing reoffending? A meta-analysis of evaluations in four countries. *Psychology, Crime & Law*, **12**, 3–24.

Tucker, M. & Oei, T. P. S. (2007) Is group more cost effective than individual cognitive behaviour therapy? The evidence is not solid yet. *Behavioural and Cognitive Psychotherapy*, **35**, 77–91.

Van Etten, M. L. & Taylor, S. (1998) Comparative efficacy of treatments for post-traumatic stress disorder: A meta-analysis. *Clinical Psychology and Psychotherapy*, **5**, 126–145.

Van Voorhis, P., Spruance, L. M., Ritchey, P. N., Listwan, S. W. & Seabrook, R. (2004) The Georgia cognitive skills experiment: A replication of reasoning and rehabilitation. *Criminal Justice and Behaviour*, **31**, 282–305.

Ward, T. & Brown, M. (2004) The Good Lives model and conceptual issues in offender rehabilitation. *Psychology, Crime & Law*, **10**, 243–257.

Ward, T. & Maruna, S. (2006) *Rehabilitation (Key ideas in criminology)*. New York: Routledge.

Ward, T. & Stewart, C. (2003) Good lives and the rehabilitation of sexual offenders. In T. Ward, D. R. Laws & S. M. Hudson (Eds.) *Sexual deviance: Issues and controversies* (pp. 21–44).Thousand Oaks, CA: Sage.

Warren, F. & Dolan, B. (1996) Treating the 'untreatable': a therapeutic community is the personality disorder. *International Journal of Therapeutic Communities*, **17**, 205–215.

Williamson, P., Day, A., Howells, K., Bubner, S. & Jauncey, S. (2003) Assessing offender motivation to address problems with anger, *Psychology, Crime and Law*, **9**, 295–307.

Willmot, P. (2009) Sex offender group manual: A rolling treatment programme for patients with a diagnosis of personality disorder. Unpublished. Nottingham: Nottinghamshire Healthcare Trust.

Wilson, D. B., Bouffard, L. A. & MacKenzie, D. L. (2005) A quantitative review of structured, group-oriented, cognitive-behavioral programs for offenders. *Journal of Criminal Justice & Behaviour*, **32**, 172–204.

Wong, S. & Gordon, A. (2001) *The violence risk scale*. Saskatoon: University of Saskatchewan.

Wong, S., Olver, M., Nicholaichuk, T. & Gordon, A. (2006) *Violence risk scale: Sexual offender version*. Saskatoon: University of Saskatchewan.

Young, J. E. (1990) *Cognitive therapy for personality disorders: A schema focused approach.* Sarasota, FL: Professional Resource Exchange.
Young, J. E., Klosko, J. S. & Weishaar, M. E. (2003) *Schema therapy: A practitioner's guide.* New York: Guilford Press.

Appendix 5.1   Treatments addressing motivation and therapy interference needs

Motivational interviewing

The first core input on the treatment pathway occurs on an individual basis and begins with the assessment process. The motivational interviewing approach taken is based on that developed by Rollnick & Miller (1995). Motivational interviewing is not a programme or a set of techniques. Rather, it is an interpersonal style, applied in all dealings with patients when their enthusiasm for change starts to flag. Whilst this style is, in fact, applied throughout patients' stay in the service, there is a clear focus to motivate them to change during the assessment and early treatment stages. There are a number of therapist behaviours characteristic of this approach, including seeking to understand the patient's frame of reference, expressing acceptance and affirmation, eliciting and reinforcing self-motivational statements, working within the patient's readiness to change and affirming the patient's freedom of choice.

Staff use the trans-theoretical model of change (Prochaska & DiClemente, 1984) to guide their input. The model hypothesizes that change occurs in a series of six identifiable stages from 'pre-contemplation' (no wish to change/no recognition of a problem) to 'termination' (change process is complete/no further need to prevent relapse). The model proposes that the content of the therapist input should match the patient's assessed stage of change to maximize therapeutic effect. The motivational approach is not time-limited and continues throughout the patient's stay in the service. However, patients will be encouraged to attend the next series of programmes once they are assessed as having reached the 'contemplation' (intention to change problem behaviour within the next six months) stage of change.

Introduction to the Therapy and Personality Disorder Group

This is the first of the pathway's group programmes, and it is only offered within a closed group setting. Individual sessions are offered to patients who request additional support, although they are not a core part of this programme. The 10–15-week programme is designed for patients who have had little experience, or a negative experience, of psychological treatment. The programme examines and practises therapy 'survival skills', particularly those related to group work, including communication, feedback and cooperation skills, through a variety of activities common to therapeutic groups. The group also contains a short psycho-educational component on the nature of personality disorder. The programme ends with input about the different components of the treatment pathway from each programme's lead clinician. Patients are asked to produce an action plan reflecting their treatment needs to present to their clinical teams as a means of promoting commitment to specific treatments.

Men Talking Group

This programme acts as a pre-therapy group to introduce the experience of a dynamic or process-focused group. It is offered to patients who have not undertaken (or who have had a negative experience of) insight-based therapy before. This group has been adapted from a module in the *Stop, think and change: An integrated and progressive programme of change for high risk offenders* (Chapman & Maitland, 1995). The programme is a guided discussion programme which lasts 10–12 weeks and encourages patients to explore their experiences of being a man and their journey from childhood to adulthood. It looks at the difficulties of trying to live up to a 'masculine image' and how this impacts on others. Again, the programme is only offered in a closed group setting; while individual sessions are offered to patients who request additional support, these are not a core part of this programme.

Stop and Think Programme

The aim of this social problem-solving programme is to change patients' criminogenic thinking. Cognitive skills are taught to enable offenders to react more appropriately to situations that trigger their criminal behaviour. The programme consists of seven steps: orientation; problem definition; goal-setting; generation of alternatives; decision-making; action; and evaluation. Patients are selected using a social problem-solving assessment. The programme is offered in the form of a 10–12-week closed group, with individual sessions offered to patients who request additional support. However, it can be undertaken on an individual basis. The programme also functions as an introduction to the cognitive behavioural style of therapy.

Appendix 5.2   Treatments addressing personality disorder needs

Dialectical Behaviour Therapy

Dialectical behaviour therapy (DBT) (Linehan, 1993a, b) combines weekly skills training in a group setting, with *in vivo* skills practice and individual behavioural psychotherapy. The agenda for the individual session is set by the patient's behaviour since the last session. The treatment is structured and hierarchical in that the treatment targets receiving most attention are those that are most serious (i.e., life-threatening or therapy interfering). As a whole, DBT blends validation and acceptance strategies (e.g., distress tolerance and mindfulness) with change-focused cognitive behavioural therapy, including problem-solving, contingency management, cognitive modification, exposure procedures and skills training.

DBT in the PDS pathway has been adapted in three ways to take account of our population's needs and environment. Many of the men have a tendency to behave violently in addition to engaging in self-harming behaviour. Thus violent behaviour, violent ideation and anger are additional treatment targets and hence individual therapy focuses on violent behaviour as well as self-harm and therapy interfering behaviour in the early stages of therapy. The skills coaching system of telephone consultation has been omitted in favour of ward-based skills coaching. This was seen to be preferable in that it was hoped to produce the same effect (the availability of skills coaching for the patients in times of distress or crisis) without undermining the role of the ward nursing staff. Finally, some minor alterations have been made to the materials used in the skills group to make them more applicable to male inpatients. For example, the original self-soothing lists contained items that were not feasible in a high security environment ('go for a walk') and items that the men felt were 'too female' ('have a facial'). These have been omitted, and more appropriate items have been substituted (e.g., 'watch a football match on TV').

No additional skills are taught, and apart from the extra treatment targets, individual therapy is conducted in the same way as in the original programme. Each patient attends weekly group skills session, offered in a rolling programme, and weekly sessions with an individual therapist. Treatment lasts 12–18 months.

Schema therapy

Schema therapy (ST) (Young, 1990) is an integrative therapy, combining aspects of cognitive, behavioural, psychodynamic (especially object relations), attachment and Gestalt models. It sees the cognitive and behavioural aspects as vital to treatment, as in standard cognitive behavioural treatment, but gives equal weight to emotional change, experiential techniques and the therapeutic relationship. Like cognitive behavioural treatment, it is structured, systematic and specific. It follows a sequence of assessment and treatment procedures. The model outlines specific schemas, coping styles and modes. Perhaps most importantly, it normalizes rather than pathologizes personality disorders in its assumption that everyone has schemas, coping styles and modes; but they are more rigid and extreme in the patients we treat.

ST is based on the premise that personality pathology develops from unmet core emotional needs in childhood, leading to the development of early maladaptive schemas. Young (1990) defines early maladaptive schemas as self-defeating emotional and cognitive patterns that develop early in childhood and are strengthened and elaborated throughout life. Maladaptive behaviours are thought to be driven by schemas. According to the model, schemas are dimensional, that is, they have different levels of severity and pervasiveness. The more severe the schema, the greater number of situations that activate it, the more intense the negative affect and the longer it lasts. Offending behaviour, like self-harm and suicide, can be understood in terms of extreme schema activation.

While schemas are trait-like entities, that is, enduring features of the personality, schema modes are the state-like, changeable manifestations of schemas. Schema modes are defined as 'self-states' which temporarily come to the fore and dominate a person's presentation, and are made up of clusters of schemas and coping strategies. In patients with severe personality disorders, whose personalities are poorly integrated, these states are relatively dissociated from one another. As a result, schema modes can shift rapidly from one state to another.

Key therapeutic strategies are empathic confrontation (validating the development and continued perpetuation of schemas whilst simultaneously confronting the necessity to change) and limited re-parenting (providing what an individual needed but did not get from their parents as children) within the boundaries of the therapy relationship. Imagery work and Gestalt techniques are also used extensively in order to access and work with emotional experiences.

ST is a long-term intervention (2–3 years) and does not subscribe to a fixed protocol for session structure. Following assessment, the emphasis is on psychoeducation regarding the ST model. The focus is then on helping the patient make cognitive and emotional changes to their current situation in order to bolster the 'healthy adult mode' before engaging in more in-depth work regarding the childhood origins of their current difficulties. Finally, the focus is weighted further towards behavioural pattern-breaking and preparing for the ending of therapy.

There are modifications to the phases of therapy for different personality disorder types (Bernstein, Arntz & Vos, 2007; Young *et al.*, 2003). In the PDS the approach has also been adapted for group work (Beckley & Gordon, 2010).

Eye movement desensitization reprocessing

Eye movement desensitization reprocessing (EMDR) (Shapiro, 1989) aims to help patients process traumatic events that cause severe distress. It also works to reduce the distress surrounding the traumatic event so that patients can cope with the once traumatized and emotionally difficult memory. EMDR begins with a detailed history-taking of traumatic experiences, exploring the associated images and memories, triggers, cognitions and emotions. Later sessions involve the patient eliciting specific images to stimulate the traumatic memories, feelings and negative thoughts. Patients are asked to focus on these traumatic images and associations while attending to bilateral physical stimulation. This usually involves eye movements: the therapist holds his fingers about 18 inches from the patient's face and moves them back and forth with the patient tracking the movements. When the memory is brought to mind, the feelings are re-experienced in a new way and the patient is able to achieve the self-knowledge and perspective to allow him to choose his response, rather than feeling powerless. EMDR continues until the traumatic memories and emotions are relieved and the event is associated with more positive thoughts and feelings.

EMDR is a relatively short-term intervention and is often combined with other interventions (usually ST). Sessions last 60–90 minutes depending on the severity of the trauma and other factors. The history-taking is usually completed in a few sessions. In standard EMDR only a few (6–12) sessions are required to reprocess the trauma. For our patients, however, who have generally experienced multiple painful experiences and years of feeling bad about them, treatment can take up to six months.

Appendix 5.3 Treatments addressing criminogenic and offence-related needs

Sex Offender Group

The Sex Offender Group (Willmot, 2009) is offered as a rolling programme with a modular structure that builds on previous stages in the treatment pathway. The emphasis is on patients integrating their learning from previous treatment. After the first module, which is about establishing the group, group members look at their life histories and relate them to their core schemas and personality traits. They then work on their own offence formulations, again linking their offending to core schemas, before looking at other domains of personality functioning that relate to sexual offending – emotion regulation, attachments, sex and intimacy – before finishing with modules on victim empathy and relapse prevention, using a good lives framework. Treatment usually lasts 18–24 months.

The programme utilizes the good lives model, which describes three classes of primary goods: those relating to the body (physiological needs for sex, food, warmth, water, sleep and health); self (autonomy, relatedness and competence); and social life (social support, family life, meaningful work and recreation). Sexual offenders with a personality disorder will, by definition, find it harder than others to achieve these 'primary goods'. It is therefore all the more important that treatment improves their ability to meet these goals. There is often a tension in relapse prevention-based programmes between the therapist's focus on the patient as perpetrator and the patient's perception of himself as a victim with many other problems. This model provides a framework which can integrate offenders' experiences as victims/survivors of abuse with their behaviour as perpetrators of abuse.

The programme involves a number of specific adaptations from standard programmes to meet the particular needs of its target population. The most contentious of these is that the most distressing material (offence disclosures, personal victim empathy work) have been removed from group setting. This reduces the potential distress and risk of disengagement that conducting these activities in the group might cause (Jones, 2009). It also reduces group members' anxieties about breaches of confidentiality and minimizes the risk of group members being retraumatized by others' offence accounts or role plays, or of group members using other group members' offence accounts in their own fantasies. This allows facilitators to use a wider range of activities, such as psychodrama or imagery in offence disclosures.

Violence Reduction Programme

The Violent Reduction Programme (VRP) (Gordon & Wong, 2000) is a highly structured treatment programme that uses a cognitive behavioural approach to effect a reduction in patients' risk of violent reoffending. It was designed for those who are institutionalized because their risk of violence is deemed to be too high for release to the community. It employs multiple therapy modes to target a variety of factors. Behavioural and social learning approaches are used to strengthen pro-social behaviours and attitudes; cognitive behavioural approaches aim to modify pro-violent cognition and behaviours. Risk, need and responsivity principles (Andrews & Bonta, 1998) and the trans-theoretical model of change (Prochaska & DiClemente, 1984) guide therapists and patients in the selection of coping strategies at different stages in the programme.

Individual work supplements the group programme, focusing on motivating patients to stay in therapy and to make changes, the personalization of learning to the individual patient and their offence paralleling behaviours, the generalization of skills to different settings and the reduction of therapy interference. Treatment generally lasts 12–18 months.

Arson Treatment Programme

Although this programme (Swaffer, Haggett & Oxley, 2001) uses a model based on a cognitive behavioural approach, the process within treatment is much more interactive and dynamic. The core group programme runs as four distinct modules: the dangers of fire; skills development; insight and self-awareness; and relapse prevention. The group process is also underpinned by specialized individual work aimed at maintaining motivation and engagement in the programme, and individualizing and personalizing the programme content.

The broad aims of the treatment programme are to encourage responsibility and 'ownership' of offence behaviour and to educate patients about the volatile and dangerous propensities of fire. The development of insight with regard to offence behaviour assists with the identification of individual risk factors related to the setting of fires, and of relapse prevention strategies to reduce risk. Treatment generally lasts 12–18 months.

Substance Misuse Programme

This programme (Thomas & O'Rourke, 2002) works to increase self-awareness in relation to substance misuse and its impact on mental health and lifestyle. The programme aims to empower patients to make informed choices about substance use and misuse. It assists in the identification of risk areas, identifies existing coping strategies and builds new ones, and encourages the practice of skills with particular emphasis on cue exposure and relapse prevention.

The programme employs motivational interviewing techniques incorporating motivational interviewing strategies with the Stages of Change model (Prochaska & DiClemente, 1984), The programme has cognitive behavioural therapy as its foundation and incorporates a module on relapse prevention (again, a CBT-based intervention).

Individual sessions are an integral part of the programme to offer support and personalization of the material, and to maintain motivation and engagement. The programme generally lasts about 12 months.

Section Three

The Therapeutic Relationship

Chapter Six

Attachment Theory and the Therapeutic Relationship in the Treatment of Personality Disorder

Louise Sainsbury

Introduction

Attachment theory is about personality development (e.g., Ainsworth, Blehar, Waters & Wall, 1978; Bowlby, 1977; Grossman, Grossman & Waters, 2005; Main, Kaplan & Cassidy, 1985; Mikulincer & Shaver, 2008). Through empirical studies attachment theory has conceptualized how individuals' emotional, cognitive, behavioural, self and interpersonal systems develop through interactions with the infant's attachment figures, with the primary function of maintaining safety through managed proximity to the attachment figure (Ainsworth *et al.*, 1978; Bowlby, 1973, 1980; Main, Kaplan & Cassidy, 1985). Problems within these systems have been identified as core features of personality disorder (McLemore & Brokaw, 1987; Widiger & Frances, 1985) and are consistent with some of the dynamic risk factors within the risk assessment literature (e.g., emotional control, cognitive distortions, relationship stability, etc.). This could begin to explain the findings that the therapeutic relationship is the strongest predictor of change in psychotherapy (e.g., Martin, Garske & Davis, 2000).

Attachment theory's evidence has been developed in child and adult populations, focusing on both normal and abnormal development. Numerous studies have found high rates of insecure attachment styles in at-risk groups, people with a range of mental health problems, patients with a range of personality disorders (e.g., Patrick, Hobson, Castle, Howard & Maughan, 1994; Van Ijzendoorn, Feldbrugge, Derks, de Ruiterm, Verhagen, Philipse, Van der Staak & Riksen-Walraven, 1997; Fossati, Feeney, Donati, Donini, Novella, Bagnato, Carretta,

Leonardi, Mirabelli & Maffei, 2003) and in forensic mental health and prison populations (e.g., Hudson & Ward, 1997; Van IJzendoorn *et al.*, 1997).

The primary areas of difficulty in personality disorder manifest predominantly within interpersonal relationships. These areas of difficulty pose significant interpersonal challenges to therapists who may find themselves working with individuals intent on sabotaging the therapeutic relationship and rejecting the help being offered (Hinshelwood, 2002). Those working with patients with these problems will have experienced the different ways in which patients dismiss, sabotage or avoid treatment.

Attachment theory is not another psychotherapy; it can be used to understand how and why individuals with insecure attachments and personality disorder relate to others and how to develop a secure attachment relationship – a core factor in treating personality disorder. Attachment theory is beginning to be incorporated into therapies including schema therapy (Young, Klosko & Weishaar, 2003) and psychoanalytic psychotherapy (Holmes, 2001; Wallin, 2007) by focusing on the importance of the therapeutic relationship as the context and method of change. For example, schema therapy has used attachment theory to help us make sense of the interpersonal dynamics at the core of the 'abandonment schema' and in the conceptualization of borderline personality disorder, as well as highlighting the overlap between internal working models and schemas. There has been increasing focus on integrating attachment theory into psychoanalytic (Holmes, 2001) and psychodynamic (Wallin, 2007) psychotherapies, as both emphasize the conceptual similarities between attachment and object relations theory.

In this chapter the focus is on two core aspects of attachment theory: the development of emotional regulation and reflective (thinking) capacity; and their utility in understanding and treating personality disorder.

Summary of attachment patterns

In this section I will summarize the core features of four attachment patterns identified within the clinical research literature in both child and adult studies. The child attachment patterns were identified by Ainsworth and colleagues (1978), using the stranger situation to trigger the attachment system in infants. Three coherent patterns of behaviour in the infants were identified – one secure and two insecure (avoidant and resistant). Subsequently a fourth pattern – disorganized/disoriented – was identified in infants whose behaviour did not fit into any of the other three categories (Main & Soloman, 1990). All the attachment patterns function to maintain contact with the attachment figure, with the insecure attachment patterns arising out of the need to maintain contact with an attachment figure that is rejecting (the avoidant strategy), inconsistent (the ambivalent strategy) or frightening (the disorganized strategy).

Bowlby (1969, 1973, 1980) proposed that infants' early experiences with their attachment figure form the basis of internal working models, which govern how they behave and what they think, feel, want and remember (Main, Kaplan & Cassidy, 1985). Main and colleagues developed the Adult Attachment Interview (AAI) to assess adults' attachment system in relation to their childhood experiences at the level of representation or accessing their attachment internal working models (George, Kaplan & Main, 1984). Using the AAI, which evokes 'states of mind with respect of attachment', Main and colleagues initially found three coherent attachment classifications, which were consistent with Ainsworth's child attachment patterns. The secure-autonomous adult category maps to the secure child category; the dismissing adult category to the avoidant child category; and the preoccupied adult category to the resistant child category. Further consistency was found in that a number of the AAI transcripts did not fit a coherent pattern and were described as 'cannot classify'. Main, Hesse and Kaplan (2005) described this category as having global disorganization throughout the interview and appears consistent with the disorganized/disoriented child category.

Child and adult attachment assessments have been used to research the stability of attachment patterns. Longitudinal studies summarized by Fonagy and colleagues have found that secure versus insecure classifications at 12 months old match analogous AAI classifications in adulthood 68–75% of the time (Fonagy, Gergeleym, Jurist & Target, 2002). Main's original longitudinal study demonstrated a consistency of well over 80% from infancy to age 19 years, when participants with intervening trauma were excluded from the analysis. The intervening trauma in that study was not abuse, but other traumas such as death of a parent, and these tended to change things for the worse (Main, Hesse & Kaplan, 2005). These findings highlight that generally attachment patterns remain stable, but that intervening trauma can change the attachment pattern. In the other direction, marriage to a secure partner or therapy has been found to transform insecure to securely attached adults (Crowell, Treboux & Waters, 2002; Egeland, Jacobvitz & Sroufe, 1988; Levy, Meehan, Kelly, Reyoso, Weber, Clarkin & Kernberg, 2006; Travis, Bliwise, Binder & Horne-Moyer, 2001). Wallin (2007) has described attachment styles as stable patterns not rigid structures.

Secure attachment is characterized by being open to the full range of emotions, combined with open exploration and reflection of the external and internal worlds. Securely attached adults can attend to all their emotions and events and acknowledge the impact and importance of their attachment relationships. They can rely on themselves and on others. A balanced perspective is maintained when talking about painful experiences with their own parents, which reflects their efforts to understand their parents. Main (1991) called the ability both to have the experience and to consider it from different perspectives 'metacognitive monitoring'. It has been further researched and developed by Fonagy and colleagues who use the terms reflective functioning or mentalization (e.g., Fonagy, Steele, Steele, Moran & Higgit, 1991). Reflective functioning is considered the central capacity to enable open, flexible self-monitoring and receptivity to the full range of interpersonal communications, including from one's own infant (i.e., sensitively attuned, as described by Ainsworth *et al.*, 1978), which enables the person to provide a secure base from which their infant can develop reflective functioning. In this situation internal working models include a positive sense of self and positive expectations of acceptance, care and support from others.

Insecure-avoidant attachment style is characterized by exclusion of emotional expression and, at the extreme of the felt experience of emotions,[1] is combined

---

[1] Physiological measures of avoidant infants and dismissing adults highlight the presence of high anxiety when the attachment system is triggered, although not overtly seen in their presentation (Spangler & Grossmann, 1993).

with partial withdrawal from others and over-independence. The infant stops seeking close proximity and maintains a distance proximity with limited explora-tion, in other words they deactivate their attachment system. As this avoidant behaviour does not trigger withdrawal by the typically dismissive attachment figure, a degree of safety is maintained, though at the cost of intimacy and accept-ance by another. Adults with a dismissing attachment style minimize the value or impact of attachment relationships and overemphasize independence, which high-lights their limited capacity for reflective functioning and the defensive exclusion of emotions, not 'knowing' what they feel or others may be feeling. Internal working models include a defensively positive view of self, which protects them from a sense of self that is unlovable, and negative expectations of others' capacity or willingness to care. Detachment from others and from their own feelings func-tions to protect them from their hopelessness about others accepting and caring for them. Those with an insecure dismissive attachment style will typically maintain emotional distance within the therapeutic relationship, often by a combination of avoidant or dismissing interactions that reduce proximity, often leaving the thera-pist feeling unduly demanding and not needed, although within inpatient sessions the patient will often attend all or most of the sessions. This attachment pattern is consistent with avoidant and schizoid personality disorder traits.

Case example: John

John was one of five siblings whose father had left shortly after his birth. His recol-lection of his childhood is sparse and one of his main memories was of being left to look after his one-year-old brother when he was five years old. His brother fell and cut his head and John was punished by his mother for not looking after him. John is very matter of fact when describing this, as he is when describing being thrown out when he was fifteen and living on the streets. He states that he does not have any feelings about this; it just happened. However, he looked paler than usual and his facial expression was somewhat constricted. His time in the hospital was char-acterized by a distant presence on the ward, with occasional verbal aggression.

The insecure preoccupied attachment style is characterized by overwhelming emotions and emotional expression, reduced exploration and a hyper-focus and over-reliance on the attachment figure. People with this attachment style fluctuate between being passive and helpless and being clinging and angrily resistant to their attachment figures, in other words they hyperactivate their attachment system. In childhood, hyperactivating their emotions was necessary to gain the response of an unpredictable and erratic attachment figure, who also discouraged exploration, typically having a preoccupied attachment style themselves. Their overwhelming emotions compromised the development of reflective functioning or capacity to mentalize about themselves or others (Main, 1995, 2000). Internal working models consist of negative expectations of self and conditional expectations of others (e.g., that others are inconsistent in providing care). Those with a preoc-cupied attachment style can present as demanding of the therapist and the thera-pist's time, be emotionally overwhelming and protest when the therapist ends the session or takes annual leave. This pattern of emotions and behaviour will be very familiar to those working with patients with borderline personality disorder.

Case example: Pete

Pete presented as very ambivalently engaged in therapy. He fluctuated between angrily telling me that therapy didn't work, that there was nothing for him out there and that he didn't want to see me; and, often in the same session, saying that I should be more committed to the therapy and should see him several times a week, and berating me for not being more effective. When attempting to work on his severe self-harm, he quickly became focused on how staff had let him down and not done as they had promised. He rigidly 'believed' they were punishing him and struggled to think more flexibly about his and their internal states.

The insecure-disorganized/disoriented style is characterized by a seemingly chaotic mix of approach and avoidance strategies, with approach strategies being inhibited as they are undertaken (e.g., approaching their attachment figure with their head and gaze averted); and include dissociation and bizarre behaviours such as freeze with a trance-like expression and hands in the air. This attachment style is typically associated with unresolved trauma, abusive parents or parents with mental health problems (Main *et al.*, 1985); the parent is either frightening or frightened. In either case, the biologically-driven source of security for the infant is also the source of their fear and thus the infant cannot escape from fear. Dissociation is highly associated with this category, probably as it is the only escape when there is no escape (Putnam, 1992: 173). Furthermore, the experience of a frightening attachment figure is too overwhelming to be integrated and is instead excluded. Internal working models consist of negative beliefs that others harm them or are frightening and that they are worthless. This attachment pattern is consistent with a combination of avoidant, borderline and schizotypal personality disorders.

Case example: Harry

I had just begun individual therapy with Harry, who had a diagnosis of severe personality disorder, including avoidant, borderline and schizoid traits. He frequently dissociated in session, particularly when asked about his feelings. Discussing his childhood experiences was curtailed as he appeared overwhelmed by emotions and would begin picking at his scars. He maintained that he needed to see me and when in the session he appeared lost, fluctuating between not seeming to know what to say and at other times talking rapidly and incoherently, jumping from one current issue to another, without any sense of how to manage these issues.

Insecure attachment styles are adaptations to an attachment figure in order to maintain safety by defensively excluding the aspects of themselves that do not gain an accepting response, either exploration and independence (preoccupied attachment pattern) or intimacy, emotion and dependence (avoidant dismissive attachment pattern). These adaptations or rules are initially developed at the pre-verbal stage of development, and these experiences are registered as implicit relational memories (implicit or procedural memory), which form the basis of insecure internal working models. These implicit memories are about how to be in relationships rather than knowledge of something and are about familiarity rather than recollection. Hence the likelihood that attachment systems are at least partly activated through the similarities of an interaction or situation. As verbal abilities develop, an explicit memory becomes a parallel part of the internal working model (Lyons-Ruth, 1998).

Wallin (2007) has helpfully described a shorthand for attachment strategies: secure individuals both feel and deal with, and are free to connect, explore and reflect. Insecure dismissing individuals do not feel but do deal with, and are not as comfortable in isolation as they present. Insecure preoccupied individuals feel and don't deal with, and have no mind of their own, but feel solely reliant on others, including for their sense of self. Insecure disorganized or unresolved are neither able to feel nor deal with.

These patterns of managing attachment needs, emotional regulation, reflective capacity and internal working models of self and others in interaction provide an understanding of why and what the patient is coping with in their interpersonal relationships. At the extremes this provides an understanding of the development of personality disorder and treatment needs. It also needs to be remembered that these insecure patterns of attachment are attempts to connect with the therapist (and others), though in a highly guarded manner. It is also well to remember that, as Holmes (2001: 21) evocatively wrote, 'what is *felt* is not an attachment bond – still less one that is, say, anxious, avoidant or ambivalent – but a self, problematic or otherwise, in relation to an other.'

The therapeutic relationship as a secure attachment relationship

Within therapy for personality disorder the development of the secure therapeutic relationship is not just a prerequisite or necessary condition, it is the treatment (Linehan, 1993: 514). Being able to experience the therapist as a secure base, to trust, to experience acceptance and emotional containment, to be able to collaborate and protest, and to know the therapist as they are, are the outcome goals of treatment (Eagle & Wolitzky, 2009: 353).

The therapeutic relationship has been conceptualized as a secure base relationship (Ainsworth 1991; Bowlby, 1988) in which the patient can experience a strong and wise other who attempts to understand and contain all aspects of them. Attachment theory provides a framework from which to formulate the patient's interactions with the therapist, based on the assumption that their insecure attachment system is triggered within the therapeutic relationship, as the therapist attempts to know the patient and to help him develop, as a secure parent does. The insecure pattern of relating has the potential to influence the nature of transference and counter transference responses within the therapeutic relationship (Holmes, 2001; Wallin, 2007). Parish and Eagle (2003) have found some evidence for the therapist as a secure base; while Geller and Farber (1993) found evidence for the internalization of the therapist being used to regulate painful affects, assuage feelings of loneliness and facilitate problem-solving and conflict resolution. Farber, Lippert and Nevas (1995) have also highlighted the differences in that the therapeutic relationship has a function that is distinctive and is defined by unique temporal, logistic and ethical boundaries.

There is considerable overlap between parental or secure base behaviours and those aspects of the therapeutic relationship that have been shown to be predictive of a positive outcome in the psychotherapy literature (Brisch, 2002: 76), including the importance of the 'unspoken affective harmony' between patient and therapist and the 'affective climate'. Further aspects identified as crucial to the development of a secure base therapeutic relationship include the therapist providing constancy, availability and sensitivity, being predictably responsive to the needs of the patient, being attuned to the patient's affective world and attending to both verbal and non-verbal material (Farber, Lippert & Nevas, 1995; Leiper & Casares, 2000). Central to this is the therapist's capacity to attune to the patient's underlying emotions and fears, and to contain and communicate about them in order to enable the patient to experience being understood, accurately responded to and thus soothed. In this way a secure base develops. In the longer term the patient internalizes and develops his capacity to emotionally regulate and reflect on himself and others.

The role of the therapist in providing a secure base therapeutic relationship depends on the therapist's state of mind in relation to attachment. Therapists with insecure attachment patterns have been found to have greater difficulty maintaining a strong therapeutic alliance (Sauer, Lopez & Gormley, 2003) and tend to respond to clients less empathically (Rubino, Barker, Roth & Fearon, 2000) and to collude with their insecure attachment style (Dozier, Cue & Barnett, 1994).

The development of an attachment relationship with patients with severe personality disorders is, as one patient eloquently described, 'Like trying to prise a nail out of a plank of wood with a pair of tweezers.' It requires delicate handling of the tweezers, combined with strength and persistence. This is because, from the point of view of the patient with severe personality disorder, seeking to know them is associated with either withdrawal and abandonment or humiliation and abuse.

Furthermore, therapy requires insecure patients to do what they have spent most of their energy not doing: trusting another person with their vulnerability. From an attachment perspective this is not so much a choice, but a response driven implicitly from their insecure internal working models of themselves and others, Thus therapy asks them to do what their first relationships discouraged: to share emotions (dismissing pattern) or to use the relationship to increase independence (preoccupied pattern). Wallin (2007: 245) has described this as a 'rendezvous with an old threat', which triggers their insecure patterns of relating to others.

Initially, the patient responds to the new therapist in the same way as they responded to previous insecure attachment figures. This provides the therapist with firsthand experience of the patient's attachment behaviours.

Case example: Shaun

During the initial months of working with Shaun, he related to me as he did with others, his willingness to engage was distorted through his suspicion, and guardedness, resulting in him being focused on engaging in therapy on his terms, guided by his insecure attachment style, such that he could not talk about aspect of his past that triggered vulnerable emotions. When I raised his potential feelings of hurt, rejection and shame, he reacted with hostility, demanding that I change the subject or he would leave the session.

To repair the impact of damaging early relationships the therapist has the task of deconstructing the patient's established insecure ways of relating to others and, at the same time, facilitating the development of new secure ways of relating to others (Lyons-Ruth, 1999: 582; Dozier & Tyrrell, 1998). The therapeutic relationship must not reinforce their insecure methods of relating, but consistently provide attuned responses; in other words, be inclusive of all aspects of the patient, especially those they have had to exclude to maintain the primary attachment relationship. The therapist must also set limits and provide feedback to enable the patient to experience their emotions and behaviours being contained, which provides the stability to enable them to explore themselves and develop.

Slade (2008) described responding to patients with insecure attachment patterns with 'in style' (the same as the attachment style) or 'out of style' responses (opposite to their attachment style), highlighting that secure therapists respond with a mix of in and out of style, depending on the needs of the patients at different points in therapy. While developing a secure base relationship and when the patient has limited capacity to manage affect, the therapist responds with more in style responses to facilitate engagement. As the therapeutic relationship strengthens the therapist gradually increases the out of style responses, which aim to increase the patient's capacity to tolerate emotions effectively and to begin considering alternative perceptions of themselves and others (Mallinckrodt, Daly & Wang, 2009; Slade, 2008).

Case example: Tom

Working with Tom's persistent denial and blocking any focus on his emotions led to feelings of anxiety about trying to proceed and was highly frustrating. This demonstrated to me the strength of his defence against his painful emotions and the likely frustration he felt in not having his needs met as a child. The therapy process was one of fluctuating between short bursts of focusing on his emotions (out of style responses) and focusing on the aspects of the issues he would talk about. Combined with this, I acknowledged his frustration and anger at my focus on his emotions, as well as explaining why I was focusing on his emotions. This proceeded over many months, with a gradual increase in the amount of time he could remain focused on his painful emotions and a reduction in the intensity of his hostile response when it got past his capacity at that time.

Wallin (2007) has described how a sense of a secure base arises from the therapist's effectiveness in helping the patient to tolerate, modulate and communicate difficult feelings, including the ones that they had to exclude.

Patients' responses to the therapist provide the therapist with the experience of their attachment style. Having knowledge of the patterns of attachment and identifying the patient's state of mind to attachments can provide a tentative indication of the patient's internal working models, defences and what patients may be excluding, suppressing or dissociating. It is important that the therapist is able to contain and not be drawn into repeating 'old experiences' or 'old threats' of withdrawing, punishing or rescuing. This represents the balance of remaining in close enough proximity to provide the secure base, without becoming enmeshed or taking over, which prevents exploration and development. As with the secure parent, it is the reflective capacity of the therapist that maintains or pulls the therapist back into freely thinking about the patient's internal state and what they are struggling with, and how they can respond 'securely' to that.

Case example: Jon

Jon, a patient in individual and group schema therapy with me, had a dismissing attachment style and over the previous two years had been slowly increasing his capacity to experience his emotions and to share them with me. Within the group, the focus was on the importance of relationships and managing reactions to loss in role play. Jon chose to role play managing his reactions to the hypothetical imminent loss of his therapist, choosing myself to play his therapist. At the time I had an uncomfortable feeling that his dismissing attachment style was going to escalate, possibly in response to the increasing openness, almost feeling like an 'interpersonal' extinction burst. In the role play he was supposed to be practising openly communicating his feelings of loss. He focused on dismissing the importance of the therapeutic relationship in a hostile manner and vociferously denying his attachment to the therapist, blocking my attempts to acknowledge the difficulties of attachments, as well the attempts of the group after the role play. I felt considerable annoyance and frustration, as well as inadequacy and being punished. In the following individual session he initially maintained there was nothing significant about that role play. In response to my persistence in focusing on the role play he withdrew, refusing to acknowledge any difficulties and then remained silent with an averted gaze for the remainder of the session, but not leaving early (very similar to the avoidant infant who focuses solely on toys, showing limited exploration when the attachment system is activated in the stranger situation).

The next session was after the Christmas break, during which time his previously increased engagement with the ward staff was maintained. During the break I had gained some emotional distance from the role play and subsequent session, and recalled the extent to which his experience of attachment figures was about rejection and abuse and how he could not be angry with his mother for her neglect and lack of protection. I wondered whether I might have been feeling some of what he had felt as a child. In the first session after the break I expressed some of what I had been feeling and that I had been wondering if this was how has felt. He acknowledged his anger both in the role play and in the subsequent session at my persistence, whilst I listened and accepted his anger and acknowledged my persistence.

This session was a turning point in Jon's therapy. It was the first time he had expressed anger directly and it felt like the final test of my safety that allowed him to begin to directly express and reflect on the pain and fear of his childhood.

The threat of pain and loss are key triggers for the activation of the attachment system. In the case described above of the insecure-avoidant attachment style, this involves minimizing needs and problems, making few, if any, requests of the therapist, and the suppression of emotions, whereas those with an insecure preoccupied attachment style exaggerate their emotions, helplessness and problems, demanding that their needs are met and overwhelming the therapist so as not to be forgotten.

Case example: Dan

Dan had been in several inpatient setting, but each time was unable to contain his emotions and reacted with impulsive aggression and self-harm, eventually being transferred to a high security hospital. In my initial session with him, he stated that I was his last hope. Needless to say, this raised some anxiety on my part, with concerns about his expectations and my abilities; and was very effective in gaining my attention.

This is a classic example of a preoccupied attachment strategy, in which the patient's sense of helplessness and fears of independence drove him quickly to place all responsibility for him on his therapist. As the sessions continued it became clear from his behaviours that he was disorganized and unresolved in his state of mind to attachment, verbally approaching me and then veering off in avoidance in the next breath.

A secure attachment does not mean perfect understanding and communication. Disruptions in understanding between the parent and infant are a natural part of the relationship, and it is through tolerating and repairing misunderstandings that the infant develops confidence that these can be resolved and that distress is tolerable and it will end (Beebe & Lachmann, 2002). In this way the infant is able to develop positive beliefs in their ability to influence others and in the responses of others (Tronick, 1989). This is consistent with the view that working through ruptures in the therapeutic relationship is a significant method of change (e.g., Safran & Muran, 2000).

As described by James (this volume, Chapter 10), the constant, regular presence of the therapist who maintains a focus on being present with the patient and all their difficulties and is able to reflect on all their contributions to the relationship provides a sense of safety sufficient for the patient to begin to trust that they can be accepted, which in turn leads to them trusting themselves.

Attachment and affect regulation

Affect regulation is a central difficultly in all personality disorders. Similarly, a core aspect of attachment theory is the regulation of affect, both in developing secure attachment and the secure attachment, leading to the development of an internal capacity to regulate affect (e.g., Fonagy *et al.*, 2002). The primary attachment strategy to regulate affect is to seek proximity to a stronger, wiser other (Main, 1990). In adulthood this can be through actual physical proximity or the evoking of internal representations, including thoughts, memories, sensations or schemas of real attachment figures (Mikulincer & Shaver, 2008).

Affect regulation develops in infancy through the attachment figure's attunement to and acceptance of the infant's emotional expression, and their soothing of the infant's distress and amplification of their positive emotions. This is encoded at an implicit level in procedural memory (Lyons-Ruth, 1999), which forms the basis of their internal working model. Thus the infant learns that she or he can have an impact on others and begins to gain a sense of agency (Fonagy *et al.*, 2002). When the caregiver is not able to meet the infant's emotional needs, the infant will adapt to the insecure caregiver's defensive exclusions with responses that reflect either the avoidant, deactivating emotional strategy or the ambivalent, preoccupied, hyperactivating emotional strategy (Main, 1995).

In therapy with patients with personality disorder the task is to provide the patient with the experience that their affects can be recognized (despite being suppressed or exaggerated) and labelled; and that these affects can be contained by the therapist and thus potentially by the patient. This requires the therapist to adopt a reflective stance and an ability not to be over- or under-whelmed by the patient's emotional dysregulation. It is the therapist's capacity to regulate the patient's affect that initially creates the internal state from which the patient can begin to mentalize or reflect on themselves and others.

Avoidant attachment patterns and the deactivating of emotions

Individuals with an avoidant dismissing attachment have internalized others as rejecting of their emotions and regard these as unacceptable. At a clinical level this is frequently seen in patients with avoidant, schizoid, antisocial and paranoid traits.

Case example: Sam

Sam talked in a monotone about the death of his father when he was seven years old. There was no emotional expression in his voice and his posture appeared frozen. However, there was tension in his face and I had a strong feeling of sadness that was not there moments earlier. I asked him about how he was feeling in the moment, to which he replied 'nothing' and appeared surprised when I described the tension in his face and the sadness I had suddenly felt.

A key part of working with patients who deactivate their emotions is greater attention to subtle changes in their non-verbal behaviours and to the emotions they may evoke in the therapist. The most obvious sign is the lack of acknowledgment or denial of emotions about significant events, as Sam did with the death of his father.

Other patients will give very clear responses that distressing emotions will not be acknowledged by their refusal to discuss events triggering such emotions, sometimes in a hostile and aggressive manner, which has typically been effective in keeping others at a distance.

Case example: Shaun

Shaun continued to maintain emotional distance in therapeutic relationships, which often led to the therapy ending either at his insistence or that of the therapist, due to his refusal to discuss central issues. He defended against triggers for vulnerability by responding aggressively. Within individual therapy he initially responded to any comments I made about how painful it must have been being bullied as a child and having no one to turn to, with aggressive denial that he was bullied as he did not let others bully him. Despite his sometimes hostile responses, I continued to include a focus on his difficulties in acknowledging past feelings of vulnerability, each time warning him that I was going to raise this and not taking him by surprise, as the bullies had. Over the course of many months, as we progressed in discussing his emotions, his ability to reflect on his difficulties in allowing him to experience and acknowledge a range of emotions increased and he began to acknowledge past feelings of vulnerability. As this occurred there was a corresponding reduction in his hostile outbursts on the ward. Within the therapy I ensured there was room for his emotions, something his past attachment figures were unable to do.

The ending of therapy and the therapeutic relationship will trigger past experiences of loss. Patients with a dismissing attachment style can try to avoid the feelings of loss in a variety of ways. One patient described that when his previous therapist raised the need to start planning for the end of the therapy, he told the therapist that it was better to end it with this session and he refused to see him again, so as to avoid having to say goodbye and the loss this entailed. Trying to block premature ending by dismissing patients is difficult, given their tendency to withdraw. Exploring previous endings prior to the end of the therapeutic relationship has proved useful in having a distanced ending experience to work through, as well as highlighting potential ending issues early.

Case example: Michael

I was the third psychologist in seven years to work with Michael. His previous two psychologists had left due to pregnancy in one case and the end of a temporary contract in the other, which meant he had concrete evidence that he was not rejected on these occasions, yet he also used this to deny that the endings triggered any feelings of loss or abandonment, both of which were prevalent in his history. I remained aware of the potential for him to avoid reflecting on the ending of this therapeutic relationship as he had done with his other therapists. Much of the work relating to endings was focused on encouraging him to talk about his emotions about his previous psychologist, who was now working in different parts of the hospital. This provided him with a semi-distance means of allowing them to know how he felt about them. At this point he raised his likely avoidance of discussing the ending of this therapeutic relationship. This felt as if he was reminding me to not let him avoid. The ending of his therapeutic relationship was decided by his being referred to medium security and, possibly for the first time, a relationship was ending for 'natural' and positive reasons. We discussed the process of ending and he wrote a therapeutic ending letter, in which he noted that he needed my persistence to be able to make the changes he had and he commented on his determination to not avoid saying how important this therapeutic relationship was to him.

Preoccupied attachment and the hyperactivating of emotions

Individuals with ambivalent preoccupied attachment have internalized that others are unpredictable and not attuned to their emotions and that increasing the intensity of their emotions is likely to get others' attention. However, this does not meet their needs effectively as the hyperactivation of their emotions prevents them from developing mutual relationships and autonomy (Wallin, 2007). This is consistent with the extreme displays of affect common in borderline personality disorder, whose function has been hypothesized as gaining a helpful response from an unhelpful environment (Linehan, 1993). As Wallin (2007: 205) described, patients with hyperactivating emotions 'need us neither to write off their emotions as manipulation and not be knocked off centre by them. We have to make room for their protest – tears and anger – without ratifying their sense that, on their own, they are helpless.'

In adulthood the hyperactivation of emotions frequently has the opposite effect, with others distancing themselves, finding these extreme displays of emotion as false and exhausting, especially when part of a helpless response to another crisis. This can happen within inpatient settings where the patient's emotions become seen as superficial and fabricated. This can create a vicious circle, where staff withdraw in the belief that this will discourage the patient's over-the-top expression of emotions and neediness, yet presents as similar to the unpredictable attachment figure so that the patient responds with ever-increasing displays of emotions, their only learnt strategy to gain the support they need. Being able to remain with the patient, acknowledging their emotions and fears and supporting them in managing them themselves with encouragement from staff or their therapist, can break the insecure pattern of hyperactivating emotions.

The fear of loss and rejection for preoccupied patients with personality disorder is often triggered by breaks in sessions and will be familiar to many clinicians. Typically the patient 'protests', as the ambivalent infant protests at her or his attachment figure on their return in the strange situation. This can feel like an exaggeration of their emotions, potentially triggering a misattuned response from the therapist, similar to likely responses from friends and partners unable to cope with the strength of their emotions. Breaks in sessions often trigger fears of abandonment, and the hyperactivating strategy provides the opportunity to work with the patient by connecting with the fears underneath the hyperactivating behaviour and supporting them in regulating their affect. Being able to stay with their emotions and reflecting on the underlying belief that others will not recognize or help soothe their emotions if it is not communicated loudly provides experience that begins to challenge their internal working models.

It is the good-enough capacity of the therapist to be open to the patient's full range of emotions (sometimes only faintly expressed non-verbally) and repeatedly acknowledging or containing these emotions for the patient that provides the experiences that are internalized as beliefs that their emotions are accepted, bearable and understandable. With patients with personality disorders, which include the hyperactivation of emotions to gain an attuned response from others, this can involve many months of 'scraping them off the ceiling' and quickly commenting on quieter expressions of emotions, so they can experience that you will notice 'normal' expressions of emotions and attachment needs.

The importance of holding the knowledge of the severity of the attachment anxiety is crucial in maintaining hope that they will progress, particularly as the patient's insecure internal working models will contain experiences that prevent them from experiencing optimism in themselves or others (see this volume, Chapter 10, for the patient's perspective).

The unthought known, reflective function and mentalization

As described in previous sections, insecure attachments involve excluding that which is not accepted or tolerated, or is actively punished by the caregiver. Thus infants have experiences that are encoded in procedural memory (Lyons-Ruth 1999), but that they cannot develop or integrate. Wallin has highlighted Bollas's (1987, cited in Wallin, 2007: 115) phrase 'the unthought known' as representing that which is experienced and excluded and thus consciously unknown and unavailable to think or talk about. Attempts within therapy to consider potential unknown thoughts are perceived as a threat to the attachment relationship as they were when the patient was an infant.

Mentalization, or reflective functioning, is the hallmark of secure attachments and is compromised in insecure attachments (Fonagy *et al.*, 1991). When not mentalizing about our own and others' mental states it is as if our thoughts, feelings and sensations are reality or facts, rather than representations of reality. Thus we have only a single perspective on our experience, typically driven by our internal working models. When we cannot mentalize we are not able to take a step back to consider what we are thinking and feeling. This limits our ability to regulate our emotions and maintains negative internal working models as potential new information is blocked from awareness. A reduced capacity to mentalize is likely to play a significant role in at least some impulsive behaviours. Mentalization is the capacity to consider that our perspectives and feelings are one of a range of reactions or interpretations of experiences. It is the awareness that our thoughts, feelings and emotions are just our responses and not facts. This enhances our ability to understand and regulate our affects and thus be open to new experiences which can revise our internal working models. The ability to distinguish thoughts as one of a number of possible ways of thinking about something is compromised in personality disorder, underpinning the cognitive distortions and contributing to interpersonal difficulties and transference within the therapeutic relationship.

Bateman and Fonagy (2001, 2004) have developed mentalization-based therapy for borderline personality disorder, and have shown significant positive outcomes. Furthermore, cognitive distortions, or the limited capacity to mentalize, have been identified as a contributing factor in offending and several offending treatment programmes, including Reasoning and Rehabilitation (Ross & Fabiano, 1991) and the Violence Reduction Programme (Gordon & Wong, 2000), aim to increase perspective taking. Reflective capacity can vary along a continuum, with some secure adults showing a lack of reflective capacity only when talking about specific trauma, through to a significantly continuous lack of capacity in personality and dissociative identity disorder.

Fonagy and Bateman (2006) highlighted the relevance of lack of mentalization capacity to borderline personality disorder and as underpinning the central characteristics of the disorder, including affect regulation and cognitive dysregulation. Following neurological research (Bartels & Zeki, 2004) Fonagy and colleagues revised their conceptualization of borderline pathology, and theorized that it is not so much that patients with BPD lack the capacity to mentalize, but that their capacity to mentalize becomes inhibited by the heightened activation of the attachment system (Fonagy & Bateman, 2006). Jurist and Meehan (2009) have highlighted that patients with BPD have developed a hyperactivating attachment system, which is triggered precisely when being able to mentalize would regulate their emotions and reduce their acting-out behaviours. Fonagy and Bateman (2006) suggest that individuals with a constitutional vulnerability and/or a history of neglect or maltreatment in infancy are more likely to react to the trauma by decoupling their capacity to deal with their own and others' mental states comprehensively. Such decoupling may be considered an adaptive response to avoid the distress in the mind of the perpetrator of maltreatment. Thus certain aspects of maltreatment are excluded from consciousness and not integrated, consistent with the unthought known.

Case example: Jack

I had been working with Jack on his difficulties in relating to others and managing his emotions. He was diagnosed with severe personality disorder, with predominant paranoid and borderline traits and a predominantly avoidant attachment style. When trying to reflect on a difficult interaction he would frequently respond to follow-on questions with hostility and repeatedly telling me he didn't know and that I was to stop asking him. With validation of his annoyance at my persistence, he articulated his belief that I wouldn't accept that he didn't know because I thought he was lying. For him this was a fact, not a belief, and initially my

> *explanation that asking him these questions was to help us reflect on his experience had no impact. It felt that the combination of containment of his emotions, explanation and my tentative suggestions as to his feelings over several months provided him with the repeated experience of being thought about in way that made sense and gradually led to an increase in his capacity to mentalize, which further increased his ability to manage his affect.*

Fonagy (2006) identified that what moves people from feeling that their perceptions are facts and into mentalization is an attachment relationship that provides first a full measure of affect regulation and then a modicum of play (or exploration) in the presence of a reflective other – in other words, a secure therapeutic relationship. Within the therapy with Jack, my initial aim was to provide an experience in which I contained and accepted his affects, gave him external affect regulation and sought to understand his feelings, which meant he could experience his feelings being knowable, nameable, shareable and changeable (Wallin, 2007: 146). However, when faced with both the patient's unregulated affect and their non-mentalizing and embedded stance, which underpins their severe personality disorder, there are times when this is an overwhelming demand on the therapist's capacity to mentalize. In Jack's therapy, when he was embedded in his experience, I tried to maintain an awareness of my affect, in particular my frustration at his hostile responses to my attempts to help and to focus my attention on his underlying internal experience and not become solely focused on his manifest dismissing behaviours.

Within a secure therapeutic relationship the therapist provides the patient with a picture of themselves being mirrored back to them. With a secure therapist, what is mirrored back is consistent with the patient's internal state. This enables the patient to experience themselves through another, in which they are accepted and thought about (mentalized), and are not humiliated, attacked or neglected. This is hypothesized to be the process in which their distorted internal working models about themselves and others begin to be developed and thus reduce the extent to which they have to rely on insecure attachment strategies (Lyons-Ruth & the Boston Change Process Study Group, 2001; Main, 1991).

Mentalization can enable people to develop new meaning in old affects. By reflecting on past painful interpersonal experiences within the context of a secure therapeutic relationship patients can come to a new understanding of their past.

Case example: Tom

Tom had been in high security hospital for many years, and having had several therapies, he had presented in the last few years as over-controlled in emotions and behaviour. I was his individual schema therapist and he had been engaged in discussing schemas that were currently relevant to him and how they presently manifest, but he was reluctant to discuss their developmental origins. I was ten minutes late for a session, and following my apology and explanation, Tom appeared tense whilst stating that he accepted my apology and that he understood that I was busy. As the session progressed he became focused on how staff expected patients to do things immediately they are asked and yet staff expected patients to wait for them. He said this in a more terse and distant manner than typical for him when describing annoyances and I wondered whether my lateness and his having to wait was also triggering something else. I asked him whether my lateness, on top of being annoying in itself, was also triggering some old feelings and if there was a double effect on him. He denied this, stating that he had talked about his past many times; he was fine with it. His non-verbal behaviour was tenser. I wondered with him about how tense he appeared and whether his tension also reflected his tension between now having a better relationship with his family and possibly feeling that he was risking the loss of his family again by recalling the abuse and rejection in his childhood. He responded with a sigh and looked tearful (for the first in therapy), he then talked about his family repeatedly arranging a day to come to see him in his early years in a secure psychiatric hospital, then didn't turn up and didn't let him know why; and he would end up ringing them. Tom looked extremely uncomfortable whilst talking about this and stated that he did not like to think about those times now that he has a better relationship with his family. This was the start of several sessions in which he connected with his emotions of his past abuse and rejection by his parents. As he re-experienced and shared his hurt and pain, he began to acknowledge more easily the abusive behaviours and the impact on him, and began to reflect on why his parents acted in that manner from a broader perspective and reduced self-blame.

When Tom talked about his experiences with his mother, it triggered old and current attachment anxiety. This activation of his attachment system reduced his capacity to mentalize about his relationship with his family. This maintained his split feelings that he was bad and needed punishing, and that his family were good, which was further confirmed for him by his index offence. The developing secure therapeutic relationship encouraged Tom to mentalize by modelling through my mentalizing about his anxieties of betraying and losing his family again, which drove his current distance and anger with others. In this way Tom began to integrate his pain and anger towards his family with his happiness at the improved relationships in last few years. As described before, supporting the patient in mentalizing further develops the secure therapeutic relationship. In Tom's case my not excluding aspects of his experience or his family's behaviour towards him may have provided a corrective emotional experience that was encoded in his internal working models of self and others.

Holmes (2009) has argued that mentalization can be easily confused with intellectualization, which can be conceptualized as a defence against, rather than an embracing and regulation of, troubling emotions. Tom's initial arguments for why he did not need to work through his childhood experiences were intellectually coherent. However, in his case it was apparent from the tension and fragility of his non-verbal behaviour and the constriction of his emotions that this was a defensive strategy. With other patients it has been more difficult to distinguish between intellectualization and mentalization.

Case example: Ben

Ben had a diagnosis of avoidant and schizoid personality disorders, and demonstrated an insecure avoidant attachment style and repeated rejections and separations in childhood. He was very quiet on the ward, in ward rounds and in groups, however, in individual sessions he was very talkative and it was very difficult to get a word in, much to my surprise. He spoke about his difficulties with insight. I was struck by the contrast between his presentation in our sessions and elsewhere. I began to be aware that his talkativeness and insight were controlling. His talking a lot reduced the space for me to comment or ask questions and his insight kept me feeling that he was working. As the sessions continued I became increasingly aware of the restricted and controlled nature of his insight. His insight and his talkativeness were initially very effective in distracting me for his lack of emotion. It seemed that he had perfected a way of maintaining his avoidance in situations where more openly avoiding would draw more attention to him. When reflecting with Ben on how he was relating to me, he was aware of reducing my opportunities to explore his experiences further, which he said he did to prevent me getting near the 'really painful stuff' – things that he felt unable to talk about. His strategy of trying to talk about some of his difficult experiences was to prevent his expectation that I would terminate the therapy if he wasn't able to talk about everything. At that point he could not identify an alternative perspective in which I did not reject him.

Lyons-Ruth *et al.* (2001) observed that changes in implicit relational knowing occur primarily as a function of what is enacted in the intersubjective field of patient and therapist and that when the relationship alters, it shifts the patient's sense of who the therapist is, who the patient is to the therapist and who they are to each other. In others words, through implicit and explicit mentalization, patients can reintegrate aspects of themselves and others, which updates their internal working models of self and others.

Case example: Simon

Simon was coming to the end of schema therapy, which had focused on his avoidant personality and attachment pattern. The latter months had focused on his past relationships, their endings and the imminent ending of this relationship. In his therapeutic ending letter to me he described how he had changed for the better, that this had come about because of our therapeutic relationship and how he had come to see me as someone he had needed rather than someone to be very wary of.

These repeated new attachment experiences of the therapist thinking about the patient's internal states extends their internal working model of attachment relationships to include the possibility of closeness without either abuse or abandonment, and with negotiation and reflection. These repeated moments within the therapeutic relationship are examples of what Wallin (2007: 125) has described as a 'moment of meeting that offers the patient a glimpse into new ways of being, beyond the constraints of pre-existing ... implicit relational knowing', or internal working models of attachment.

Conclusions

Attachment theory provides an empirically-driven theory of personality development and specifically of the emotional and cognitive development and interpersonal relationships that are the central features of personality disorder and likely contribute to offending. This extends the understanding of the development of the emotional and cognitive feature of personality disorder, contributing to the treatment of personality disorder, including specifying the functions of the therapeutic relationship in treatment.

References

Ainsworth, M. D. S. (1991) Attachments and other affectional bonds across the life cycle. In C. M. Parkes, J. Stevenson-Hinde & P. Marris (Eds.) *Attachment across the life cycle* (pp. 33–51). New York: Routledge.

Ainsworth, M. D. S., Blehar, M. C., Waters, E. & Wall, S. (1978) *Patterns of attachment: A psychological study of the strange situation.* Hillsdale, NJ: Lawrence Erlbaum.

Bartels, A. & Zeki, S. (2004) The neural correlates of maternal and romantic love. *NeuroImage*, **21**, 1155–1166.

Bateman, A. W. & Fonagy, P. (2001) Treatment for borderline personality disorder with psychoanalytically orientated partial hospitalization: An 18-month follow up. *American Journal of Psychiatry*, **158**, 36–42.

Bateman, A. W. & Fonagy, P. (2004) *Psychotherapy for borderline personality disorder: Mentalization-based treatment.* Oxford: Oxford University Press.

Beebe, B. & Lachmann, F. (2002) *Infant research and adult treatment: Co-constructing interactions.* Hillsdale, NJ: Analytic Press.

Bowlby, J. (1969/1982) *Attachment and loss. Vol. 1, Attachment.* New York: Basic Books.

Bowlby, J. (1973) *Attachment and loss. Vol. 2, Anxiety and anger.* New York: Basic Books.

Bowlby, J. (1977) The making and breaking of affectional bonds: I. Aetiology and psychopathology in the light of attachment theory. *British Journal of Psychiatry*, **130**, 201–210.

Bowlby, J. (1980) *Attachment and loss. Vol. 3, Loss: Sadness and depression.* New York: Basic Books.

Bowlby, J. (1988) *A secure base: Clinical applications of attachment theory.* New York: Routledge.

Brisch, K. H. (2002) *Treating attachment disorders: From theory to therapy.* New York: Guilford Press.

Crowell, J. A., Fraley, R. C. & Shaver, P. R. (2008). Measurement of individual differences in adolescent and adult attachment. In J. Cassidy & P. R. Shaver (Eds.) *Handbook of attachment: Theory, research and clinical applications* (pp. 599–634). New York: Guildford Press.

Crowell, J. A., Treboux, D. & Waters, E. (2002) Stability of attachment representations: The transition to marriage. *Developmental Psychology*, **38**, 467–479.

Dozier, M., Cue, K. & Barnett, L. (1994) Clinician as caregivers: Role of attachment organisation in treatment. *Journal of Consulting and Clinical Psychology*, **62**, 793–800.

Dozier, M. & Tyrrell, C. (1998) The role of attachment in therapeutic relationships. In J. A. Simpson & W. S. Rholes (Eds.) *Attachment theory and close relationships* (pp. 221–248). New York: Guilford Press.

Eagle, M. & Wolitzky, D. L. (2009) Adult psychotherapy from the perspective of attachment theory and psychoanalysis. In J. H. Obegi & E. Berant (Eds.) *Attachment theory and research in clinical work with adults* (pp. 351–378). New York: Guilford Press.

Egeland, B., Jacobvitz, D. & Sroufe, L. A. (1988) Breaking the cycle of abuse. *Child Development*, **59**, 1080–1088.

Farber, B. A., Lippert, R. A. & Nevas, D. B. (1995) The therapist as an attachment figure. *Psychotherapy*, **32**, 204–212.

Fonagy, P. (2006) The mentalization approach to social development. In G. Allen & P. Fonagy (Eds.), *Handbook of mentalization-based treatments* (pp. 53–101). Hoboken, NJ: Wiley.

Fonagy P. & Bateman, A. W. (2006) Mechanisms of change in mentalization-based treatment of BPD. *Journal of Clinical Psychology*, **62**, 411–430.

Fonagy, P., Gergeleym G., Jurist, E. J. & Target, M. I. (2002) *Affect regulation, mentalization and the development of self.* New York: Other Press.

Fonagy, P., Steele, M., Steele, H., Moran, G. S. & Higgit, A. C. (1991) The capacity for understanding mental states: The reflective self in parent and child and its significance for security of attachment. *Infant Mental Health Journal*, **12**, 201–218.

Fossati, A., Feeney, J., Donati, D., Donini, M., Novella, L., Bagnato, M., Carretta, I., Leonardi, B., Mirabelli, S. & Maffei, C. (2003) Personality disorders and adult attachment dimensions in a mixed psychiatric sample: A multivariate study. *The Journal of Nervous and Mental Disease*, **191**, 30–37.

Geller, J. D. & Farber, B. A. (1993) Factors influencing the process of internalisation in psychotherapy. *Psychotherapy Research*, **3**, 166–180.

George, C., Kaplan, N. & Main, M. (1984) Adult attachment interview protocol. Unpublished. University of California, Berkeley.

Gordon, A. & Wong, S. C. P. (2000) Violence reduction program: Facilitator's manual. Unpublished.

Grossman, K. E., Grossman, K. & Waters, E. (Eds.) (2005) *Attachment from infancy to adulthood: The major longitudinal studies.* New York: Guilford Press.

Hinshelwood, R. D. (2002) Abusive help – helping abuse: The psychodynamic impact of severe personality disorder on caring institutions. *Criminal Behaviour and Mental Health*, **12 (2 Suppl)**, S20–S30.

Holmes, J. (2001) *The search for the secure base: Attachment theory and psychotherapy.* New York: Brunner-Routledge.

Holmes, J. (2009) From attachment research to clinical practice: Getting it together. In J. H. Obegi & E. Berant (Eds.) *Attachment theory and research in clinical work with adults* (pp. 490–514). New York: Guilford Press.

Horvath, A. O. & Greenberg, A. S. (1989) Development and validation of the Working Alliance Inventory. *Journal of Counseling Psychology*, **36**, 223–233.

Hudson, S. M. & Ward, T. (1997) Intimacy, loneliness and attachment style in sexual offenders. *Journal of Interpersonal Violence*, **12**, 323–339.

Jurist, E. L. & Meehan, K. B. (2009) Attachment, mentalization and reflective functioning. In J. H. Obegi & E. Berant (Eds.) *Attachment theory and research in clinical work with adults* (pp. 71–93). New York: Guilford Press.

Leiper, R. & Casares, P. (2000) An investigation of the attachment organization of clinical psychologists and its relationship to clinical practice. *British Journal of Medical Psychology*, **74**, 449–464.

Levy, K. N., Meehan, K. B., Kelly, K. M., Reyoso, J. S., Weber, M., Clarkin, J. F. & Kernberg, O. F. (2006) Change in attachment patterns and reflective function in a randomised control trial of transference focused psychotherapy for borderline personality disorder. *Journal of Consulting and Clinical Psychology*, **74**, 1027–1040.

Linehan, M. M. (1993) *Cognitive-behavioural treatment of borderline personality disorder.* New York: Guilford Press.

Lyons-Ruth, K. (1998) Implicit relational knowing: Its role in development and psychoanalytic treatment. *Infant Mental Health Journal*, **19**, 282–289.

Lyons-Ruth, K. (1999) The two-person unconscious: Intersubjective dialogue, enactive relational representation and the emergence of new forms of relational organisation. *Psychoanalytic Inquiry*, **19**, 576–617.

Lyons-Ruth, K. & the Boston Change Process Study Group (2001) The emergence of new experiences: Relational improvisation, recognition process, and non linear change in psychoanalytic psychotherapy. *Psychologist/Psychoanalyst*, **21**, 13–17.

Main, M. (1990) Cross-cultural studies of attachment organisation: Recent studies and, changing methodologies and the concept of conditional strategies. *Human Development*, **33**, 48–61.

Main, M. (1991) Metacognitive knowledge, metacognitive monitoring and singular (coherent) versus multiple (incoherent) models of attachment: Findings and directions for future research. In C. M. Parkes, J. Stevenson-Hinde & P. Marris (Eds.) *Attachment across the life cycle* (pp. 127–159). London: Routledge.

Main, M. (1995) Recent studies in attachment: Overview, with selected implications for clinical work. In S. Goldberg, R. Muir & J. Kerr (Eds.) *Attachment theory: Social, developmental and clinical perspectives* (pp. 407–474). Hillsdale, NJ: Analytic Press.

Main, M. (2000) The organized categories of infant, child and adult attachment: Flexible vs. inflexible attention under attachment-related stress. *Journal of the American Psychoanalytic Association*, **48**, 1055–1096.

Main, M., Hesse, E. & Kaplan, N. (2005) Predictability of attachment behaviour and representational processes. In K. E. Grossman, K. Grossman & E. Waters (Eds.) *Attachment from infancy to adulthood: Lessons from longitudinal studies* (pp. 245–304). New York: Guilford Press.

Main, M., Kaplan, N. & Cassidy, J. (1985) Security in infancy, childhood and adulthood: A move to the level of representation. In I. Bretherton & E. Waters (Eds.) *Growing points of attachment theory and research. Monographs of the Society for Research in Child Development*, **50** (1–2), Serial No. 209, 66–104.

Main, M. & Soloman, J. (1990) Procedures of identifying infants as disorganized/disoriented during the Ainsworth strange situation. In M. Greenberg, D. Cicchetti & E. M. Cummings (Eds.) *Attachment during the preschool years: Theory, research and intervention* (pp. 121–160). Chicago: University of Chicago Press.

Mallinckrodt, B., Daly, K. & Wang, C-C. D. C. (2009) An attachment approach to adult psychotherapy. In J. H. Obegi & E. Berant (Eds.) *Attachment theory and research in clinical work with adults* (pp. 234–268). New York: Guilford Press.

Martin, D. J., Garske, J. P. & Davis, M. K. (2000) Relation of the therapeutic alliance with outcome and other variables: A meta-analytic review. *Journal of Consulting and Clinical Psychology*, **68**, 438–450.

McLemore, C. W. & Brokaw, D. W. (1987) Personality disorders as dysfunctional interpersonal behaviours. *Journal of Personality Disorders*, **1**, 270–285.

Mikulincer, M. & Shaver, P. R. (2008) Adult attachment and affect regulation. In J. Cassidy & P. R. Shaver (Eds.) *Handbook of attachment: Theory, research and clinical applications* (pp. 503–531). New York: Guilford Press.

Modestin, J., Oberson, B. & Erni, T. (1998) Possible antecedents of DSM-III-R personality disorders. *Acta Psychiatrica Scandinavica*, **97**, 260–266.

Parish, M. & Eagle, M. N. (2003) Attachment to the therapist. *Psychoanalytic Psychology*, **20**, 271–286.

Patrick, M., Hobson, P., Castle, D., Howard, R. & Maughan, B. (1994) Personality disorder and the mental representation of early social experience. *Developmental Psychopathology*, **6**, 375–388.

Putnam, F. W. (1992) Discussion: Are alter personalities fragments or figments? *Psychoanalytic Inquiry*, **12**, 95–111.

Ross, R. and Fabiano, E. (1991) *Reasoning and rehabilitation: A handbook for teaching cognitive skills*, Ottawa, Ontario: T3 Associates.

Rubino, G., Barker, C., Roth, T. & Fearon, P. (2000) Therapist empathy and depth of interpretation in response to potential alliance ruptures: The role of the therapist and patient attachment styles. *Psychotherapy Research*, **10**, 408–420.

Safran, J. D. & Muran, J. C. (2000) *Negotiating the therapeutic alliance: A relational treatment guide*. New York: Guilford Press.

Sauer, E. M., Lopez, F. G. & Gormley, B. (2003) Respective contributions of therapist and client adult attachment orientations to the development of the early working alliance: A preliminary growth modeling study. *Psychotherapy Research*, **13**, 371–382.

Slade, A. (2008) The implications of attachment theory and research to adult psychotherapy: Research and clinical perspectives. In J. Cassidy & P. R. Shaver (Eds.) *Handbook of attachment: theory, research and clinical applications* (pp. 762–782). New York: Guilford Press.

Spangler, G. & Grossmann, K. E. (1993) Biobehavioural organisation in securely and insecurely attached infants. *Child Development*, **64**, 1439–1450.

Travis, L. A., Bliwise, N. G., Binder, J. L. & Horne-Moyer, H. L. (2001) Changes in clients' attachment styles over the course of time-limited dynamic psychotherapy. *Psychotherapy: Theory, Research, Practice, Training*, **38**, 149–159.

Tronick, E. (1989) Emotions and emotional communication in infants. *American Psychologist*, **44**, 112–119.

Van IJzendoorn, M. H., Feldbrugge, J. T. T. M., Derks, F. C. H., de Ruiterm, C., Verhagen, M. F. M., Philipse, M. W. G., Van der Staak, C. P. F. & Riksen-Walraven, J. M. A. (1997) Attachment representations of personality-disordered criminal offenders. *American Journal of Orthopsychiatry*, **67**, 449–459.

Wallin, D. J. (2007) *Attachment in psychotherapy*. New York: Guilford Press.

Widiger, T. A. & Frances, A. (1985) The DSM-III personality disorders: Perspectives from psychology. *Archives of General Psychiatry*, **42**, 615–623.

Wong, S. C. P. & Gordon, A. (2000) Violence Reduction Programme. Unpublished.

Young, J. E., Klosko, J. S. & Weishaar, M. E. (2003) *Schema therapy: A practitioner's guide*. New York: Guilford Press.

Chapter Seven

Therapeutic Style and Adapting Approaches to Therapy

Kerry Beckley

Introduction

The aim of this chapter is to outline the principles that underpin our approach to treatment within the Personality Disorder Service (PDS) at Rampton Hospital. The content of this chapter is unashamedly drawn from the 'real-world' experience of working within this setting. At times, what has, in the light of clinical experience, felt to be the most effective course of action has been in contrast to what is purported to be best practice within national guidelines (e.g., National Institute for Health and Clinical Excellence, 2009a, b). My own training as a clinical psychologist has taught me to place value on what is known to be effective, over what is thought to be. Taking the evidence-based stance is undoubtedly a logical one, but it can result in the assumption that the clinical judgement of the practitioner is of limited value. This is something one has to be particularly mindful of when working with populations where the evidence is still emerging.

The question remains as to how practitioners should approach their clinical work. Drawing on literature from both criminal justice and mental health perspectives is undoubtedly useful, but does not provide a definitive framework for practitioners working in forensic personality disorder services. Treatment developed from a criminal justice perspective does not specifically consider personality disorder and is solely focused on offending behaviour and criminogenic need (Dowsett & Craissati, 2008). Perry, Banon and Ianni (1999) argued that effective treatment for personality disorder should include a focus on clear structures, enhancing compliance, clearly differentiating between problem behaviours and interpersonal

Working Positively with Personality Disorder in Secure Settings: A Practitioner's Perspective
Edited by Phil Willmot and Neil Gordon
© 2011 John Wiley & Sons, Ltd.

relationship patterns, be theoretically highly coherent, relatively long term and well integrated with other services to the patient. They also argued that there was little to be gained from seeking to establish the superiority of one model over another as these non-specific factors were more important in determining effectiveness.

The psychotherapy integration movement went a step further in suggesting that there was greater value in selecting techniques and methods from different schools of thought as it was 'clinically wise to do what works' (Goldfried, 2001). Fernandez-Alvarez. Clarkin, del Carmen Salguerio and Critchfield (2006) highlighted the negative influence of a rigid adherence to a theory or technique on the quality of the therapeutic alliance and suggested that it would be more effective for the therapist to concentrate on their clinical experience of a particular presentation. This position, known as technical eclecticism, presents significant challenges to the researcher, but is undoubtedly more representative of the realities of clinical practice as delivered by experienced practitioners working with extremely heterogeneous patient groups. If this stance is accepted, randomized control trials (RCTs) are arguably of limited utility as a stand-alone methodology in establishing an evidence base for personality disordered offenders, given the comorbidity of disorders and significant clinical complexity that exist. Alternative methodologies which promote the value of service user and practitioner experiences (Morgan, 2004) are of particular relevance with this population.

Even within specialist personality disorder services, access to treatment can be variable. Some services have chosen to narrow their admission criteria (e.g., only admitting patients with DSM-IV cluster B personality disorder diagnoses) in order to focus resources for those where there is a more established evidence base (e.g., patients with a diagnosis of borderline personality disorder). The PDS does not have a restricted remit; most patients meet the criteria for several personality disorders and frequently have comorbid mental health difficulties and/or neurological impairment. Our approach, therefore, is to adopt an integrative approach to treatment. Practitioners within our service are trained in a range of treatment approaches in order to most effectively work with such a heterogeneous population. This has enabled us to move beyond our original theoretical orientations as the process of cross-fertilization continues to evolve. This chapter aims to highlight some of the common factors that are accepted principles in our service, and which may aid other practitioners in approaching their work in this field. The case examples used within the chapter are fictitious, but are representative of common issues.

Taking a developmental focus

The importance of focusing on childhood experiences as a way of making sense of personality development is a central tenet of our work. This is inherent in many therapeutic approaches, such as schema focused therapy (SFT) (Young, 1990), cognitive analytic therapy (CAT) (Ryle, 1990) and mentalization based therapy (MBT) (Bateman & Fonagy, 2004). A basic assumption made explicit through the treatment pathway is that the person needs to resolve their own victimization and modify their personality difficulties before offence-focused treatment can be optimally effective. This would suggest that only when the person can accept that the perpetrators of their own abuse are responsible for their actions can they truly accept responsibility for their own victimization of others. This dialectic of 'acceptance and change' is a central theme of psychotherapy with personality disorder (e.g., Linehan, 1993). Standard cognitive behavioural therapy (CBT) is of limited clinical utility in treating personality disorder (Young, 1990) and so it is postulated that offence-focused treatments which are based on such principles will be inadequate as a 'stand-alone' treatment to reduce the risk of recidivism. Providing the person with a narrative about their life that is developmentally coherent helps them to place all of their experiences within a meaningful context. When personality disorder is conceptualized in this way, offending behaviour can be understood as one of a range of behavioural manifestations that are functionally linked to core difficulties in relating to self and others, and are context-dependent.

Management of shame

Taking a developmental focus within the context of a validating and trusting therapeutic relationship enables the person to achieve an adaptive emotional distance from their offending. Models such as SFT and CAT provide the practitioner with formulation tools which place offending behaviour within the context of a personality disorder formulation rather than as a stand-alone behaviour. This has proved to be particularly useful in cases where a high degree of shame and guilt is experienced as a consequence of the person's offending and/or childhood abuse. The importance of reducing shame-inducing activity when managing offenders has been well documented within the restorative justice literature (Ahmed, Harris, Braithwaite & Braithwaite, 2001), but this is often not explicitly considered by services involved in their management and treatment. Focusing on offending behaviour in isolation arguably increases the person's experience of shame and therefore serves to interfere with their ability to engage in interventions designed to reduce their risk of recidivism. Both individual and group interventions can provide powerful opportunities to reduce and manage the effects of shame if the therapeutic alliance is attended to with this explicitly in mind.

Motivation

Patients with personality disorders are commonly regarded as hard to engage, the implicit assumption being that there is something inherent in the individual that makes them resistant to treatment. Such an assumption may be conceptualized as therapy interfering behaviour (Linehan, 1993) on the part of the clinician, as it can result in unhelpful and anti-therapeutic assumptions about the patient. There are a multitude of factors which can present obstacles to effective therapy and a significant number of them arguably reside in the culture of the service and in the practitioners themselves. Having appropriately trained clinicians working in a favourable therapeutic context is likely to result in the majority of patients being motivated for treatment. However, these factors are rarely mentioned within individualistic approaches to assessing motivation. This is not to say that the process of therapy is straightforward. Clearly, the interpersonal difficulties inherent in personality disorder mean that engagement can be challenging. Within the PDS, the clear structure to the treatment pathway, therapeutic optimism and the emphasis placed on the therapeutic relationship are considered key factors to our high levels of engagement and psychological treatment being highly regarded by the majority of patients. The high level of individual motivation undoubtedly has a positive influence upon the wider population.

Practitioners' motivation to facilitate the change process is made explicit though their perseverance in therapy, particularly with those individuals who struggle to maintain therapeutic optimism or who present with significant therapy interfering behaviours. The persistence of the practitioners does not go unnoticed by the patient group (see this volume, Chapter 15 on patients' experiences of therapy). It is extremely unusual for a patient to be considered 'untreatable' and we take the position that failure in treatment is more likely to be attributable to the timing or appropriateness of the intervention. The purpose of therapy is to enhance the person's motivation sufficiently in order for them to achieve in its aims.

This position can be particularly powerful with the patient who feels that he does not deserve help or is incapable of change. Within long-term psychotherapy, it can be frustrating for the therapist when there is little sign of observable change. Gordon (2003) has described working therapeutically in a high secure context as 'swamp work', due to the complex difficulties experienced by the patient group and the uncertain and unpredictable nature of the therapeutic work. It is often the case that, just when the therapist is on the verge of giving up, a glimmer of change is observed, albeit a subtle shift in presentation or an acknowledgement that the therapist is valued. The formal and informal support (see this volume, Chapter 13 on staff supervision) which exists among practitioners contributes in no small way to this capacity to persist, or at times endure the nature of this work, particularly when working with patients who are overtly hostile and denigrating of the therapist.

Case example: Jack

Jack was in his fifties and had spent a decade in high security after a very violent offence and was resigned to spending the rest of his life there. Many therapists had tried to engage him during this time, and were met with hostility and derision, leading them to conclude that he was not amenable to psychological intervention and as such had become 'stuck' in high secure care. He was a man of great intellect and could be very effective in engaging others in meaningless intellectual debates about the futility of treatment and relationships with professionals generally, often resulting in therapists and named nurses withdrawing on the basis that they felt they had no meaningful role to play. However, there was evidence that he gained something from his therapeutic encounters and so it was decided to continue offering him weekly sessions, the only goal being for him to have some form of sustained contact with a member of his clinical team. The absence of an agenda or pressure to 'conform' to what he considered other people's needs enabled Jack to start to shift from his cynical and denigrating stance. Due to his previous reluctance to engage in therapy or psychological assessment he had never really had the opportunity to tell his story. He responded to his therapist's curiosity about his life and was soon bringing photo albums to the sessions and providing increasing amounts of detail

> *about his past life which had been characterized by emotional neglect and inhibition. Over time, he became increasingly able to tolerate 'curious questions' and tentative hypothesizing regarding his personality development and offending behaviour. Jack was never going to be amenable to group intervention and formalized forms of therapy, but the ability to progress with a different approach led to a greater understanding of him being achieved and to him demonstrating the capacity to engage meaningfully with a treating professional, as a consequence of which he was able to achieve a move to lesser security.*

There are clearly times when continuing to work with a patient may be detrimental to either or both parties and there are ethical issues about where to draw the line between working with resistance and imposing unwanted treatment. Persistence needs to be balanced with respecting the wishes of the patient, which often requires a judgement to be made on the part of the practitioner. It is also important that the practitioner is aware of when perseverance may be potentially harmful to themselves and to know when to withdraw.

Case example: Colin

Colin had been working with his therapist for three years and always maintained that he was not prepared to work with another therapist, due to the difficulty he had experienced in developing a meaningful attachment with his current therapist, John. The therapist was torn between continuing to work with him, recognizing that his early childhood experiences had impacted significantly upon his ability to form relationships with others, and encouraging Colin to develop other therapeutic relationships in order to generalize the progress he had made with his current therapist. External influences on the relationship resulted in Colin becoming increasingly demanding and denigrating in his behaviour towards John. This was understood as a consequence of him re-enacting a very difficult relationship with his father, perceiving his therapist's consideration of ending their relationship as abusive. Attempts to resolve this within the relationship were persisted with for a long time, but it was increasingly apparent that John was losing the capacity for therapeutic optimism in the face of Colin's hostility. Although this interaction was understood as Colin's way of maintaining his stance that others would ultimately abandon him, the ferocity with which he engaged in this interpersonal pattern paralleled his offending. He was not able to tolerate trying to make sense of this with another therapist and subsequently disengaged from therapy at that time.

Although this does not appear to be an example of effective therapy, there were many indications that Colin was able to benefit from treatment and it was important that the service as a whole did not become engaged in this difficult interaction with Colin in response to his actions. A period of time away from therapy could prove useful to Colin for him to reflect on what he has achieved and also what he hopes to continue to achieve with another therapist.

The therapeutic alliance

Within the personality disorder literature, it is generally accepted that the therapist needs to be relatively active within therapy, providing a structure that makes sense to both parties and setting limits in an attempt to contain maladaptive behaviours (e.g., Benjamin & Karpiak, 2002; Linehan, 1993). It has also been demonstrated that the alliance is a key indicator of treatment outcome (Horvath, 2001) and that it is likely to be most difficult to achieve when the patient has more severe difficulties. Although establishing relationships with those who are considered to have a severe personality disorder can be challenging, this is not always the case. While the extent to which this is attributable to the containment of the environment or the expertise of the practitioner is not clear, both are likely to contribute significantly to successful alliance-building.

Goals of therapy

As with other clinical populations (e.g., Tryon & Winograd, 2002), a clear understanding of the goals of therapy is crucial when working with patients with a diagnosis of personality disorder. All too commonly there are well-meaning attempts to engage patients in more effective ways of coping in the absence of a functional understanding of the behaviour. Approaches such as dialectical behaviour therapy (DBT) (Linehan, 2003) have been shown to be effective in achieving behaviour change within the context of weekly chain analysis, which requires the patient to examine their own cycles of behaviour in great detail. DBT is also very useful in providing a hierarchy of goals (targeting life-threatening, therapy interfering and quality of life interfering behaviours in order of importance) that make explicit to the patient how and why the session will be structured. Although it may be necessary to structure the initial goals of therapy where life-threatening behaviours are present, it is important not to make assumptions regarding their quality of life goals. It may be that the person does not want to achieve future release, but wants to be able to establish and maintain a positive relationship with another person, who may be their therapist. For some, being able to construct a narrative regarding their life in order to make sense of their actions is enough. Making incorrect assumptions regarding the individual's goals is likely to result in disengagement and hopelessness for both patient and therapist. However, it is also imperative that the patient's expressed goals are not simply taken at face value or assumed to remain static, as the process of therapy is likely to impact on their ability to evaluate the future.

Caring for the patient

Emotional connectedness to the patient's experience is a key feature of effective therapy. The therapist's capacity to be empathic has been found to have a stronger impact on outcome than the therapeutic alliance itself (Bohart, Elliott, Greenberg & Watson, 2002). Positive regard has been demonstrated to have a similarly important role on retention in therapy (Farber & Lane, 2002), which is of particular importance in the longer-term treatment timeframe for this population (Smith, Barrett, Benjamin & Barber, 2006). Most therapeutic approaches to personality disorder are explicit about the importance of these factors in both developing and maintaining the alliance, but their direct impact on risk reduction in offenders has been a neglected area within the research. SFT is a core personality disorder treatment within our service and 'limited reparenting', where the therapist provides corrective emotional experiences, within appropriate boundaries, for adverse early attachment experiences, is a key element and aims to provide a more active experience of being cared for. The more damaging negative experiences the person has experienced, the greater the sense of defectiveness and mistrust of others they often hold and so the harder the therapist has to work in order for the patient to truly experience feeling accepted or validated. Clearly this approach would be in direct conflict with certain psychodynamic approaches in particular, but SFT has been found to be significantly more effective in treating patients with borderline personality disorder than transference-focused therapy (Giesen-Bloo, van Dyck, Spinhoven, van Tilburg, Dirksen, van Asselt, Kremers, Nardort & Arntz, 2006).

Difficulties in caring for the patient are exacerbated by both the negative characteristics of the individual which have contributed to their offending (e.g., sense of entitlement, hostility or sadism), their behaviour towards the therapist at times and their offending history. Therapeutic approaches such as SFT and CAT assist in providing a degree of separation between the person and their behaviour, and can provide a forum in which genuine warmth and concern for the patient can be experienced. Effective therapy will prove difficult when the therapist cannot find the patient likeable or worthwhile and, although this is a relatively rare occurrence within our service, it would be reason enough for that therapist to consider not commencing or continuing in therapy with them.

Limited self-disclosure

Self-disclosure is a controversial issue within the general clinical literature but particularly within forensic services. Barrett and Berman (2001) found that self-disclosure was related to lower levels of client distress (in a non-personality disordered sample), although such disclosures were relatively infrequent within sessions. Limited self-disclosure is encouraged to be used by those who have an understanding of how and why it can be used effectively. For example, it has an explicit place within certain treatment models which have been adapted for use within the service (Beckley & Gordon, 2010). Clinical experience would suggest that it is helpful for a number of reasons; as a way of minimizing the power imbalance within therapy, in providing individuals with a sense of being trusted and to provide a more 'normal' experience of human relationships. It also enables the therapist to model being 'imperfect' by acknowledging her/his own mistakes and vulnerabilities.

It is important to note that such self-disclosures should be: (i) relevant to session content; (ii) generally more emotion-focused than information-giving; (iii) in no way contrary to security policies; and (iv) discussed within clinical supervision. Our experience of using disclosure in this way has been really positive and is seen as something which Norcross (2002) concludes is 'probably effective'. Limited self-disclosure should not exclude genuine expressions of disapproval or shock at the person's antisocial behaviours and attitudes. This can be a particularly effective strategy at the point when the patient is able to both believe in and value their therapist's regard for them. Again, care needs to be taken in how and when this is utilized, but it can be effective in getting the individual to re-evaluate aspects of their presentation in a more emotive way. SFT would use this within the context of 'empathic confrontation' where the therapist is rejecting of a particular behaviour whilst caring for the person, for example:

> *Although I understand that you are feeling really vulnerable right now, it is difficult for me to be able to support you in feeling safer when you are talking to me in such a demeaning way as I am noticing my own reaction of anger. I need you to stop putting me down so we can focus on helping you deal with the hurt you feel by your sister not wanting contact right now.*

Self-disclosure in this example aims to increase the patient's understanding of the impact of their behaviour on the therapist at the same time as conveying an understanding of why they are acting in this way.

Delivery of treatment

It is not uncommon in forensic settings for group work to be regarded as 'superior' to individual work, the implicit or sometimes explicit message being that individual therapy is not as effective in addressing the needs of this population. This has stemmed from the predominance of group-based interventions within the prison service. One might assume that many of our patients represent the 'unsuccessful' within prison service statistics due to the nature or extent of their personality problems. Therefore, trying to recreate the same treatment for this population would seem likely to be ineffective, or worse, harmful.

Dealing with clinical heterogeneity brings with it both opportunities and challenges to delivering therapeutic interventions. A combination of group and individual therapy is considered best practice with personality disordered populations (Livesley, 2003) and our treatment pathway incorporates both modalities. However, it is not uncommon for patients to undertake part or all of their treatment on an individual basis if this is considered appropriate. This may be due to patient choice in some circumstances, known difficulties for the person in engaging in group work at a point in time or issues related to treatment delivery (e.g., a long delay before the start of the next group). All of these factors are valid in certain circumstances but can increase the practitioner's workload.

One way in which this challenge has been met is to incorporate a wider range of staff into treatment delivery. Nursing staff make up part of all group facilitator teams and are selected on the basis of their suitability to deliver different interventions. Core group therapy skills are required by all and training is offered to assist the development of these skills. New facilitators take an observer role initially and will contribute more as their confidence and expertise develop. Some groups require external training (e.g., DBT, SFT) and there is the opportunity for those who are committed and capable to develop a particular expertise in an approach. For some, there will be a limit to the role they can take due to the requirement for core therapy training and qualifications (e.g., SFT), but this usually impacts on individual therapy more than group facilitation.

There are wider benefits for the service in utilizing nursing staff and/or other professionals in group facilitation. These individuals are able to engage in continuing professional development in order to equip them for this role. Not only are these skills used in the particular groups, they are also integrated onto the ward as the individual nursing staff can act as advisers or coaches to both patients and staff at the ward level. This is crucial if the benefits of treatment are to be generalized. This also facilitates the development and embedding of a therapeutic culture within the service through its impact on both staff and patients' perceptions of the nursing role and the importance of psychological treatment.

The impact of the environment is considered to contribute significantly to the presentation of personality disorder traits (Livesley, 2003), yet this area is often neglected in treatment planning. When the aim of treatment is to increase the person's ability to recognize and express their emotional needs, tension can arise between the institution's need to contain emotional distress (do not disturb any further), and the patient's need to explore and test out new ways of experiencing themselves and others. If this is not communicated effectively to the wider clinical team, they may be in danger of invalidating the progress made in achieving such goals which may present initially as more 'unsettled' behaviour on the ward.

Case example: Simon

Simon had spent many years in high secure hospitals and although considered at very high risk of reoffending, his institutional presentation was one of compliance and controlled emotional reactions to situations. He could always provide logical and well-considered reasons why he was so controlled in his response to provocation. However, his conformity was often viewed with suspicion by some staff as it was markedly different from the serious nature of his previous offending and his very occasional hostile outbursts within hospital. An understanding of how his risk related to his personality was key to making sense of his presentation. For many years as a child, he had responded to his emotionally neglectful childhood by subjugating his own needs in response to them not being met adequately by his parents. Whenever he had tried to assert his needs, he was punished. His offending was understood as a response to years of his needs being subjugated, resulting in a build-up of frustration and anger towards others, with his offending functioning as a way of getting his need for care and a sense of identity met. This oscillation between two extremes is understood as the way the individual tries to cope with core needs through maladaptive coping strategies (avoidance of needs and overcompensation of getting his needs met through antisocial means).

> *Simon's behaviour within hospital paralleled his earlier life. He was a 'model patient' as he was compliant, wary that even appropriate requests for getting his needs met could be construed as him being overly demanding. As a consequence, his anger and frustration would 'bottle up', resulting in the occasional hostile outburst. This would be construed as further evidence of his lack of progress. The challenge for his therapist was to highlight these parallels and to negotiate with his clinical team the opportunity for him to be appropriately assertive and express frustration without this being construed as a problem or challenge.*

External challenges to treatment adaptation

One of the main limitations to adapting treatment approaches is how this is viewed by external agencies. If the patient is considered ready to return to prison after being 'successfully treated', his progress is often invalidated due to the prison service's reliance on a narrower understanding of what constitutes effective treatment, based on the risk–needs–responsivity literature (e.g., Andrews & Bonta, 2006). This can result in prison service clinicians disregarding the highly specialized treatment for which the patient was originally sent to the PDS to receive. Another important consideration is that prison treatment programmes will often exclude individuals from treatment if they are considered to have significant personality difficulties or high levels of psychopathy, so that patients who return to prison can encounter ongoing problems in accessing appropriate treatments.

Medium secure units create similar challenges for the 'treated patient'. All have different admission criteria, both implicit and explicit. They also offer vastly different types of treatment and these may be at variance with the approaches used within the PDS. One solution may be to provide more support to patients undergoing the transition to lesser security. However, the financial implications and the clinical pressures within the service often prohibit this. In addition, receiving services differ in their view of such 'support', with some seeing it as a failure to maintain boundaries and an inability to 'let go' in both the patient and the practitioner, and regarding continuing contact as a barrier to their own engagement with the patient. Our own view is that the service has acted as a 'home' to the individual for an extended period, and limited ongoing contact could facilitate the transition process.

Summary

Forensic personality disorder services need to be guided, but not restricted, by the evidence to date. By virtue of the history of therapeutic nihilism surrounding this patient population and which is only now starting to change, a clear focus on treatment development and adaption is a necessity. Experienced practitioners in the field must endeavour to find ways to take what is thought into the realms of what is known if we and others are to be effective in our clinical endeavours.

References

Ahmed, E., Harris, N, Braithwaite, J. & Braithwaite, V. (2001) *Shame management through reintegration*. Cambridge: Cambridge University Press.

Andrews, D. A. & Bonta, J. (2006) *The psychology of criminal conduct*, 4th edition. Cincinnati, OH: Anderson.

Barrett, M. S. & Berman, S. (2001) Is psychotherapy more effective when therapists disclose information about themselves? *Journal of Consulting and Clinical Psychology*, **69**, 597–603.

Bateman, A. & Fonagy, P. (2003) *Psychotherapy for borderline personality disorder: Mentalisation-based treatment*. Oxford: Oxford University Press.

Beckley, K. & Gordon, N. (2009) Schema therapy group manual, Rampton Hospital, Nottinghamshire.

Benjamin, L. S. & Karpiak, C. (2002) Personality disorders. In J. C. Norcross (Ed.) *Psychotherapy relationships that work: Therapists' contributions and responsiveness to patients* (pp. 423–438). New York: Oxford University Press.

Bohart, A. C., Elliott, R., Greenberg, L. S. & Watson, J. C. (2002) Empathy. In J. C. Norcross (Ed.) *Psychotherapy relationships that work: Therapist contributions and responsiveness to patients* (pp. 89–108). New York: Oxford University Press.

Dowsett, J. & Craissati, J. (2008) *Managing personality disordered offenders in the community: A psychological approach*. London: Routledge.

Farber, B. A. & Lane, J. S. (2002) Positive regard. In J. C. Norcross (Ed.) *Psychotherapy relationships that work: Therapist contributions and responsiveness to patients* (pp. 175–194). New York: Oxford University Press.

Fernandez-Alvarez, H. Clarkin, J. F., del Carmen Salguerio, M. & Critchfield, K. L. (2006) Participant factors in treating personality disorders. In L. G. Castonguay & L. E. Beutler (Eds.) *Principles of therapeutic change that work* (pp. 203–218). New York: Oxford University Press.

Giesen-Bloo, J., van Dyck, R, Spinhoven, P., van Tilburg, W., Dirksen, C., van Asselt, T., Kremers, I., Nardort, M. & Arntz, A. (2006) Outpatient psychotherapy for borderline personality disorder: randomized trial of schema-focused therapy vs. transference-focused therapy. *Archives of General Psychiatry*, **63**, 649–658.

Goldfried, M. R. (2001) *How therapists change: Personal and professional reflections*. Washington, DC: American Psychological Association.

Gordon, N. S. (2003) *The swamp workers' stories: An exploration of practitioners perspectives as a foundation for the development of a context sensitive development programme in a forensic setting*. Unpublished PhD dissertation. Metanoia Institute/Middlesex University.

Horvath, A. O. (2001) The alliance. *Psychotherapy*, **38**, 365–372.

Linehan, M. (1993) *Cognitive behavioural treatment of borderline personality disorder*. New York: Guilford Press.

Livesley, W. J. (2003) *Practical management of personality disorder*. New York: Guilford Press.

Morgan, S. (2004) Practice based evidence. In P. Ryan & S. Morgan (Eds.) *Assertive outreach: A strengths approach to policy and practice* (pp. 247–268). Hong Kong: Elsevier Science.

National Institute for Health and Clinical Excellence (2009a) *Antisocial personality disorder: Treatment, management and prevention*. Clinical Guideline 77. London: NICE.

National Institute for Health and Clinical Excellence (2009b) *Borderline personality disorder: Treatment, management and prevention*. Clinical Guideline 78. London: NICE.

Norcross, J. C. (2002) *Psychotherapy relationships that work: Therapists' contributions and responsiveness to patients*. New York: Oxford University Press.

Perry, J. C., Banon, E. & Ianni, F. (1999) Effectiveness of psychotherapy for personality disorders. *American Journal of Psychiatry*, **156**, 1312–1321.

Ryle, A. (1990) *Cognitive analytic therapy: Active participation in change*. Chichester: Wiley.

Smith, T. L., Barrett, M. S., Benjamin, L. S. & Barber, J. P. (2006) Relationship factors in treating personality disorders. In L. G. Castonguay & L. E. Beutler (Eds.) *Principles of therapeutic change that work* (pp. 219–238). New York: Oxford University Press.

Tryon, G. S. & Winograd, G. (2002) Goal consensus and collaboration. In J. C. Norcross (Ed.) *Psychotherapy relationships that work: Therapist' contributions and responsiveness to patients* (pp. 109–125). New York: Oxford University Press.

Young, J. E. (1990) *Cognitive therapy for personality disorders: A schema-focused approach*. New York: Professional Resource Exchange.

Chapter Eight

The Grey Areas of Boundary Issues When Working with Forensic Patients Who Have a Personality Disorder

Sue Evershed

The nature of the problem

> *It's a difficult and painful session as the patient before me tells me about finding his mother dead in bed when he was 13. I resist the urge to reach across and squeeze his arm to offer some comfort, knowing that if I did so the gesture might be misinterpreted by him or by others.*
>
> *I return to my office as an ex-patient telephones from prison. He is desperately unhappy and tells me he is finding it impossible to access the treatment he needs. I want to try to help but I am wary of stepping on toes.*

Much of the day-to-day clinical work we undertake with our patients will inevitably involve managing dilemmas such as these. Therapeutic work is generally fraught with the difficulties of negotiating and maintaining therapeutic boundaries in order to keep the patient and the clinician safe in both the short and the long term. Within the intense situation of a therapeutic session, the decisions we make about what we do and say, and how we do and say it, can be misinterpreted by patients and staff alike. Therapeutic work with forensic patients with personality disorder is even more challenging when so many of them have underlying attachment problems and a history of dangerous behaviour triggered by interpersonal difficulties.

Working Positively with Personality Disorder in Secure Settings: A Practitioner's Perspective
Edited by Phil Willmot and Neil Gordon
© 2011 John Wiley & Sons, Ltd.

For staff members who are ward based, the situation can be even more complex. Ward staff do not have the structure or the containment of the therapeutic session to help in boundary maintenance. Their interactions are inevitably more informal and spontaneous, and the settings and contexts are diverse. Simply being in a ward setting with a group of others for a number of hours requires the staff member to interact socially, and every interaction brings with it the possibility of boundary dilemmas. It is both extraordinarily difficult and probably unnatural to limit interaction to therapeutic topics for eight hours or longer. Thus staff are required to 'make small talk' in order to model appropriate social behaviour, and in doing so inevitably put themselves at risk of disclosing information about themselves. The opportunity for such dilemmas to arise increases exponentially with every patient and every staff member on the ward, and every hour spent in contact with them. Moreover, the dynamics within and between the two groups and the observations and interpretations that each individual makes regarding others all pose possibilities for boundary breaches.

Furthermore, the relationship between a ward-based staff member and a patient is multifaceted. Ward staff have several different roles, apart from a therapeutic one. They are carers, assisting with domestic activities and administering medication; they are companions and are encouraged to join in social and leisure activities with patients; they have a security role in searching patients and their rooms; and they have a hospitality role, serving food and providing ward amenities. Each aspect of the role brings with it a different set of expectations on the part of the patient and other staff, and this mix of expectations can again bring risks of boundary breach.

With the introduction of clinical governance across mental health sites, managers of clinical services and practitioners have become more concerned with safe delivery of services and standards of care. As a result, the issue of therapeutic boundaries in clinical practice has become more pertinent and is scrutinized more carefully than ever before. Services are actively looking for sensible guidance on how to ensure safe practice regarding boundaries and how to manage boundary issues when they arise. Boundary violations, when they do occur, often have calamitous results for the patient, the clinician and the service. In forensic settings, they can be headline news and sensationalized to the point that one could be forgiven for thinking that such violations occur on an almost daily basis.

Researching the area or simply trying to collate information about the extent of the problem is extraordinarily difficult. Staff and services are reluctant to talk about it and averse to giving information which might harm reputations. Nevertheless, it would seem that in most organizations there are actually very few formal investigations into boundary-related problems. For example, over the last five years in one high secure hospital there have been, on average, only four investigations into boundary-related problems each year. A breakdown of these incidents shows that:

- 80% involved female staff (staff demographics would predict 55%).
- 90% involved male patients (patient demographics would predict 85%).
- 60% involved unqualified staff (staff demographics would predict 40%).
- 55% were regarding overly intimate relationships (with 75% of these involving non-qualified staff).

These figures would imply that the hospital experiences particular problems with unqualified female staff members engaging in inappropriate relationships with male patients. However, only 55% of investigations found any evidence of a problem. It would appear that boundary problems are not just about clinicians breaking boundaries, but may also be about differing perceptions and expectations of therapeutic relationships.

> *Later that week, a junior member of staff tells me in supervision that she accepted a 'thank you' token of four homemade paper flowers from a patient. The flowers had no monetary value and she felt that to refuse might cause him to feel rejected. She took advice from the ward manager at the time. However, another member of the clinical team was very critical of her behaviour, suggesting that she had violated a therapeutic boundary by accepting a gift.*

It would seem that there are different opinions about what constitutes appropriate and inappropriate therapeutic behaviour. Whilst most clinicians would agree that more extreme behaviours are clearly outside the boundaries of appropriate behaviour, the everyday dilemmas that occur in our therapy relationships are rarely clear-cut or straightforward. Most such dilemmas represent the grey areas of therapeutic boundaries in which the most appropriate action may not be immediately obvious.

What is a boundary problem?

Perhaps some of the problem lies with the definition of therapeutic boundaries themselves. A great deal has been written on the notion of therapeutic boundaries. A literature search reveals that the topic has occurred in the title of over 1,500 books, articles or dissertations, and there are almost as many definitions of boundaries as there are books on the subject. Unsurprisingly, then, surveys among practitioners show a lack of agreement as to what constitutes a boundary violation.

> *In discussing boundary crossings, a senior medical colleague tells me that he still occasionally corresponds with three ex-patients ten years after he has finished working with them. Most of his colleagues engage in similar 'courteous correspondence' but his behaviour has been challenged by the production of a draft policy paper.*

Marzillier and Gardner (1994) found that UK psychologists only really agreed on the most serious boundary violations such as sexual relations with patients or the giving and receiving of gifts of high monetary value. In all other circumstances, there were wide differences of opinion. Research in the United States surveying more than 2,000 psychiatrists, psychologists and social workers yielded similar findings (Borys & Pope, 1989). The study asked about the participants' behaviour as well as their beliefs about boundary issues and again wide differences in beliefs and behaviours were observed in all but the most serious boundary violations. The authors highlighted ten factors which affect our engagement in boundary violations and our beliefs about the appropriateness of boundary situations. These include the theoretical orientation of the clinician, the therapeutic setting, clinician gender and patient gender.

Gutheil and Gabbard (1993) tried to categorize boundary situations in terms of the different aspects relating to the role of the clinician and the tasks expected of them: the time afforded to the patient, the place and space given to sessions, the language and tone used in the therapeutic relationships, the amount of self-disclosure and the utility of that self-disclosure, any money exchanged for services, the nature of any gifts given and services rendered (by the clinician or the client), the way the clinician and the patient dress, and the nature, frequency and degree of any physical contact. Gutheil and Gabbard proposed that boundary dilemmas can arise in all the above areas and they suggest that the category list can serve as a useful aid to reflection (and planning) for clinicians wanting to focus on boundary problems.

A recent seminal work by Gutheil and Brodsky (2008) made an attempt to take into account the factors that seem to impact on our views about boundaries by defining therapeutic boundaries as 'the edges of appropriate behaviour in a given moment as governed by the therapeutic context and contract'. This implies that boundaries are not hard-and-fast 'rules' for behaviour, but can change according to the situation. Llewelyn and Gardner (2009) took this further when they talked about boundaries as social constructs which define the therapeutic relationship and the social roles within it. Often, however, these constructs are not formally defined or even discussed. They remain as tacit expectations about how we should behave as clinician and patient, and how we should relate to each other. Thus the real boundaries in a relationship are difficult to identify and manage simply because of their lack of clarity.

> *A colleague tells me that she has worked with a very difficult, hostile patient for six months. He routinely refuses to attend ward rounds or to speak to anyone else on the clinical team. The team feel that she should stop working with him because by continuing she is condoning his team-splitting behaviour. She feels he will withdraw altogether if she stops.*

Even if the clinician spends time at the start of therapy working up a therapeutic contract discussing just these issues, the discussion is likely to focus on the overarching aspects of the roles and the relationship (e.g., the differences between friendship and a therapy relationship) rather than the specific behaviours that are likely to be played out during the therapeutic process. Misunderstandings and crises, small or large, are therefore highly likely to occur between the clinician and the patient. Moreover, therapy relationships usually occur within a therapeutic system where other clinicians and managers also work. Whilst it is not unusual for clinicians to talk to their patients about the relationship, it is rare for specific discussions to take place about the social construct that is the relationship amongst teams or within the wider organization. Thus, disagreements about what is and is not OK between the clinician and the wider organization are even more likely to occur.

In an effort to help resolve these differences of opinion about boundary situations, Gutheil and Gabbard (1993) distinguished between boundary crossings and boundary violations. In these terms, a boundary violation would be defined as a behaviour that is inevitably harmful to the patient. As seen above, there is much closer agreement about the most harmful boundary situations amongst clinicians. A boundary crossing, however, would be defined as any departure from normal practice within a therapeutic situation. If the clinician behaves in a way that they would not normally behave with a particular patient, this would be seen as a boundary crossing. Such behaviour would not necessarily be seen as harmful or wrong; indeed, there are arguments that boundary crossings can be useful. Boundary crossings constitute most of the dilemmas facing clinicians in everyday work, and these are the issues where there is most disagreement.

Defining the boundaries

The context of the situation is also important to bear in mind; the culture, the setting and what is happening in the immediate environment will inevitably influence clinician and patient behaviour. A patient who is taken ill in the session is likely to (and probably should) elicit clinician responses that are different from the usual ones. The personalities of the individuals, the needs of the patient and the patient's own history will also affect the clinician's response. Thus, reaching out and patting someone on the hand to alleviate distress may be more appropriate in a community environment than in a forensic inpatient setting; but not if the patient has been sexually abused.

The stage of treatment is also important because most clinicians say that they will tolerate more boundary crossings by the patient early in therapy as a trade-off for developing a working relationship. Often patients come to therapy without therapeutic skills, not knowing what to expect or how to behave. Clinicians tend to tolerate more patient boundary breaking in the early stages, with the idea that relationship skills are shaped up as therapy progresses.

Weighing up these options is difficult at the best of times, but frequently the clinician will have to make a decision about how to respond, with no preparation or thinking time. Finally, it would seem that the only way to determine whether a response was a boundary crossing or a violation (harmful) is by looking at the end result of the response (the outcome) or by examining the meaning of the particular behaviour to the patient, in the moment. Neither method is readily available to the clinician at the time. Hence the resolution of boundary situations depends on the judgement of the clinician in what can be a difficult and stressful situation.

> *A staff member stops me as I go onto the ward to say that he thinks my patient is turned on by the way I dress. Do I carry on to see the patient or postpone? Do I alter my style of dress? Do I check this out with my patient?*

Additionally, behaviour in and outside the session can be misinterpreted by others, especially if the contextual factors are not recognized. This can lead to rumour or direct confrontation from a prejudged perspective which can damage the reputation of both the clinician and the service. To some extent it matters less what the clinician and the patient actually do in the session; what matters far more is how other people perceive the behaviour and what this signifies to them. An additional difficulty here is the fact that there is often a degree of avoidance in clinicians and others about addressing possible boundary violations directly (Pope, Sonne & Green, 2006). This is true in most settings, but possibly more so in the forensic arena where many clinicians are operating in a close and closed inpatient setting, but also as the forensic community itself is a small world. The result can be that a clinician is subject to rumours about their practice but is unaware of it, and, more worryingly, that more serious boundary violations may be taking place, but no one will talk about them.

Apart from the difficulties in defining what is and what is not acceptable in therapeutic practice generally, what is it that makes boundary issues so difficult to manage? From a clinician's perspective, perhaps it is because in most cases there is an awareness that every possible response is likely to elicit both positive and negative consequences. Often the response chosen will be the least unacceptable rather than the 'best'. From a manager's perspective, boundary issues are difficult because they generate so many different views and opinions alongside very strong feelings.

Why do boundary crossings occur?

A look into history reveals that boundary crossing is not a new phenomenon. The heroes of our therapeutic past gave very mixed messages on the subject. Freud, Winnicott, Klein and others are cited as having engaged in behaviours that most of us would see as questionable, from sending patients postcards and providing them with financial support to treating family members, taking patients on holiday and inviting patients to stay in their homes as a part of treatment (Gutheil & Gabbard, 1993).

> *My patient has been talking about his childhood. Time is running out in the session and he remains distressed. Do I finish the session on time as usual or allow the session to run overtime until he is calmer?*

From the surveys outlined above (Borys & Pope, 1989; Marzillier & Gardner, 1993), it would seem that boundary crossing is not uncommon. These surveys suggest that apart from the immediate difficulty of determining the best response when faced with a boundary dilemma, clinicians will sometimes knowingly cross boundaries and will feel justified in doing so. Lewellyn and Gardner (2009) attributed many boundary crossings to the drive to be compassionate and the desire to be helpful and alleviate suffering. This, after all, is why most clinicians enter their professions in the first place. Hence clinicians will frequently alter their usual style of responding when dealing with a distressed patient. Such breaches may range from simply offering additional session time to departures from the usual therapeutic style or behaviour (e.g., holding a patient's hand to comfort them).

It is also recognized by many clinicians that boundary crossings can sometimes promote beneficial outcomes in patient work: 'Nonsexual boundary crossings can enrich psychotherapy, serve the treatment plan, and strengthen the therapist-client working relationship' (Pope & Keith-Spiegel, 2008: 638). For example, boundary crossings, especially in the early stages of therapy, can be used to cement a warm therapeutic alliance. Most clinicians are aware that a strong therapeutic alliance is a prerequisite for successful therapy. The crossing of a boundary in response to patient need or distress can strengthen the therapeutic bond either because the patient feels that the clinician is giving more, or the patient feels more at ease in the relationship because the clinician allows boundary breaches to go unchallenged.

> *Within the session my patient repeatedly questions me about how I cope with, and how I feel about, different social situations. The situations are relevant to the topics discussed, but should I answer his questions? And if so, how much detail should I give?*

Breaches of boundary can also assist in the completion of psychological tasks. For example, clinicians may consider going for a walk with an agoraphobic patient. Boundary breaches on the part of the patient can also become a focus of therapy (e.g., if a patient becomes controlling and hostile in a session and has a history of aggression). In a forensic setting, patients are rule-breakers by definition, so it is highly likely that this patient population will themselves break boundaries. At some point the focus of therapy is likely to be the idea of compliance to social norms. Boundary breaches within the therapy relationship provide a useful source of therapeutic material.

Patients who have a diagnosis of personality disorder are also likely to have interpersonal or attachment difficulties. Many have a history of chaotic and difficult relationships (Linehan, 1993; Young, 1994) and have no 'blueprint' for effective relationships. Thus forming and maintaining a therapeutic alliance is likely to be difficult for them. Also for those who have suffered sexual abuse, there may be confusions about sexual identity and a tendency to sexualize relationships, including the therapy relationship. Thus the likelihood of boundary breaches by patients in this population, especially those who have borderline personality disorder features, is high (Phillips, 2003). Safran and Muran's (2003) concept of a 'rupture' (a breakdown or challenge) within the working alliance will inevitably include instances of boundary crossings by the patient. Safran and Muran argue that such ruptures are the vehicles for therapeutic progress: that by working through the ruptures or crossings with the patient, a better understanding of relationships is formed.

The treatment process for forensic patients with personality disorders tends to be longer than those in other contexts. This is partly because patients often have numerous treatment targets, but also because the treatments themselves are not short in duration. Writers on treatments for personality disorder suggest that clinicians should remain in therapeutic relationships with patients for long periods (e.g. Linehan, 1993; Young, 1994). This means that very close therapeutic relationships are built up, and so there is a greater potential for boundary breaking.

All of the above instances could be seen as boundary breaches arising from a benign intent on the part of the clinician to meet the needs of the patient. However, breaches can also occur when clinicians are acting according to their own needs and agenda. In some instances the clinician may not be fully aware of what is happening. Populations of forensic patients with personality disorder inevitably include patients who engage in extreme behaviours. Parasuicidal and violent behaviour can engender feelings of hopelessness and stress in the clinician, which in turn can lead to an urge to avoid or to punish the patient in some way (Fallon, 1983; Goodman, 1997; Maier, Stava, Morrow, van Rybroek & Bauman, 1987). Thus clinicians may behave differently in sessions where they feel threatened or at risk in some way. Boundary breaches in these circumstances could include simply failing to challenge or confront as they would normally, shortening or missing appointments, or failing to develop empathy and becoming more punitive with patients.

Sadly, boundary breaches may also derive from clinicians working to their own agenda in a conscious way. Such breaches occur when the clinician knowingly behaves, at the expense of the patient, in a manner that meets their own needs (e.g., financial, sexual, relationship, status/self-esteem).

Risks of boundary crossings

As noted above, boundary crossings can have beneficial outcomes. However, they can also have difficult and damaging consequences to the patient, to the clinician and to the services within which the clinician is working. The negative consequences to the patient can range from, at best, a failure to achieve therapeutic goals to, at worst, patients' problems being exacerbated so they end up feeling abused and exploited. Damage to the patient can arise even when the crossing is made with the best of intentions. For example, the compassionate act of reaching out to pat the arm of a distressed patient can become a 'boundary gremlin' with traumatic consequences if the patient is unable to tolerate or reacts badly to touch (e.g., if they have a have a history of sexual abuse, or if the gesture is likely to trigger deviant sexual fantasies).

The obvious conclusion is that boundary crossings are safer if the clinician knows the patient and their history well. However, there is a body of research which indicates that serious boundary violations have often been preceded by a series of smaller and apparently benign boundary crossings. This suggests that, for some clinicians, boundary crossings become easier to make with every instance until there is a risk of a serious violation (Pope *et al.*, 2006). Thus it seems important that every departure from normal practice, however benign it may appear, should be thought through carefully and the likely consequences explored.

Boundary crossings can also have serious consequences for the member of staff involved, regardless of the intention behind the action. Staff integrity and practice can be questioned, and if the incident is seen as serious, investigations can result which threaten both job and career.

The negative consequences of boundary crossings can also extend to entire services which can suffer disruption if staff members are suspended from clinical practice. Additionally, such incidents and their consequences can promote fear and resentment in other staff; resentment of the system and of the individual who crossed the boundary; and fear of being 'tarred with the same brush'. This can in turn lead to further boundary breaches if staff members distance themselves from close therapeutic alliances with patients as a means of protecting themselves from accusations of getting too close.

Obstacles to safety regarding boundaries

Even the most virtuous and meticulous of clinicians can struggle with the complexity of therapy relationships and boundary problems. In addition to the difficulties in identifying and managing the therapy dyad, there are other pitfalls in the environment that can cause difficulties.

The mental health system exists within, and is part of, the modern culture of regulation. Much of what we do is regulated and checked through clinical governance processes. Clinical work, training and supervision, in particular, are often monitored by organizations as a means to ensure competent and safe practice. One might hope that clinical governance processes of this sort could be employed to help prevent, identify and manage boundary crossings. Regrettably, in most establishments the clinical governance procedures tend to measure the quantity rather than the quality of what we do: counting chickens rather than judging the quality of their meat. This simplistic way of scrutinizing clinical services is inherently dangerous. It can generate a false sense of security about the standards of our practice and can result in us relying on existing ways of monitoring so that we fail to check the quality of our services.

Every organization operates its own stereotyping subcultures. In forensic settings where most patients are male, it is common to find age and gender stereotyping. Thus, although there is no agreement in the literature about which characteristics are predictive of boundary violation (Norris, Gutheil & Strasburger, 2003), young, attractive women are more likely to come under scrutiny for boundary crossings than other categories of staff. Their dress will be commented upon and their behaviour within the session will be questioned because they are deemed by colleagues to be sexually attractive to the patients and therefore at risk of boundary breach. Repeated criticism and constant scrutiny can make these clinicians feel exposed and lead them to behave in an overly risk-conscious manner, so that patients' needs are not adequately met. At the same time, whilst the organization's focus is on young female clinicians, it may miss the potential for boundary breaches from other members of staff.

This problem is exacerbated when the organization is risk-averse, as many forensic establishments tend to be. Generally, an intolerance of mistakes within an establishment leads to a culture of blame rather than a learning culture. Poor practice (real or suspected) in a blame culture tends to be covered up and minimized, which limits any chance of improving practice for patients.

The assistance of a cohesive team is vital if the clinician is facing boundary issues. At their best, teams can offer invaluable support and guidance to a clinician working with continuing boundary dilemmas. However, some teams can be toxic rather than supportive. Fixed and rigid opinions within teams, professional jealousies, the inability to accept different perspectives, stereotyping and discriminatory attitudes, and even simple 'personality clashes' can lead to team splits or at worst, the scapegoating of individual team members. If clinicians are alienated through team splitting, their opinions are likely to become polarized, they are less likely to communicate effectively with their team and less likely to ask for or reflect on the feedback of that team. Clinicians on both 'sides' of the split thus become even more vulnerable to boundary breaches.

Probably the biggest obstacle to safety in regard to boundary breaches, however, is clinicians' defensiveness and shame about such issues. There are expectations and myths regarding therapy staff, which are held, not just by organizations, patients and non-clinical staff, but by clinicians themselves at times. Staff and patient expectations about clinicians generally tend to be unrealistically positive: clinicians are often seen as perfect beings who are warm and empathic, who do not have their own problems and who do not make mistakes (Pope *et al.*, 2006). When clinicians fall from grace they can fall badly and often there is little tolerance when mistakes are made from organizations and in their own eyes. Thus it can be very difficult for a member of staff to raise concerns about boundary issues with individual clinicians, and clinicians themselves may avoid raising such issues about their own practice.

Where are the guidelines on boundaries?

Thus far we have noted that boundary crossings are potentially harmful to services, staff and patients. However, boundary dilemmas are also both commonplace and complex. So where can the virtuous clinician find guidance about boundary recognition and management?

Organizational policy

Most organizations have policies which focus on staff and patient behaviour, including staff–patient relationships. The better policies outline an acceptance that therapeutic relationships are essential to patient treatment, whilst recognizing that close personal friendships or intimate relationships are inappropriate. The best policies also attempt to delineate the actions staff should take if they become aware of a potential or actual boundary breach. This usually involves the staff member reporting the breach to a clinical supervisor or manager.

Unfortunately, many policies reflect the fact that organizations tend to see any boundary crossing as problematic (Gutheil & Gabbard, 1998) and such a stance can lead to overreactions and misapplications of sanctions to what is, in reality, perfectly acceptable behaviour. The result of such organizational overreaction can be that staff members resort to very rigid interactions to protect themselves (Pope & Vasquez, 2007), which in turn can adversely affect patients. Lazarus (1994) made the point that policies about boundaries are designed to protect patients, not create situations that damage them: 'one of the worst ethical violations is that of permitting current risk management principles to take precedence over humane intervention' (1994: 260).

Gutheil and Gabbard (1998) argued that clarity about where boundaries lie should not mean rigidity; that policies need to be written in such a way that acknowledges that every patient and every clinician in every situation is unique. However, this means that policies cannot be specific about the behaviours constituting anything but the most serious of boundary breaches and thus can provide little by way of guidance to staff members or their managers and supervisors.

Professional codes of conduct

The problems relating to organizational policy also pertain to codes of conduct. In the UK, professional codes of conduct exist for most mental health professionals, including psychologists, psychiatrists, social workers and nurses. All are very clear, outlining the key areas of concern, the responsibility of clinicians to observe such boundaries in their own practice and that of their colleagues, and the procedures and sanctions that may occur if a non-benign boundary breach is reported.

Unfortunately, not all staff members working directly with patients are covered by professional codes of conduct. Non-clinical staff (e.g., domestic or estate staff) may provide vital services and come into contact with patients on a daily basis, but may have no professional affiliations. Other unqualified clinical staff members (e.g., healthcare assistants and assistant psychologists) also fall outside the reach of the sanctions of professional bodies although organizations and professions rely on their clinical supervisors ensuring adherence to the codes of conduct.

However, even when professional codes of conduct do apply to staff members, there is a recognition from the professional bodies that they cannot reflect the complexity of motivations in therapeutic interactions or the contextual or social nature of boundaries. The British Psychological Society Code of Ethics and Conduct reflects this and exhorts psychologists not to rely on codes of conduct alone: 'No code can replace the need for psychologists to use their professional and ethical judgement' (British Psychological Society, 2009: 4). Llewelyn and Gardner go further, suggesting that if psychologists do not use their own judgement they may not give their best to their patients: 'If we simply rely on rules or codes, we are likely to act woodenly, and to lose the opportunity to make a real difference to our clients' (Llewelyn & Gardner, 2009: 7).

Training

Most qualified clinical staff will have undergone professional training at undergraduate and often at postgraduate level. Such training is scrutinized and accredited by the professional bodies and is designed to fit them for practice. It might be assumed that the training would incorporate significant input on professional issues, including developing an awareness of boundaries and guidance on boundary management. However, for most trainees, there is only minimal teaching on boundary issues or on ethics generally. Standard training for psychiatrists and psychologists includes only one formal session on professional ethics in the whole of their training. Of course, most trainee professionals are offered more extensive input, often delivered through case consultation and supervision when ethical issues arise in clinical practice. However, this is neither standardized nor formalized. Thus it is impossible to determine the amount or the quality of ethics training that staff members have received.

Organizations also have a responsibility to provide training in ethical and safe practice, especially since some staff will have received no training in this area at all. Most forensic mental health employers appear to provide some training on generic induction courses for all staff, but this is often limited to an hour at most. Given the small amount of time allotted to it, the training tends to simplify the issues. There is a clear focus on accepted boundary violations (sexual and financial indiscretions) rather than the grey areas, and the training tends to emphasize the risks to staff of being groomed or conditioned by patients. There tends to be very little on the risks of staff themselves initiating boundary violations and boundary crossings, or why this might happen.

More worryingly perhaps, ongoing 'top-up' training in boundary awareness and management seems to be the exception. Consultation across several high and medium secure hospitals suggests that training on boundary issues is not included as continuing essential training for staff, and is often not available at all within organizations.

Supervision

Most organizations require that clinical staff participate in supervision of their practice to the extent that many have set key performance indicators to evidence its occurrence. Based on the key performance indicators in a number of forensic services, it would seem that such organizations believe that they are performing within acceptable limits if 80% of their staff members are receiving clinical supervision once a month. Needless to say, this would mean that 20% of the staff members were not receiving any supervision in their clinical practice, suggesting that clinical supervision is not as embedded a process as organizations might hope. Given that it is likely that this 20% will comprise staff members who are 'supervision avoidant', it is logical to assume that these are the staff whose practice, above all others, may most require supervision to keep them safe.

One group of professionals, at least, should be able to use supervision in this way. Psychologists as a professional body have recognized the need and the benefits of clinical supervision to support good practice from trainee status and (somewhat unusually) throughout a clinician's professional career. It was, therefore, concerning that Gardner (1993), in a rare survey of British qualified psychologists, found that three-quarters of those surveyed said that were supervised on less than 10% of their caseload and a third received no supervision at all. Since then much has changed. The British Psychological Society some ten years later required that practising clinical psychologists receive supervision on a regular and frequent basis (Division of Clinical Psychology, 2003).

So, has this impacted on practice? Unfortunately, we can only assume that clinical psychologists now access regular and frequent supervision because there does not appear to have been an evaluation of this policy. However, this only relates to clinical psychologists. What of forensic psychologists? Sadly there seems to be little by way of guidelines in support of regular supervision for this group. More worryingly, perhaps, in the recent move from the British Psychological Society to the Health Professions Council as the regulatory body for practitioner psychologists, the policies regarding supervision have been abandoned (Health Professions Council, 2008). Thus it would appear that post-qualification supervision is no longer mandatory. Clearly, if boundary issues do arise for these staff, supervision cannot be relied on to provide guidelines or support.

There are also implicit assumptions in supervision that the supervisee will bring relevant issues to supervision for discussion. However, boundary problems can lead staff to feel very ashamed of their practice and they can be reluctant to raise them for scrutiny in supervision. It is possible, then, that the very issues that should be raised for guidance will not be brought to supervision. One assumes that a good supervisor will work to reduce this concern and will endeavour to ensure that boundary issues are discussed when required. Unfortunately, Gardner (1993) found that only 10% of staff discussed boundary issues with any frequency.

Of course, even when supervision does take place and the supervisor does manage to create an environment where boundary issues can be discussed, there is no guarantee that supervision will be effective in managing or preventing or boundary problems. Evaluative studies of the effectiveness of supervision are rare, but those that do exist suggest that its primary benefit is to prevent staff burnout. There is very little evidence to suggest that it has any impact on clinical practice or therapeutic outcome (Feltham, 2000).

Treatment manuals

A number of treatment manuals exist for use with mentally disordered offenders, and over the last 10–15 years there has been an increase in the number of treatments developed for use with patients who have a personality disorder in particular. Some (but by no means all) of these manuals deal with boundary issues, although few cover the topic fully. For example, one manual contains significant discussion and guidance about how staff might maintain their own 'personal limits' (Linehan, 1993), but gives little guidance on how the clinician might identify these limits. Another manual includes a self-rating questionnaire for practitioners to examine their practice regarding clinical boundaries (Gordon & Wong, 2000), but little help is given as to how the boundaries might be maintained. Neither manual discusses the impact of different situations on the relationship and the therapeutic boundaries.

Not only do the manuals vary in terms of the depth and breadth of the coverage, but the different therapy approaches vary in the way they view boundaries and boundary maintenance. What is appropriate behaviour within some treatment approaches may be seen as very detached and remote, or overly involved from the viewpoint of another treatment style. For example, within dialectical behaviour therapy, the treatment strategy of telephone consultation (where the patient is allowed to call the clinician throughout the day or night if they are in crisis) was seen by psychodynamic therapists as a serious breach of boundaries. On the other hand, Young (1994), in describing schema therapy, argues that patients require an intense and involved relationship with the clinician (limited reparenting) rather than the detached and passive style of the psychodynamic therapists. For patients and clinicians undertaking multiple treatments, this variation can be very confusing. It would be unreasonable to expect therapy dyads to radically alter the quality of the relationship and behave differently as they switch from one treatment to another, but this may place both participants at risk.

So how can we do better?

As may be obvious from the argument so far, there are a number of areas that, if addressed, could assist in the prevention and management of boundary issues. The responsibility for implementing these lies with a variety of bodies.

Employers and organizations

Much of the responsibility for managing boundary issues will inevitably fall to employers or employing organizations. They can assist in a number of ways. First, the production of flexible and sensible policies and procedures will serve to provide the infrastructure for the way in which the organization operates on boundary issues. Policies and procedures need to acknowledge that strong therapeutic relationships are to be encouraged and that, as a result, boundary dilemmas are an inevitable part of our work.

The difficulty faced by a writer of policy trying to improve boundary crossing definition is how to define clearly what constitutes an appropriate or an inappropriate therapeutic relationship, whilst still allowing that every therapeutic situation is unique. Pope and Vasquez (2007) went further, arguing that, when investigating potential boundary breaches, organizations need to make decisions 'with the greatest possible clarity about the potential benefits and harm, the client's needs and well-being, informed consent and informed refusal, and the therapist's knowledge and competence' (2007: 218). The better policies attempt to do this. One organization has adopted a 'traffic light' approach, highlighting examples of red (clear boundary violations), green (clearly appropriate relationship) and amber (more difficult to determine) behaviours to illustrate the need to take context into account.

Policies should also set out in detail what support is available for staff members who are embroiled in boundary dilemmas, and should specify what staff should do if they become aware of a potential or actual boundary breach.

Organizations would also benefit from moving towards a learning culture and away from a culture of blame. Starting from the premise that boundary dilemmas and crossings are inevitable, the safety of the organization will depend upon limiting the harm arising from the boundary crossings. This is more easily done if the organization is able to understand fully the triggers and motivations of the individuals concerned and contexts in which the crossings occurred. An organizational structure that makes it easier and less anxiety-provoking to raise boundary issues, and an organizational culture that accepts that staff members will make mistakes, will make it more likely that the organization is able to learn from those mistakes and not repeat them in the future. However, this can only be achieved if the organization accepts that the goal of the policies and procedures is not to avoid all violations, but is instead to ensure that violations are managed in a way that minimizes harm and maximizes benefits.

An open, informed and understanding culture will minimize the damage that can arise from boundary issues. However, in order to achieve this fully, the organization needs to make full use of information. In forensic settings, security information is often kept 'secret' or held on a 'need to know' only basis. This frequently means that clinical teams and managers of staff under suspicion are not given the relevant information and are thus limited in their ability to support, protect or manage the staff and patients involved effectively.

Certainly, organizations need to provide more sophisticated initial training for staff about the complexities of boundary issues and how to manage them. Training needs to cover a variety of topics rather than simply concentrating on the possibility of patients manipulating or attempting to condition staff. Perhaps a deeper understanding of the complexities of boundary issues could be achieved by group consideration of common boundary dilemmas and discussions about the options available to staff. Training could also include looking at how to formulate boundary pushing by patients and how to support clinicians who are working with these dilemmas.

Elton Wilson (2002) suggested that all staff should be trained in the rudiments of ethical thinking to overcome stereotypical or black-and-white thinking about boundary issues so that they are aware of the need for human relatedness and compassion. It would also assist them in understanding the human tendency to adapt and change in response to our own and others' needs and pressures (and hence our ability to violate boundaries). Training related to ethical thinking and practice would increase awareness that values are contextual and arise from the powerful effect of conditioning. This type of development would also focus on the reality that ethical decisions are difficult and may involve dissonance with personal values and the aspirations of codes.

The lack of ongoing training in this area also needs to be addressed. If organizations aim to retain staff for a number of years, they need to ensure that staff are safe and competent to manage risky situations. Apart from the benefits to patients if staff members are able to manage boundaries effectively, it has long been recognized that the relational or dynamic security of an establishment rests on the quality of relationships between staff and patients. Boundary breaches, therefore, constitute a real threat to the security and control of the establishment. There is, then, a very cogent argument for making ongoing training on boundary management mandatory for all staff.

Organizations also need to ensure that all clinical staff have access to regular supervision, and that the supervision is of suitable quality and focused on addressing boundary issues. The provision of training in supervision skills for staff members would help, but more importantly, organizations need to truly prioritize supervision and ensure that staff members have the time available to attend.

Professional bodies

The mental health professional bodies certainly have some responsibility to address boundary issues. The development of the therapeutic alliance and the management of the boundaries are central to all contact with patients, yet currently very little formal time is allocated to this. The professions maintain the standards for the training of staff and should be demanding that this course prioritize the understanding of boundary issues.

The professional bodies also define the guidelines for continuing professional development, including clinical supervision. The Health Professions Council seems to have taken a step backward in its decision not to enforce the guidelines on supervision for clinical psychologists, but in fact all mental health professional bodies could help to ensure that regular supervision occurs and so could provide support for staff. Substance misuse workers in Wisconsin, for example, have taken this issue very seriously and have recently revised the contract for the certification of staff, making supervisors ethically and legally responsible for the behaviour of their supervisees (Wisconsin Department of Regulation and Licensing, 2007). If supervisors are aware that they could be held to account for the work of their supervisees, they are likely to work harder to ensure the breadth and depth of their supervision.

Clinical supervisors

Supervisors have a responsibility to ensure the provision of high quality clinical supervision for their supervisees. Since the therapeutic alliance and boundary management are central to working with patients, this should take a high priority within supervision. Supervisors can promote ethical thinking in supervisees as boundary issues are discussed, looking at the complexity of the situation and weighing up the benefits and costs of each possible course of action.

Boundary issues are probably best addressed by reviewing transference and countertransference themes that have arisen within the therapeutic sessions. Most models of supervision incorporate this (Hawkins & Shohet, 2000; Inskipp & Proctor, 1995; Page & Wosket, 1994; Scaife, 2001), but it is all too easy for supervisors, when facing reluctance by the supervisee, to focus purely on the content of the session rather than the process because it is more comfortable for both parties.

Since supervisees may be reluctant to bring boundary issues to supervision, the patients who are not raised for discussion by supervisees may well be the ones with whom there is most risk. Thus, supervisors need to monitor the caseload of supervisees and make sure that the entire caseload is discussed in supervision on a regular basis. There also needs to be a focus on the very end of supervision – the period 'between the chair and the door' when most boundary issues seem to occur (Gutheil & Simon, 1995). As in therapy, supervisors need also to focus on any slips and omissions in the supervisee's account of their work, including material that is raised in an unusual way or that has a degree of emotion attached to it.

Clinical teams

Clinical teams can play a part in minimizing the risks of boundary crossings by supporting and guiding individual clinicians. If the team has an understanding of the difficulties of working with individual patients and is supportive of the clinicians working with them, then boundary issues are much more likely to be raised and discussed. This makes it much easier for teams to offer support and assistance.

A system of initial and ongoing assessment and formulation of patients in terms of likely boundary issues ensures that the team is prepared and can plan for potential difficulties. Differences of opinion will be highlighted at an early stage, and this will also help to ensure that any potential team splits can be managed and minimized before dilemmas arise. Again, it is helpful if the team can operate within a philosophy of harm-minimization rather than an expectation that boundary crossings should be completely eradicated.

Patients

The use of therapy contracts (written or verbal) with patients allows the subject of boundary management to be raised and discussed with patients. Contracts which allow discussion of the 'rules of engagement' are especially useful with patients who have not engaged in therapy before. Some patients may still continue to push boundaries, either wilfully to achieve their own ends or as a result of their particular needs and deficits, but others will comply and assist in boundary management. However, contracts can be helpful even when working with patients who continue to push boundaries because the contract enables the clinician to challenge and explore attempts at boundary crossings. Such discussions can be beneficial in terms of maintaining the therapy relationship itself, but they can also form the focus of the therapy itself (Safran & Muran, 2003).

Clinicians

Ultimately, however, it is the individual clinician who clearly has a responsibility to keep themselves and their patients safe. Clinicians spend many hours assessing their patients in terms of clinical and offending needs. The formulation of individual patients in terms of potential boundary difficulties is also important in that it serves to allow planning and reduces the likelihood that difficult decisions will have to be made 'in the moment'.

The requirement to be open about practice issues in teams, and especially in supervision, is vital. Clinicians have a responsibility to seek guidance about therapeutic boundary management, recognizing the possibility of 'blind spots' and noting their vulnerabilities. Should discussion or supervision reveal unmet needs in the clinician which make them vulnerable to boundary crossing or violation, the clinician also has a responsibility to take steps to address these needs (e.g., through training, additional experience or therapy).

There are a number of self-assessment tools that assist the clinician in reflecting on practice. Hamilton and Spruill's (1999) *Risk management checklist for trainees and supervisors* is one of many designed for use by psychologists and psychotherapists. Other tools (e.g., Pilette, Berck & Achber, 1995) are available for nursing staff, including ward-based staff.

Final note

This chapter has attempted to look at the grey areas of boundary maintenance and management: the boundary crossings that are unlikely to result in significant harm.

Serious boundary violations are rare, but they do occur. Unfortunately, there are clinicians who place their own needs and desires above the welfare of their patients and the services in which they work. Some of these clinicians are predatory in their boundary violations, but most are more likely to be responding to a temporary vulnerability to the powerful countertransference that can occur in therapy. In both cases, the clinician is likely to make cognitive errors that give permission for such violations to occur. They will minimize their responsibility for the decisions they are making; rationalize their behaviour; avoid those resources designed to help prevent boundary problems; and work to evade scrutiny (Pope & Keith-Spiegel, 2008). Thus, when serious boundary violations occur, they are often unexpected, leaving colleagues, patients and staff shocked. The only clues that a violation is taking place may be a pattern of departures from usual practice, including the timing, frequency and location of sessions, and the way in which sessions are documented.

The individual clinician is therefore central to the maintenance of clinical boundaries and the prevention of harm. This is simply because, if clinicians are unwilling to engage in the systems and processes outlined in this chapter, these systems and processes are rendered ineffective. This is not to suggest that organizations, professional bodies, staff teams and supervisors should not strive to improve the safeguarding systems. On the contrary, reviews of the literature demonstrate that supportive and open supervision, focused training in boundaries and greater awareness of professional guidelines and sanctions all serve to reduce the likelihood of boundary violation (Halter, Brown & Stone, 2007).

References

Borys, D. S. & Pope, K. S. (1989) Dual relationships between therapist and client: A national study of psychologists, psychiatrists, and social workers. *Professional Psychology: Research & Practice*, **20**, 283–293.

British Psychological Society (2009) *Code of ethics and conduct.* Leicester: British Psychological Society.

Division of Clinical Psychology (2003) *Policy guidelines on supervision in the practice of clinical psychology.* Leicester: British Psychological Society.

Elton Wilson, J. (2002) *Ethical thinking.* Presentation at POPAN Round Table meeting, 18 March, London.

Fallon, E. (1983) Helping Direct care workers manage self-injurious behaviour. *Milieu Therapy*, **3**, 45–52.

Feltham, C. (2000) Counselling supervision: Baseline, problems & possibilities. In B. Lawton & C. Feltham (Eds.) *Taking supervision forward: Enquiries and trends in counselling & psychotherapy* (pp. 5–24). London: Sage.

Gardner, D. J. (1993) Day-to-day ethical practice in clinical psychology in the UK: A preliminary investigation. Research dissertation for BPS Diploma in Clinical Psychology.

Goodman, J. H. (1997) How therapists cope with client suicidal behavior. *Dissertation Abstracts International: Section B: the Sciences & Engineering*, **57**, 9–13.

Gordon, A. & Wong, S. (2000) The violence reduction program. Unpublished manual.

Gutheil, T. G. & Brodsky, A. (2008) *Preventing boundary violations in clinical practice.* New York: Guilford Press.

Gutheil, T. G. & Gabbard, G. O. (1993) The concept of boundaries in clinical practice: Theoretical and risk-management dimensions. *American Journal of Psychiatry*, **150**, 188–196.

Gutheil, T. G. & Gabbard, G. O. (1998) Misuses and misunderstandings of boundary theory in clinical and regulatory settings. *American Journal of Psychiatry*, **155**, 409–414.

Gutheil, T. G. & Simon, R. I. (1995). Between the chair and the door: boundary issues in the therapeutic 'transition zone'. *Harvard Review of Psychiatry*, **2**, 336–340.

Halter, M., Brown, H. & Stone, J. (2007) *Sexual boundary violations by health professionals – An overview of the published empirical literature*. London: Council for Healthcare Regulatory Excellence.

Hamilton, J. C. & Spruill, J. (1999) Identifying and reducing risk factors related to trainee – client sexual misconduct. *Professional Psychology: Research and Practice*, **30**, 318–327.

Hawkins, P. & Shohet, R. (2000) *Supervision in the helping professions*, 2nd edition. Milton Keynes: Open University Press.

Health Professions Council (2008) *Standards of conduct, performance and ethics*. London: Health Professions Council.

Inskipp, F. & Proctor, B. (1995) *The art, craft and tasks of counselling supervision. Part Two – Becoming a supervisor*. Twickenham: Cascade Publications.

Lazarus, A. A. (1994) How certain boundaries and ethics diminish therapeutic effectiveness. *Ethical Behavior*, **4**, 255–261.

Linehan, M. M. (1993) *Cognitive-behavioral treatment of borderline personality disorder*. New York: Guilford Press.

Llewelyn, S. & Gardner, D. (2009) Boundary issues in clinical psychology. *Clinical Psychology Forum*, **193**, 9.

Maier, G., Stava, L., Morrow, B., van Rybroek, G. & Bauman, K. (1987) A model for understanding and managing cycles of aggressive psychiatric in clients. *Hospital and Community Psychiatry*, **38**, 520–524.

Marzillier, J. & Gardner, D. (1994) Boundaries in professional relationships: Conference workshop. *Clinical Psychology Forum*, **72**, 20–24.

Norris, D. M., Gutheil, T. G. & Strasburger, L. H. (2003) This couldn't happen to me: Boundary problems and sexual misconduct in the psychotherapy relationship. *Psychiatric Services*, **54**(4), 517–522.

Page, S. & Wosket, V. (1994) *Supervising the counsellor: A cyclical model*. London: Routledge.

Phillips, D. G. (2003). Dangers of boundary violations in the treatment of borderline patients. *Clinical Social Work Journal*, **31**, 315–326.

Pilette, P. C., Berck, C. B. & Achber, L. C. (1995) Therapeutic management of helping boundaries. *Journal of Psychosocial Nursing*, **33**, 40–47.

Pope, K. S. & Keith-Spiegel, P. (2008) A practical approach to boundaries in psycho-therapy: Making decisions, bypassing blunders, and mending fences. *Journal of Clinical Psychology: In Session*, **64**, 638–652.

Pope, K. S., Sonne, J. L. & Green, B. (2006) *What therapists don't talk about and why: understanding taboos that hurt us and our clients*. Washington, DC: American Psychological Association.

Pope, K. S. & Vasquez, M. (2007) *Ethics in psychotherapy and counseling: a practical guide*, 3rd edition. San Francisco: Jossey-Bass.

Safran, J. D. & Muran, J.C. (2003) *Negotiating the therapeutic alliance: A relational treatment guide*. New York: Guilford Press.

Scaife, J. (2001) *Supervision in the mental health professions: A practitioner's guide*. Hove: Brunner-Routledge.

Wisconsin Department of Regulation & Licensing (2007) *The changing regulation of substance abuse counselors*. Madison, WI: State of Wisconsin.

Young, J. (1994) *Cognitive therapy for personality disorders: A schema-focused approach, revised edition*. Sarasota, FL: Professional Resource Exchange.

Chapter Nine

One Patient's Therapeutic Journey

'James' and Louise Sainsbury

Introduction

Phil Willmot and Neil Gordon

James was a patient in the Personality Disorder Service at Rampton. His name and details have been changed, but the following is his account of his seven-year therapeutic journey through the service. At the time of writing he was about to be transferred to a medium secure unit, having successfully completed his treatment pathway. We asked James to write this account because of his degree of insight and his positive response to therapy, but we would not want to give readers the impression that this is typical of patients' experiences in the service; for many the therapeutic journey can be more of a struggle than it was for James. Nevertheless, we believe this is a rare and valuable insight into a patient's perspective.

James's account is followed by the parallel account by Dr Louise Sainsbury of the same therapeutic journey. Louise was James's psychologist and primary therapist for four years.

The patient's story

During my time in prison on remand I was terrified, depressed and lonely. I just couldn't cope with the busyness and crowds on the wing. I wanted to go to the hospital wing and I tried to hang myself; but people wouldn't listen to me and told me I was just looking for attention. I didn't know what was going on. I was angry and I ended up taking another prisoner hostage. I saw some psychiatrists

Working Positively with Personality Disorder in Secure Settings: A Practitioner's Perspective
Edited by Phil Willmot and Neil Gordon
© 2011 John Wiley & Sons, Ltd.

before my trial. One said I had a psychopathic disorder and recommended I go to a medium secure unit; another recommended I go to a medium secure unit, but not his, and a third said I was untreatable. My trial had to be stopped because of my poor mental health; I just couldn't stop crying or shaking. Eventually, I was convicted and given a life sentence.

To begin with I was on the hospital wing. I was trying to appeal against my conviction. I was still really emotional and being disruptive; kicking off and smashing up my cell. I tried again to take another prisoner hostage. I was in a right mess. Some of the staff in that prison were helpful and supportive; they looked after me and got me on some medication that helped to settle me down. A psychiatrist came to see me from a medium secure unit and said I was too dangerous for medium security and recommended me to the Personality Disorder Service at Rampton. Rampton sent a psychiatrist to see me, and also a psychologist. He was supportive but also no-nonsense and he was the first person I admitted my offences to. That was the first time ever that I'd felt safe enough to say what I'd done. Before, I'd always feared that I'd be ridiculed, rejected or attacked.

It was strange when I got to Rampton. I'd heard all the horror stories they tell you in prison – that it's like Beirut – and I was really frightened at first, but it was nothing like what I expected; everyone was helpful and supportive. I had a few problems settling in, but the staff managed to get me off the ward and doing things, which helped.

After a few months I moved on to one of the treatment wards and started treatment. I did the Introduction to Group Work. I found it a bit tedious but it showed you what the other groups were about. Then I did the Men Talking Group. That was really helpful; it got you thinking about things like masculinity and stereotypes, and all the different masks people use when they're feeling threatened or uncomfortable. It also taught you how to express your feelings in a safe way and how to get on in groups.

After the Men Talking Group I started DBT, which is when I first started working with Louise, my psychologist. At that time I was a mess emotionally and she spent a lot of time scraping me off the ceiling and just reassuring me. To start with I tried to frighten her off because I'd worked with that many people who'd opened me up, left me raw and then told me I was untreatable and just abandoned me, so I'd tell her things to shock her, like saying I wanted to take a hostage or tell her something really terrible about myself, just to see how she'd react. She wasn't shocked or scared though. She still thought I was treatable and she kept coming back and slowly she managed to break down the barriers.

It was little things she did that convinced me she wasn't going to reject me, like sometimes she'd spend longer than an hour with me if I was having a really bad day. I remember I used to give her a really hard time if she turned up late for our sessions because I'd get anxious waiting and start thinking she didn't care. Then one day she turned up late and I was about to give her an earful and I saw that she was full of a cold and she was really quite poorly. That meant a lot to me; it showed she'd really made an effort to see me and that our sessions must be important to her.

As I said, I was all over the place emotionally at that time. Things weren't going well on the treatment ward. There were a lot of 'alpha male' patients there and I got bullied a bit by them. I would do stuff to get back at them; smear shit on the toilet walls, put the washing machine on boil wash, stuff like that, which just made things worse with them. I was getting more and more wound up and getting put on more and more medication. In the end I told staff that I'd got a broken CD to protect myself. That was the last straw and I got moved to another ward where things just got worse. I suppose I was angry with myself for getting into that situation and for not being able to get on with other patients, and I felt I'd been let down again by people who should have been there to look after me – this time by my clinical team. That was the story of my life up till then: as soon as things got tough, people just abandoned me. I think I also blamed my old clinical team for not being able to treat me, as well as blaming myself for not being worthy of treatment. By now I was hearing these voices that were telling me to attack staff and I ended up attacking one of them with a knife and fork and getting transferred to the Intensive Care Unit.

Being in the Intensive Care Unit was a turning point for me. I had to look at myself honestly and look at all the bad stuff I'd done in the past and I realized that there was no point in just punishing myself all the time. I couldn't make my past any better but I could make sure nothing like that ever happened again. I'd hit rock bottom and the only way was up. One thing that made a big difference at that time was that Louise, my psychologist, kept coming to see me. That meant such a lot to me because it felt like everyone else from my ward was avoiding me, but she stuck by me. That made me believe that she could see something worthwhile in me and that I was actually worthy of treatment. From there things started to get better. I got put on some different medication which helped to dampen down my thoughts and emotions a bit, and DBT also helped me to control my emotions as well as teaching me how to analyse and understand what I was thinking and feeling and doing.

Next I did the R&R [Reasoning and Rehabilitation] group. I enjoyed that and it was really useful. It gave me confidence and taught me how to express myself better and how to negotiate.

After that I started schema therapy. That's been the most important therapy I've done, though I'm glad I did other things first, like DBT, which helped me to feel safe in that group. Thanks to the Schema Group I understand myself a lot better now, and why I think and do the things I do. One of the best things about the Schema Group was that the therapists talked about their schemas too. That really helped to break down barriers and show that they're human, and they have similar schemas to me, and they think and feel the same as I do. I found that really encouraging and it boosted my self-confidence a lot.

After schema therapy I was ready to start my offence-focused therapy. That was hard to begin with because it meant switching to a new psychologist after four years of working with Louise. We spent a long time talking about it and wrote each other end-of-therapy letters to express what we thought. Ending that therapeutic relationship was scary and sad, but it was also happy in a way because the relationship had come to a natural end rather than just ending and me being left thinking I'd been dumped again and wasn't worthy or treatment

Starting with a new psychologist was frightening and to begin with I felt he wasn't being supportive enough and it wasn't going to work with him, but then I spoke to Louise and I realized I needed to give it more time and talk things through with him, and because of the experience and confidence I'd got from working with Louise I was able to sort things out with my new psychologist. If I hadn't had that previous relationship with Louise, though, I wouldn't have been able to do it.

The work I've done with my therapists and the relationships I've had with them have been the biggest thing that's helped me, but relationships with other staff have also been helpful. I've had some great named nurses who've made time for me, listened to me and fought my corner when I've needed them, and I've never felt judged by them. Some have been a bit soft and I could twist them to let me do things. To be honest, I think I had more respect for the ones I couldn't twist. I felt safer with them too because I knew they wouldn't let me go too far. That's been a really important thing with the nursing staff I've worked with; they've helped me to feel safe and contained.

Soon I'm going to be moving on to a medium secure unit. I'm looking forward to it but I'm also frightened because it's a big new move after seven years in Rampton and I know there will be a whole lot of new restrictions and rules. I know I've still got a lot of work to do – relapse prevention work and preparing me for life in the community – but it's an opportunity to demonstrate and try out all the skills that I've learnt here in a different setting.

Looking back at how I've changed over the last seven years, now I feel I'm in control of myself using my own skills rather than having to rely on other people and on drugs to control my behaviour. I've also got a thicker skin now. Before I'd get really demanding and threatening if things didn't go the way I wanted, but now I can talk to most people and discuss and negotiate things. The biggest change for me though is that now I've learnt to feel safe and relaxed in other people's company. That makes such a big difference from a few years ago when being with other people was really uncomfortable; my head was full of thoughts about what a terrible person I was and I was constantly worrying that everyone else would see that and looking out for signs that they were going to attack me or reject me. Now, for the first time in my life, I can just be comfortable being me.

The therapist's story

I first met James when I became his individual therapist for Dialectical Behaviour Therapy (DBT) (Linehan, 1993). James met the criteria for DBT, with a diagnosis of borderline personality disorder. He showed a high degree of emotional dys-regulation, impulsive acting-out behaviour, including aggression, suicide attempts and chaotic relationships. As a child he had experienced abuse and neglect, had been taken into care and had several foster placements, which had broken down due to his destructive behaviours. At the start of the individual DBT sessions he was very keen to do well in DBT, desperate to show that he was 'good' and to be accepted. James had struggled for a long time to believe that others would stick with him, based on his childhood experiences; and his eagerness to be good enough was his strategy for trying to ensure his expectation of being abandoned or abused did not occur. The initial need was to start to develop a secure thera-peutic alliance. From an attachment perspective the development of a secure base relationship is both the necessary condition and the context in which development occurs (Bowlby, 1988; Wallin, 2007). James was clear about his primary treatment targets, including reducing suicidal thoughts and urges, aggression and impulsivity; and increasing his capacity to contain his emotions, think about his and others' thinking, and contain his impulses and effectiveness in relating to others. I was immediately struck by how insightful he could be when emotionally regulated. Early on in therapy James described how, if he was worried about his safety, he did not have the space to think about changing. In some ways this increased my hope that he could benefit from therapy; however, raising my expectations also proved unhelpful in expecting too much too soon. Whilst James was aware of what he needed to do, the difficulty was in helping him to react and act differently. He needed the emotional regulation to be able to identify and rehearse strategies for regulating his emotions. In the first part of therapy I had to provide the emotional stability for him to be able to develop his capacity to regulate his emotions. The focus was to develop these capacities within the therapeutic relationship and then to generalize these to others in his environment.

For the first six months or so, much of the session time was focused on how James and I were relating to each other and our therapeutic relationship. This involved maintaining my patience and focus on his internal state underneath the acting-out behaviours. Although DBT allows for the client to telephone the therapist in times of crisis between sessions, this was not possible in the secure hospital setting. Instead, in the orientation phase of DBT, I informed James that should he need additional coaching to get him through difficulties 'in the moment', then he could ask staff to call me when I was in the hospital and I would come to the ward as soon as my other commitments would allow. I emphasized that my availability was dictated by my other commitments and that there might be times when I would not be able to see him on the same day. James appeared to appreciate this and he rarely asked for time outside of sessions. On occasion I did extend sessions to coach him in gaining some emotional regulation before I left. He was frequently overwhelmed by his emotions and fears about himself and others. This flexibility or temporary extended limits (Linehan, 1993: 325) was essential in the therapy, providing both James and me with the experience that his emotions could be contained, and these experiences provided James with a sense of predictability and consistency in this therapeutic relationship.

James's emotions were very easily triggered in the chain analyses exploring his destructive behaviours, including strong feelings of shame and fear that I would abandon him. James struggled initially to put these emotions and fear into words. My tentively guessing what his fears were (mindreading in DBT terms (Linehan, 1993) was based on his history and non-verbal behaviours. This aimed to develop positive experiences for James of openly relating to another and reducing his fear of reprisal or rejection.

James was on a ward with 14 other patients with diagnoses of personality disorder. He was feeling increasingly at odds with some of the other more dominant patients and resorted to indirect aggression, such as putting their clothes onto boil wash and smearing in the toilets. As a result he became a target for other patients, and he increasingly retaliated. I was focusing on his underlying feelings of hurt, rejection (his primary emotions) and trying to contain his anger (his secondary emotion) and help him not to act on his strong impulses for revenge. This period had the greatest tension in the therapeutic relationship for me; the pull of James's wish to be rescued and the push of his fear of being either abused or abandoned were at their strongest as he experienced further rejection from his peers. At times it was hard to stay focused on his underlying fears and pain, trying not to react to the push–pull with a push–pull response. Supervision was critical in supporting me to maintain a focus on his internal needs and trying to support him in finding an effective way through these difficult relationships by providing the space to reflect on my reactions to the 'emotional pulls', or tranference, from James.

Unfortunately, it was relatively early days in terms of James being able to toler-ate his emotions without acting on his urges. He was feeling increasingly hurt, angry and unsafe on the ward, until in one session, he falteringly told me that he had broken a CD and had a piece of it on him to protect himself and that he was worried about this. He appeared to be trying to find a way out of the situation he was in and he was able to discuss how we would tell the staff and support him in handling this, which he did.

This was one of a number of turning points in his therapy; marking an increase in his experience of what I could cope with and a reduction in therapy interfering behaviours. His history was signficantly marked by his behaviour being more than his mother, foster parents or prison staff could cope with. Whilst the ward enviro-ment could contain a significant amount, James's behaviours were challenging for the ward staff and managing their expectations, particularly of the therapy was important.

A second turning point in the therapy occurred shortly afterwards. Unfortunately, we were not able to contain his emotions and feelings sufficently or to support him, and his behaviour deteriorated. He was moved to a different ward. For James this felt like a rejection and that his clinicial team could not protect him, similar to the lack of protection in his childhood. He further deteriorated on the new ward, threatened to assault a member of staff and was sent to the intensive care ward. Unlike other professions, psychologists and other therapists within the service tend to stay with their patients when they change wards, though James did not understand this at the time and interpreted this as my 'sticking by him' while the rest of his team had 'rejected' him. He appeared very surprised to see me on the intensive care ward, as well as ashamed of himself. In later months he talked about the very positive impact on him of my 'not giving up' on him.

Returning to the ward was a difficult but very positive experience for James. His worries that the staff would be punitive towards him proved false, challenging his expectations that he would be rejected and punished.

As James developed increasing trust in me, within sessions we could focus more on developing his capacity to manage his reactions to triggering situations. He was becoming less emotionally reactive to completing the chain analysis and what we had learnt from developing our therapeutic relationship helped to identify his fears and emotions in difficult interactions on the ward. Rehearsing how to manage himself was done through role play. James was exceptionally good at this. I think it appealed to the more dramatic aspects of his personality. On an early occasion I role played him having a very angry and verbally demanding response and he was to role play me. His reaction to my role play was to look directly at me and say, 'You have a hard job'. This was probably the first time when he spontaneously took a perspective from outside himself and showed increasing capacity to consider my experience of the relationship. From my perspective it was a moment of shared understanding about both our experiences, which was very rewarding.

A further signficant experience within the therapy occurred when, after two weeks without sessions due to my being on annual leave and then at a conference, I saw James, despite having a cold. I had decided to see him due in part to thinking that it would prevent a more difficult subsequent session and in part due to my tendency not to 'give in' to a cold. James began the session by heatedly talking *at* me about the different people who had let him down and not been there for him. I sat in silence listening to him, considering the possibility that his comments about others were actually about me and thinking about how to respond, when he stopped in mid-sentence. He then said, 'But I am having that challenged right now.' He told me he appreciated my efforts and we highlighted his increasing capacity to 'see clearly' what was happening in the present and not be distracted by his past. It was also important to support James in being appropriately angry with me and being able to effectively disagree with me and to experience that relationships could survive such feelings.

As James maintained some stability and his progress was highlighted by other members of staff, he became increasingly impatient to start work addressing his offending behaviour, arguing that he could undertake this and schema therapy at the same time. I was concerned that he was rushing into his therapies and focusing on moving to medium secure services rather than on further developing his progress. He raised in a somewhat demanding manner his belief that I was holding him back. In one way he was right; I was trying to slow him down. However, at that point he could not believe that my intentions were for his benefit. His increasing capacity to cope showed in that he did not try to terminate our relationship. Instead, he expressed his beliefs that I was holding him back to his clinical team in a ward round when I was not present. This highlighted his ongoing difficulties in addressing issues directly and accepting when someone in a position of authority made a decision he did not agree with. I focused on discussing our different opinions, at the same time as trying to maintain a difficult balance of not 'giving in' to James to avoid further conflict and trying to enable him to express his frustration and mistrust towards me. As a compromise I said that I would carry out the offence assessment for the offending therapy, and we would use this to gain an indication of his capacity to cope with this work. After this was completed, James acknowledged that it was more difficult than he had anticipated, particularly as he had worried more than he had anticipated about my reactions to his offending. However, he had raised these worries directly with me, not avoiding them or subsequently testing me through difficult behaviours. He was then able to reflect on his pushing too hard for things and further highlighting his fears that others would forget about him or not want to help him.

James had shown more than six months of more stable behaviour without any aggression or suicidal urges, indicating he had gained sufficient emotional regulation to undertake work on his childhood abuse and neglect. Schema therapy (Young, Klosko & Weishaar, 2003) was undertaken to address his schemas or core beliefs consisting of memories, feelings and emotions and to help him to grieve for his childhood. Within the PDS, schema therapy comprises a combination of individual and group weekly sessions.

As James developed, his increasing capacity to contain and effectively tolerate his emotions, impulses and his internalization of myself as a secure base was becoming apparent. One example was provided by a member of the ward staff, who told me that James had started to express his anger about a decision in a somewhat aggressive manner, to which she had asked him what I would say. She described how at that point he stopped, appeared to calm quickly and said, 'Ah, probably that I am overreacting as I feel unfairly treated by the decision', and he walked away. Due to his increasing internal containment I felt it was important for him to begin to work more independently to generalize his abilities to relate more securely to others. I was keen that he work more independently. A big step in increasing his independence involved James attending a schema therapy group that I did not facilitate, whilst I continued to provide his individual schema sessions. James initially opposed this, arguing that my not seeing him in the group would lead to reduced communication between the group and individual sessions. I asked James what he was worried about as he knew that there would be communication. He looked down, and appeared sad and alone. He spoke about his worries that he would not do as well without me there to push him along and keep him on track. I thought about this in terms of separation anxiety and talked with James about his need to develop some independence now that he had developed some secure dependence on me. We spent many sessions talking about interdependence and the need to be able to do both. He was able to develop positive relationships with group facilitators and participants, as well as demonstrating increasing capacity to tolerate difficult interactions. I faciliated one of the group sessions to cover for an absence; and James commented afterwards that he felt more anxious when I was present as he felt under more pressure, given that I knew him.

Schemas relevant to James had been identified through chain analysis in DBT. These included mistrust abuse, emotional deprivation, defectiveness, abandonment instability and social isolation. (For further explanation of these schemas, modes and other schema therapy concepts, see this volume, chapter 11 on interpersonal dynamics.) Secondary coping schemas were also identified, including failure, entitlement and unrelenting standards, subjugation and punitiveness, which represented ineffective ways of trying to get his needs met. As almost all the core schemas were triggered at the same time, schema modes were introduced. James quickly identified with the child modes – vulenerable and angry little James modes – as well as healthy adult mode. He conceptualized his aggressive acting-out behavours as angry little James mode, who was protecting vulnerable little James, who was hiding behind the wall he had built around himself. We talked about the times he had hidden behind walls with myself and key moments in our interactions that had helped him to lower the wall and given him some hope that he could trust others.

James used imagery techniques very effectively to work on the origins of his core schemas. We used imagery to work through his emotions about being taken into care and in various foster placements. In the first imagery work we completed we focused on his memory of a social worker taking him into care for the first time. He described his mother standing on the pavement crying, appearing smaller and smaller as the car drove away. He described himself on the back seat thumping on the rear window. We spent a lot of time sitting with his sadness, loss and grief, and at the end of the session he joked about feeling 'Branstoned' (i.e., pickled). His ability to sit with and not react to his emotions, as well as use a mature humour defence, was a new experience for James, and one which gave him increased confidence in his ability to feel comfortable with himself. In that and subsequent imagery work, he brought in 'healthy James' who contained 'angry little James' and comforted both 'angry little James' and 'vulnerable little James'. These were particularly emotional sessions. At the start of therapy, containing his secondary emotions of anger and frustration was hard and tiring and I had to contain my own reactions to his demanding and hostile behaviours. In this stage of his therapy his primary emotions of hurt, loss, shame and grief were very honest and powerful. It seemed that James felt the strength of his emotions and their ability to be seen by another, despite their relative quietness compared to his (by then) 'old', noisy, acting-out behaviours.

When working through his experiences of abuse and betrayal, he spontaneously began to focus on how he had betrayed his victim, connecting with the shame and pain he made his victim suffer. This time, instead of defensively denying his offences when faced with the enormity of what he had done, as he did when he was first convicted, he was able to tolerate his guilt and shame and accept that he could not undo what he had done, but that he had to make sure he did not add to it. It felt at the time that all of the experiences we had shared through the previous three and half years had culmimated in his capacity to integrate the worst of what of he had done with what had been done to him, without using this as a justification, accepting that he was both an offender and a victim.

The extent to which James had internalized a sense of attachment security and positive internal working models was highlighted several times during the last year of our therapeutic relationship. Notably, after getting a new named nurse he came to session wanting to get my support for him to change the named nurse. He asked me to not say anything until he had finished saying his piece. I remained silent throughout and he intially listed his reasons for wanting to change his named nurse. As he continued he paused and said, 'I know you will say to me that I need to work at the relationship, not give up without having tried, as I still have fears that get in the way of trying in relationships.' At this point he paused again and said more calmly, 'I need to give it a try with him.' James then wanted to know why I was smiling. I shared with him my positive feelings at his new capacity to reflect on his thinking and mine. Reflective thinking is the hallmark of a secure attachment style (Fonagy, Steele, Steele, Moran & Higgitt, 1991).

As the end of schema therapy approached, we began to discuss the ending of this therapeutic relationship. We spent several months discussing this as the reality approached. In the meantime he began his offence-focused treatment with his new psychologist. He initially struggled to trust his new psychologist, and he used our therapeutic relationship to work through his worries and rehearse, through role play, how to raise these with his new psychologist. Using the therapy letter technique from cognitive analytic therapy (Ryle, 1991), I told James that I would write a therapy ending letter, covering the therapy journey – both the good points and the bad – and I asked him to do the same. These letters were read out in the final session. Both James and I had recalled some of the same key moments in the therapy: what he had gained and what I had learnt from him. He ended the sessions being able to express both the sadness at the ending and excitment at the new beginning he was undertaking.

James's account places a lot of importance on his relationship with his primary therapist, which reflects the emphasis on this relationship in much of the psycho-therapy literature (e.g., Martin, Garske & Davis, 2000; Critchfield & Benjamin, 2006). However, I think it is important to stress that therapy never takes place in a vacuum and that the progress that James made in therapy would not have been possible without the work of nursing staff and other professionals involved in his care.

Given James's developmental history it was not surprising that he began therapy with a lot of negative beliefs about people in authority. An important focus during DBT was getting him to practise interacting effectively with staff and challenging these negative beliefs using role play. This task was greatly helped by a his named nurses and other key workers who were able to understand his behaviour and respond appropriately both to his dysfunctional behaviour and to his attempts to behave differently.

Towards the latter stages of his therapy, James's relationships with other disci-plines certainly mirrored his relationship with his therapist, and the processes he describes of becoming able to feel safe and contained with me were reflected in other key relationships, such as with nurses, psychiatrists and social workers. Also, as time passed, he became easier to contain, less impulsive and demanding and more emotionally stable, and I think this reflected the consistent approach taken by his clinical teams.

References

Bowlby, J. (1988) *A secure base: Clinical applications of attachment theory.*

Critchfield, K. L. & Benjamin, L. S. (2006) Integration of therapeutic factors in treating personality disorders. In L. Castonguay & L. Beutler (Eds.) *Principles of therapeutic change that works* (pp. 253–271). New York: Oxford University Press.

Fonagy, P., Steele, M., Steele, H., Moran, G. S. & Higgitt, A. (1991) The capacity for understanding mental states: The reflective self in parent and child and its significance for security of attachment. *Infant Mental Health Journal*, **12**, 201–218.

Linehan, M. M. (1993) *Cognitive behavioural treatment of borderline personality disorder.* New York: Guilford Press.

Martin, D. J., Garske, J. P. & Davis, M. K. (2000) Relation of the therapeutic alliance with outcome and other variables: A meta-analytic review. *Journal of Consulting and Clinical Psychology*, **68**, 438–450.

Ryle. A. (1991) *Cognitive analytic therapy: Active participation in change.* New York: Wiley.

Wallin, D. J. (2007) *Attachment in psychotherapy.* New York: Guilford Press.

Young, J. E., Klosko, J. S. & Weishaar, M. E. (2003) *Schema therapy: A practitioner's guide.* New York: Guilford Press.

Section Four

Supporting and Developing the Therapeutic Workforce

Chapter Ten

Therapists' Experiences of Therapy

Neil Gordon, Kerry Beckley and Graham Lowings

Introduction

When talking with experienced mental health professionals, a common reaction
to revealing that you enjoy working therapeutically with individuals with a diagnosis of personality disorder is one of surprise, often followed by sympathy. Most
professionals in psychiatric settings have some contact with individuals considered
to be 'personality disordered' and for those working in a forensic mental health
service, this is a core element of their day-to-day experience. For many in acute
mental health services, this has not been a particularly positive experience.
Paradoxically, for those practitioners in forensic settings who have often *chosen* to
work with this client group, passionate commitment is often a feature of their
professional approach. This chapter provides a more balanced perspective on the
experience of therapists who work with personality disorder by highlighting the
challenges, while also considering the benefits and emotional richness of these
interpersonal encounters. The discussion is informed by the findings and core
themes from two interview-based qualitative research studies exploring the experiences of therapists in a high secure setting (Gordon, 2003; Lowings, 2008).
Whilst Lowings's study explored the experiences of therapists working in a range
of settings and focused on working with people labelled with a borderline personality disorder, much of this chapter centres on the context of Gordon's research
– the high secure forensic setting with complex personality disorder presentations.
The themes illuminating therapists' experiences do, however, resonate in both

Working Positively with Personality Disorder in Secure Settings: A Practitioner's Perspective
Edited by Phil Willmot and Neil Gordon
© 2011 John Wiley & Sons, Ltd.

studies, and what is presented in this chapter are insights into the working challenges and rewards of therapeutic work with individuals living with personality disorder.

For the purposes of the chapter the direct quotes from practitioners have been integrated with the personal therapeutic experiences of the authors to provide a coherent narrative of the therapist's perspective. Although this chapter is written from the perspective of forensic practitioners, it is assumed that the insights offered may also have some relevance to those working in non-forensic contexts. We recognize that any therapeutic intervention with those defined as personality disordered is interpersonal in nature and that both parties directly contribute to the quality of the interaction. However, in the chapter we wish focus on the therapist's experience.

I'm in the room too: the use of self in therapy

Clearly, our own needs and motivations impact on our decisions as to whom we choose to work with. So, why work with a clinical group widely considered the most difficult to engage and the most emotionally challenging? Contemporary approaches such as schema therapy (Young, Klosko & Weishaar, 2003) encourage therapists to use their theoretical model to assist with self-reflection, believing that an understanding of our own emotional processes and high levels of self-awareness are essential features of competent practice. We also know that many mental health professionals are drawn to working with the distress of others as a way of addressing their own needs (Aiyegbusi & Tuck, 2008). Bamber (2006) identified that clinical psychologists were more likely to have pronounced self-sacrifice schemas (i.e., excessive focus on meeting the needs of others at the expense of their own). Our own experience would indicate that the strength of the relational interaction between patient and therapist can be highly personally rewarding as the therapist can feel both very connected to the patient and in a position to really 'know' them. This position is very important and is implicitly or explicitly used by the wider clinical team in decision-making. Being closely connected to such patients, particularly in a forensic setting, can leave the therapist in a potentially vulnerable position (see this volume, Chapter 8 on boundary issues), but if the therapist is experienced, reflective and skilful, they can work effectively within appropriate boundaries and be able to fully utilize the emotional bond within the therapeutic relationship in order to take greater therapeutic risks.

Emotional connectedness to the patient's experience is a key feature of effective therapy. Therapeutic factors such as empathy and positive regard are unquestionably essential features within any effective alliance. However, it is important to maintain this position consistently in the face of boundary challenges, emotional demands, hostility or aggression, all of which can feature within the therapeutic relationship in these settings. This occurs as the majority of these patients have an acknowledged ambivalence (if not paranoid resistance in some cases) in relation to their involvement in therapeutic work. Also, because of their personality difficulties (and often histories of victimization) these patients struggle with forming relationships and find the potential demands of the therapeutic encounter a frightening prospect. They are also people who may not see the relevance of therapy and interpret it as a demand that the institution is making of them before achieving release to conditions of lesser security.

Working with such patients (who are by definition often impulsive and easily emotionally dysregulated) often means that when the therapist goes into a session they are never quite sure with what they will be presented. This is a feature of people with histories of offending behaviour, with the consequence that their relationships with those who are treating them are often characterized by dysfunction and rupture (Jones, 2002). Because these difficulties are common with these individuals, it might be assumed that the difficulty is solely in the patient. However, the reflective therapist needs to be mindful of how their interpersonal style and external stressors are impacting on a difficult interaction.

Therapist–patient fit also warrants careful consideration. Most of the work in this area has focused on gender and ethnicity, an issue identified in Lowings's (2008) work. Although these factors may be important in some circumstances, there is a danger of making assumptions about both on the basis of observable difference, and potentially ignoring other factors that can impact significantly on the therapeutic relationship. Perhaps most important in this area are the personality characteristics of the therapist and how these can impact on his or her ability to work therapeutically. (See this volume, Chapter 11 for a discussion of schema chemistry between staff and patients and Chapter 15 on patients' views of therapy for accounts of therapist behaviours and characteristics that affect the therapeutic relationship).

A common theme in many treatment approaches for personality disorder is the expectation on the therapist to 'go beyond' normal boundaries of therapy. For example, Dialectical Behaviour Therapy (DBT) allows the patient to telephone the therapist at times of crisis between formal therapy sessions, while schema therapy and mentalization-based therapy encourage a greater emotional connection and, at times, touch and self-disclosure by the therapist. These interventions would not normally feature in traditional psychodynamic approaches. Linehan's (1993) concept of 'cheerleading' and Young's concept of 'limited reparenting' (Young *et al.*, 2003) are examples of the need for the therapist to be emotionally active and explicitly positive and encouraging in their work with patients with personality disorders. Lowings (2008) refers to one of the therapists in his study sending letters of welcome to prospective clients. It is our opinion that it is an essential requirement for the therapist to be emotionally available and genuine in their therapeutic style. For many therapists, this feels like a relief in contrast to other therapeutic approaches, which can restrict the extent to which the person feels they can be human in order to retain professional boundaries.

An effective therapist can feel like a salesperson, reflecting the therapist's ability to articulate the relevance of the theory to the patient whilst maintaining motivation and engagement. The rhetorical element (Frank & Frank, 1991) relates to the therapist's ability to provide convincing arguments and rationales that encourage the patient to commit to the therapeutic work while maintaining a collaborative approach. When assuming this rhetorical role, Gordon (2003) described therapists using themselves as *imperfect examples* to establish a link with the patient, usually disclosing some aspect of their own life they had difficulties with.

Relating to the patient with a degree of humility and self-disclosure requires a willingness to acknowledge personal weakness, which can be in direct contrast to

Strategies

the dominant discourse in forensic personality disorder services. If the patient is able to see their therapist as *imperfect*, they are more able to identify with their *ordinariness* and humanity (Gordon, 2003). This capacity to disclose about selective negative aspects of one's personal life struggle is a powerful influencing factor in the development of a collaborative psychotherapy relationship and is often something that many therapists feel very uncomfortable with. Like any strategy, it will not always be appropriate or successful, but when it does work, it can be extremely powerful for both. As one therapist commented in Gordon's (2003) study:

> 'You have to be genuine and be yourself, you've got to acknowledge you don't have all the answers and that sometimes you get things wrong.'

Empathic confrontation: Being a critical friend

The role of therapists in advocating and being honest and 'up front' with the patient can be represented by the notion of being a *critical friend* (Gordon, 2003). A critical friend is someone who is both a friend and a critic. The therapist is seen as a 'friend' because of the relationship he/she provides and the commitment and concern that he/she demonstrates. Young (2003) describes this process as empathic confrontation, where the problem is identified and challenged assertively by the therapist whilst attending to the needs of the patient to be cared for and understood.

The therapist also needs to resist playing a power game by openly acknowledging his or her authority and capacity to influence the patient's situation and not pretending that the relationship is equal. As Pilgrim (1997) observed, therapists in this setting are responsible for the writing of reports and risk management assessments which can have a major impact on the individual's progress to conditions of lower security, so this needs to remain in the mind of both therapist and patient. This power issue was discussed in Lowings's (2008) work and he identified the challenge of therapists needing to overcome the power imbalance and forge trust with the client, a challenge that can be exacerbated in high secure settings.

It has been suggested that patients with a history of sexual offending may attempt to 'groom' (i.e., develop a relational contact with ulterior motives) staff (Perkins, 1991) to gain advantage over other patients and influence over staff, thus paralleling their behaviours with victims they have offended against. This concept is also commonly used, rightly or wrongly, to describe the interpersonal behaviour of personality disordered patients in general. Within the high secure setting there is often a concern that the constraint created by the controlled environment is the only factor that is inhibiting the offending behaviour of the individual, and on release the absence of this extrinsic motivator will lead to relapse. It is therefore of great importance in this setting to track and challenge cognitions (e.g., violent and sexual fantasy and thinking) and behaviours that parallel the patient's past offending behaviours (Jones, 2001). This requires the therapist to be open about risk issues and to constantly review the person's behaviour in different contexts, to establish if the 'progressing' patient is genuine. This situation has to be dealt with sensitively and openly, and the concept of the *critical friend* within the role of the therapist as a 'friend' is brought into view and they tell it how it is, not backing away from talking about these difficult and controversial issues.

A sexualized environment!

The high secure context has the potential to be a sexually charged environment as individuals are encouraged, within the intimacy of a therapeutic relationship, to talk about their sexual crimes and violent fantasies as part of the treatment process. The dimensions of this category, predominantly discussed by female therapists in Gordon's (2003) study, relate to managing these encounters and maintaining personal boundaries. Issues of self-disclosure and self-presentation are central in these accounts and relate to the increased self-consciousness experienced by female therapists in terms of how they may be perceived by certain patients. A common problem within this setting is the perception of any interest in sexuality and sexual expression by the patient as an example of *offence paralleling behaviour* (Jones, 2002), while another problem is that close and intense therapeutic relationships, particularly between therapists and patients of the opposite sex, can sometimes be misinterpreted by other staff and patients. Lowings's (2008) study showed that his participants considered that an accusation of being 'too close' can come from other staff working with the client who construe the close working relationship and therapeutic alliance as an indication of something inappropriate. Lowings (2008) suggests that educating others as to the nature of the therapeutic alliance may remove any misunderstanding between the therapist and others who also care for the personality disordered client.

A further interesting dimension of this experience relates to machismo (and misogyny), which is a well-documented aspect of the staff and patient cultures in high secure environments (Morris, 2001). It is reflected in a perception that female therapists are susceptible to over-involvement with their patients and that male staff have a need to protect them from violence and threat.

In Gordon's (2003) research, for the female therapists working in this setting, *self-presentation* issues related to their perceived need to be careful in their presentation (e.g., their choice of clothing) highlight the sexualized nature of the context. As well as their appearance, female therapists were aware of the dangers of working with this client group in relation to *self-protection*.

> 'Therapeutic work focused on sexual behaviour creates a sexualized environment where female therapists can become targets of inappropriate comments; this can easily make you vulnerable and feel isolated.'

The nature of the work itself may give rise to some wariness on the part of the therapist and can lead to female therapists continuously self-monitoring during their interactions with their patients, because of the potential for these men to misconstrue the nature of the relationship.

Gartner and Shapiro have observed that 'the sex of the therapist significantly informs the treatment of any patient but is especially influential in relation to sexually abused (or sexually offending) adults' (1999: 266). It can be seen how these female therapists are managing their self-presentation to avoid miscommunication to, or misinterpretations by, the patient. These issues, however, are not confined to female therapists. In this environment male staff at times psychologically defend themselves from the pathology of their patients by projecting a compensatory 'hyper-masculinity' where caring is viewed as 'soft and namby-pamby' (Morris, 2001: 97). This was an issue for one therapist in Gordon's (2003) study, who acknowledged:

> 'I know that some of the nurses think what I am doing with this guy is a waste of time, particularly some of the male staff, they have no time for [patient's name] and think all this therapy stuff is just wasted on him. For some of them it's just their whole attitude to therapy, they don't want to be involved with it.'

Others' negativity in Lowings's (2008) study also related to these issues. One of Lowings's (2007) participants discussed that the negativity expressed by other staff members made her clients more appreciative of therapy as it contrasted with the less therapeutic interactions of others with whom the client came into contact.

Gartner (1999) explored in detail the potential countertransference dynamics that can come into play when male survivors of abuse encounter therapists of the same sex as their abuser. He suggests that it is important for male therapists not to perpetuate gender stereotypes when engaged in teaching and learning about being men as this can undermine the sexually abused man's capacity to deal with his victimization. In this sense some therapists in a high secure setting may be providing a therapeutic counterbalance to the hyper-masculinity of the therapeutic milieu. An important aspect of this gender sensitivity theme is that these dilemmas are rarely explored or talked about, despite the obvious fact that our physical presentations and gender role behaviours permeate the therapeutic encounter (Gartner & Shapiro, 1999) and are an important dimension in high secure settings.

This silence around the themes of *self-presentation* and *self-protection* (Gordon, 2003) also prevents those working in these environments from recognizing the sexual behaviour of patients which could be seen as normal adult experience. For some of these men, therapy can be their first experience of an intimate, trusting relationship with someone who cares about them and their experiences. It is almost impossible for men in this setting to have their actions interpreted as representing 'normal' sexual behaviour as any interest in female staff can be perceived as potentially offence paralleling.

> 'In forensic mental health there's a horrible stigma and a lot of the things that people experience are normal but they get stigmatized. Sexual attraction for example is perfectly normal but it is frowned upon and is discouraged and is seen as slightly taboo.'

Hear no evil, see no evil, speak no evil

Therapists need to protect themselves from the corrosive effects of being exposed to the narratives of patients who have committed violent and sexual offences and have themselves experienced various levels of physical and sexual abuse. As Ryan and Lane observe, 'professionals who interact with dysfunctional populations are at risk personally, socially and professionally' (1997: 457). These risks stem from the realities, beliefs and attributions of each individual and how they meet the challenge of integrating these experiences into their personal worldview. Part of the process of protecting oneself from and dealing with these extremes of experience is to become *desensitized* to the horror of the story being told, as one of the therapists in Gordon's (2003) study observed:

> 'I think sometimes we become dehumanized and insensitive to the actual offences these guys have committed. It easy to see the positive side of them. We are a bit like soldiers who have to deal with death – we deny the reality of what took place.'

Therapists in this study described finding themselves minimizing and avoiding thinking about what the person had done as a way of maintaining the capacity to work with the person:

> 'A basic rule for me is that there is a huge amount of the picture that I can't hear, in the same way that I couldn't hear about abuse before [when first being exposed to narratives of abuse before it was realized how prevalent it was]. There is a lot of stuff I am not hearing now and I have got to try and keep open to these other possibilities.'

This struggle can be illuminated with reference to Houston's (1990) notion of numb, dumb, deaf and blind spots. She suggested that there were always aspects of our therapeutic experience we could not fully understand and acknowledge because we were temporarily *unable to feel* or experience certain emotions, *unable to say* what we felt because we cannot find the words to express what was going on for us, *unable to hear* what we were being told because our experience was somehow blocking it out and, finally, *unable to see* what might be happening between us and the patient. In the therapists' accounts in Gordon's (2003) study, these themes were a constant feature of the experience of working with difficult issues. One way of managing this struggle and helping to access these blind, numb, deaf and dumb spots is through supervision. However, there can be a danger of assuming that supervision is a panacea for the therapist, as the quality of supervision is determined by a similarly wide range of factors that impact on the therapeutic relationship. Having a whole network of supportive and emotionally connected relationships in the workplace is possibly of greater necessity when working with individuals with a personality disorder diagnosis than it is any other context.

An effective therapist acknowledges the need for an external perspective on their work because there are always aspects of practice that are not within their awareness. Cox provides a dramatic analysis of the potential difficulties in dealing with the demands of this patient group by deconstructing the view that our problems with patients are 'hung up with our keys at the gate' (1994: 447). As he eloquently puts it, therapists in this setting are in constant contact with experiences 'that bad dreams are made of'. Therapists who deal each day with patients struggling with their violence and fear are therefore always in need of high quality supervision to help them process and manage their own vulnerabilities.

Gordon's (2003) findings suggest a further interesting dimension of managing self in these encounters. This is where an event occurs (perhaps overt hostility or threatening behaviour by the patient) or something is spoken about, such as the crime or the abuse, and the therapist is suddenly acutely aware of the their previously denied reality of the person's experience or actions. One participant remarked:

> 'Sometimes you are not expecting the dramatic shift in the relationship, but when someone gets very angry, or threatening or distressed you suddenly become more aware of what you are actually dealing with here.'

A further way that therapists protect themselves from the demands of the encounter is the notion of suddenly *waking up in the room* (Gordon, 2003). This describes a superficial engagement with the patient in which the therapist is 'going through the motions' of therapy:

> 'It's about the danger of institutionalized relationships, which are about routinely regurgitating a theoretical model to protect you from that person, that stops you from engaging, it's like an experience of waking up [in the room], it's when you wake up from your theory and you realize, "Oh that's what I have been doing", and realize you have not heard what this person has been saying. I think we so often miss out on what the problem is because of our pet theories.'

This notion of being blinded by our theories and falling into institutionalized forms of relating is illuminated further with reference to the tendency of therapists to manage the focus of the session to avoid conflict and difficult issues by what they referred to as having *a lazy day*.

> 'Sometimes when you have not got a lot of energy you have a lazy day where you would avoid addressing emotive issues and conflicts and would focus on the superficial. It might be that you are tired or your head is so busy you cannot ask the right questions.'

This is related to the long-term nature of the work and an acceptance that the sense of urgency to effect change and resolve issues is influenced by the fact that the therapist could be working with the patient for a number of years. Therapists were very aware of the importance of remaining alert to these strategies as examples of their own 'therapy interfering behaviours' (Linehan, 1993).

A useful concept to help us understand this phenomenon comes from Young's (1994) work on schema therapy. Young talks about a self-state or mode described as the 'detached protector', which is characterized by an individual's capacity to disassociate from painful experiences and behave in a neutral and apparently unaffected way. Therapists sometimes appeared to operate in a similar way to protect themselves from the pain or distress of the patient. In acknowledging this aspect of their practice, Gordon's participants emphasized the importance of recognizing this as an indicator of their own vulnerability and acknowledged how important it was to use supervision to reflect upon and explore the dynamics of their disengagement behaviour.

A further pervasive feature of the therapists' experience can relate to their expectation that they would disappoint and be rejected by the patient as the work progressed. As Melia, Moran and Mason (1998) have suggested, when working with people in this setting it is often useful to expect the worst and not be surprised by patients' negative reactions. As one therapist pointed out:

'Most of the therapists here will have had the experience of the patient disengaging and withdrawing from therapy, and blaming them for his lack of progress; that can be crushing if you are an inexperienced member of staff.'

This relates to *managing the precarious relationship* (Gordon, 2003) and is an essential feature of coping effectively with ruptures within the therapeutic alliance. As this quote emphasizes, part of coping with this challenging experience is to anticipate motivational fluctuation. It is important, when working with personality disordered offenders, to regularly revisit motivational issues and recognize that this patient group is particularly likely to engage in therapy interfering behaviours that lead to disengagement and rejection of the therapist. Part of this issue relates to the personality disordered individual's tendency to impulsive and self-destructive interpersonal behaviour. As Morris points out, when working with personality disordered individuals, their 'psychopathology is expressed in their relationships' (2001: 97). Whereas a psychotic person's psychopathology is usually manifest in their own mind in the form of delusions and hallucinations, it is within the therapeutic encounter itself that much of the personality disordered person's distress emerges and has to be responded to and made sense of.

This is further complicated in high secure contexts by the increasingly litigious culture where patients' complaints and the involvement of solicitors are common. Therapists have a difficult line to tread in maintaining the individual's commitment and engagement with therapy while expecting periods of disenchantment and withdrawal as inevitable features of their work. Being prepared for this helps the therapist to manage their own vulnerability and encourages a complex formulation of the patient's behaviour that does not become overly personalized and detrimental to the practitioner's self-esteem.

Creating the container: Safety in risk-taking

The therapist as *physical and psychological space coordinator* (Gordon, 2003) relates to how therapists often make use of imperfect environments by rearranging the physical and psychological furniture in the room. In many ways this is determined by the environment, as there are policies and guidelines requiring therapists to sit in a particular place in high secure settings. For some therapists, the management of potential risk within the therapy context is very close to the surface. One of Gordon's (2003) participants indicated:

'If I felt vulnerable I would be more cautious about the supervision arrangements. I don't mean clinical supervision but who's around and the placement of chairs in the room. I have made arrangements in the past for people to peek in sometimes.'

The arrangement of the physical space in which therapy occurs involves the therapist in maintaining a delicate balance between risk assessment and management, and providing the patient with choice. This is described by Gordon (2003) as *in-session risk management*. The patients are in a situation where they cannot leave the secure environment and in some sense are trapped. The container of the therapy, therefore, needs to offer a different experience, where the patient can make choices and not feel constrained.

This theme is linked to being a critical friend in terms of not avoiding risk issues, as these are the primary targets of treatment in this setting. *The contained container* theme (Gordon, 2003) relates to the idea that the therapist creates a therapeutic container through the relationship that is situated in the wider container of the institution and the implications this might have for practice. As Greenwood (2001: 37) has argued, high secure environments and prisons represent the 'ultimate container' as these environments, which are specially designed to prevent escape, incarcerate individuals who exhibit behaviour that could not be contained by the society of which they are part (Morris, 2001). One therapist in Gordon's (2003) work said, when comparing working in the high secure context to community working:

> 'You can do things in here that might feel quite dangerous in the community; you can ask questions that might have a lot of emotional attachment for the person. So I can say to someone that they are likely to be very fragile and they might need a couple of hours in their room, whereas I can rely a lot on nursing staff helping me to keep the person safe by offering me an extra pair of eyes and ears. So someone can go in and see them at 10 o'clock at night, whereas in the community I might be leaving them for a week or fortnight and that's quite a scary prospect.'

This is a common feature of therapy conducted within institutional environments and emphasizes the importance of the therapist developing effective communication links with the wider team. As another of Gordon's (2003) participants said:

> 'But it's all so safe. It means that if you want to do things that are more risky you've got more control, you can influence the environment, you can influence the context.'

Noticing the flowers in the desert

The pitfalls outlined above can give a negative impression of this work. What is rarely described is the positive experience of working with individuals with a personality disorder. It is assumed that those who make an informed choice to work with individuals with a diagnosis of personality disorder do so because they either have experienced, or expect to experience, this task positively. Few therapists in this area would deny that their clinical work poses many challenges, and that in no other area does the systemic and interpersonal context warrant almost constant consideration. So what makes their experience so significantly different from the prevailing view? There is little doubt that this clinical population evokes enthusiasm and commitment in many of the practitioners who work with them. Some clinicians describe both the strength of the relationship and the opportunity for longer-term working at the 'core' of the person's difficulties as rewarding aspects of the work. This is increasingly distinct from colleagues working in general adult and primary care services which are focused on providing an effective service in increasingly shorter timeframes. This is not to say that efficient and effective practice is of no concern to those working with personality disorder, but it is widely accepted that this population needs more therapy and for longer (National Institute for Health and Clinical Excellence, 2009). However, the length of incarceration within high secure services is somewhat unusual and is one of the few places where success and effectiveness are not measured by the number of sessions. Gordon's (2003) study, however, indicated that the long-term nature of therapy in this context carries particular features:

> 'There's people who I have been working with here and there is nothing happening emotionally with them for months and months and then you suddenly have this … it's like a desert flower, it's suddenly a kind of explosion and then you get months of nothing and then another. That's just the way that person grows maybe.'

As this illustrates, many therapists have detailed knowledge of the people they work with, which they have built up over a period of years. As a consequence they have developed an understanding that there may be latent periods within the relationship where little change or development is taking place. For some therapists, this lack of observable progress over lengthy periods can be very disheartening and this has been interpreted (as frequently described in the literature) as a lack of responsivity or as the patient being 'untreatable'. For others, as Gordon's (2003) participants described, it is the importance of the 'desert flowers' that makes the work so rewarding.

Conclusion

This chapter has focused on several key themes related to therapists' experiences of providing therapy in a high secure setting. The findings from in-depth research interviews have helped us to articulate the challenges we face and provide insights into the attraction and positive dimensions of this work. Working with patients with a diagnosis of personality disorder provides a real opportunity for the therapist to experience their role as important to those they work with and effect change. For some, the experience of 'treating the untreatable', working with people no one expects to make progress in therapy, is intensely rewarding and satisfying. Many of us find the range of new and emerging therapies and approaches to understanding and treating personality disorder both exciting and challenging. Therapists in high secure settings relish the opportunity to push back the frontiers of theoretical, clinical and ethical approaches to working with this client group, including being continually confronted with finding new ways to effect change. It is exciting and rewarding work, both professionally and personally, and we feel privileged to have the opportunity to make a positive difference to the damaged lives of those we care for.

References

Aiyegbusi, A. & Tuck, G. (2008) Caring amid victims and perpetrators: Trauma and forensic mental health nursing. In J. Gordon & G. Kirtchuk (Eds.) *Psychic Assaults and frightened clinicians: Countertransference in forensic settings* (pp. 11–26). London: Karnac.

Bamber, M. R. (2006) *CBT for occupational stress in health professionals: Introducing a schema-focused approach.* London: Routledge.

Cox, M. (1994) A supervisor's view. In C. Cordess & M. Cox (Eds.) *Forensic psychotherapy: Crime psychodynamics and the offender patient* (pp. 199–224). London: Jessica Kingsley.

Frank, J. D. & Frank, J. B. (1991) *Persuasion and healing: A comparative study of psychotherapy.* Baltimore, MD: Johns Hopkins University Press.

Gartner, R. B. (Ed.) (1999) *Betrayed as boys. Psychodynamic treatment of sexually abused men.* New York: Guilford Press.

Gartner, R. B. & Shapiro, S. A. (1999) Gender and the therapeutic relationship. In R. B. Gartner (Ed.) *Betrayed as boys. Psychodynamic treatment of sexually abused men* (pp. 266–295). New York: Guilford Press.

Gordon, N. S. (2003) The swamp workers' stories: An exploration of practitioners' perspectives as a foundation for the development of a context-sensitive development programme in a forensic setting. Unpublished PhD. Metanoia Institute/Middlesex University.

Greenwood, L. (2001) Psychotherapy in prison: The ultimate container. In J. W. Saunders (Ed.) *Life within hidden worlds: Psychotherapy in prisons* (pp. 37–55). London: Karnac.

Houston, G. (1990) *Supervision and counselling.* London: Rochester Foundation.

Jones, L. F. (2001) Anticipating offence paralleling behaviour. Paper presented at Division of Forensic Psychology Conference, Birmingham.

Jones, L. F. (2002) An individual case formulation approach to the assessment of motivation. In M. McMurran (Ed.) *Motivating offenders to change* (pp. 31–54). Chichester: Wiley.

Linehan, M. (1993) *Cognitive-behavioral treatment of borderline personality disorder.* New York: Guilford Press.

Lowings, G. (2008) A study to establish what constitutes an effective therapeutic alliance and how this can be achieved and maintained with a difficult to engage client group, those with a diagnosis of borderline personality disorder. Unpublished PhD, University of Leicester.

Melia, P., Moran, T. & Mason, T. (1998) Triumvirate nursing for personality disordered persons: Crossing the boundaries safely. *Journal of Psychiatric and Mental Health Nursing,* **6**, 15–20.

Morris, M. (2001) Grendon Underwood: A psychotherapeutic prison. In J. Williams Saunders (Ed.) *Life within hidden worlds, Psychotherapy in prisons* (pp. 89–112). London: Karnac.

National Institute for Health and Clinical Excellence (2009) *Borderline personality disorder: Treatment, management and prevention.* Clinical Guideline 78. London: NICE.

Perkins, D. (1991) Clinical work with sex offenders in secure settings. In C. R. Hollin & K. Howells (Eds.) *Clinical approaches to sex offenders and their victims* (pp. 151–177). Chichester: Wiley.

Pilgrim, D. (1997) *Psychotherapy and society.* London: Sage.

Ryan, G. & Lane, S. (1997) *Juvenile sexual offending: Causes consequences and correction.* San Francisco: Jossey-Bass.

Young, J. E. (1994) *Cognitive therapy of personality disorders: A schema-focused approach.* Sarasota, FL: Professional Resource Exchange.

Young, J. E., Klosko, J. S. & Weishaar, M. E. (2003) *Schema therapy: A practitioner's guide.* New York: Guilford Press.

Chapter Eleven

Making Sense of Interpersonal Dynamics: A Schema Focused Approach

Kerry Beckley

Like it or not, we are drawn into a fierce and involving relationship that gets less and less objective.

(Hinshelwood, 1999: 189)

Introduction

Working in forensic mental health requires attention to our responses to the 'raw material' of our patients, as well as working on the raw material itself (Hinshelwood, 2008: xix). A psychodynamic perspective tries to illuminate what is going on at a systemic level and its contribution to our understanding is invaluable. This necessitates an understanding of both organizational and psychoanalytic theory in order to make sense of the insights it provides. Consequently, this approach is neither universally accessible nor easily understood by the multidisciplinary team (MDT) or wider nursing team in many services. It is unusual for professionals within this environment, in particular nursing staff, to access the available literature in order to assist them in making sense of their experiences. It is therefore necessary to consider how existing knowledge and resources within the workforce can be used effectively to increase their reflective capacities.

The clinicians' framework for understanding organizational and interpersonal dynamics will always be heavily influenced by the theoretical perspective of the service. The Personality Disorder Service (PDS) may differ from other services through the relative dominance of Schema Focused Therapy (SFT) (Young, 1990)

Working Positively with Personality Disorder in Secure Settings: A Practitioner's Perspective
Edited by Phil Willmot and Neil Gordon
© 2011 John Wiley & Sons, Ltd.

for treating personality disorder. SFT is an integrative model which provides a framework from which we can not only make sense of our patients' experiences, but also our own responses to patients. SFT was introduced to the PDS as a therapeutic intervention in 2003 (Beckley & Gordon, 2010), and staff and patients have both been enthusiastic about the model as a framework for psychological formulation. The model is particularly useful for validating patients' early experiences and enabling them to make sense of these through its developmental focus. Staff who have experience of the model in training, team formulations or schema group facilitation also report a greater understanding of patient care and increased self-awareness. This chapter uses schema theory to illustrate how interpersonal dynamics and their consequences have implications for the individuals involved, the clinical environments they inhabit and the organization that contains them. The case examples used are fictional in the sense that they are not based on specific incidents, but serve to reflect the realities of working in this context.

The schema model

Schema theory provides an alternative, but arguably complementary framework to the traditional medical model of personality disorder. Perhaps most importantly, it normalizes rather than pathologizes personality disorders with its assumption that everyone has maladaptive schemas and coping strategies, but that these are more rigid and extreme in personality disordered individuals. SFT is based on the premise that personality pathology develops from unmet core emotional needs in childhood, leading to the development of early maladaptive schemas (EMSs). Young (1990) defined EMSs as self-defeating emotional and cognitive patterns that develop early in childhood and are strengthened and elaborated throughout life. Maladaptive behaviours are underpinned by schema activation. Young has identified 18 schemas (see appendix 11.1), all of which are maladaptive, and he suggests that the person develops coping strategies in order to deal with the emotional distress associated with the schema. These coping styles take the form of *schema surrender* (giving in to the schema and accepting that the negative consequences are unavoidable); *schema avoidance* (avoiding internal and external triggers that may activate the schema); and *schema overcompensation* (acting as though the opposite were true).

While EMSs are trait-like entities (i.e., enduring features of the personality), schema modes are the state-like, changeable manifestations of schemas (see appendix 11.2). Schema modes are defined as 'self states' that temporarily come to the fore and dominate a person's presentation, and are made up of clusters of schemas and coping strategies (Young, Klosko & Weishaar, 2003). In patients with severe personality disorders, whose personalities are poorly integrated, these states are relatively dissociated. As a result, schema modes can shift rapidly from one state to another. Using the concept of schema modes enables therapists to work more effectively with these sudden and extreme emotional shifts. In the SFT model, the combination of EMSs, coping responses and modes forms the basis of personality disorders.

Bernstein, Arntz and de Vos (2007) proposed that schema modes should be the focus of SFT for forensic patients, and expanded the mode model to include the emotional states that are seen most frequently in these patients. They hypothesized that psychopathic patients make prominent use of several over-compensator modes, including those involving arrogance and superiority ('self-aggrandizer mode'), manipulation ('conning and manipulative mode'), focusing of attention on perceived threats ('paranoid over-controller mode'), intimidation and aggression ('bully and attack mode'), and cold, ruthless attempts to eliminate a threat or enemy ('predator mode'). The psychological functioning of the forensic personality disordered patient means that these modes are just as apparent within the context of institutional care is they are in the community. Patients impose themselves on others, violently, criminally or sexually, albeit often in more subtle ways, and elicit responses from staff accordingly (Ruszczynski, 2008). If SFT can modify particular aspects of personality functioning (e.g., empathy, emotional regulation, cognitive distortions) associated with risk of antisocial conduct, then arguably it can be considered an 'offence-focused' intervention.

Schema activation within the interpersonal context

A sense of constancy in self is not gained from internal reflection, but is a function of being in predictable, supportive relationships that enable the individual to receive consistent messages from others (Campbell, 2000). Models that emphasize the interpersonal manifestation of personality disorder are of more use in an institutional context where social difficulties are exacerbated and form the basis of most team discussions. The principle of 'complementarity' – the process by which an individual's behaviour can 'pull' the other into a familiar pattern of interacting (Safran & Segal, 1996) – is readily apparent in the forensic mental health arena. In terms of the SFT model, this can be described as *schema chemistry* (i.e., the interpersonal activation of schemas between individuals) (Young, 2009).

The institution's capacity both to reinforce and heal schemas within its workforce also warrants consideration. Bamber (2006) highlights how EMSs play a role in determining career choice and that schemas and coping styles are re-enacted within the work environment. The experience can be a healing one if staff members' schemas are of low-to-moderate intensity, but difficulties such as disillusionment, stress and other psychological problems occur if the schemas are more pronounced. Aiyegbusi and Tuck (2008) highlighted the inherent risks to the mental health of nursing staff who may be unconsciously drawn to working in this context due to their own unresolved trauma histories. As a profession, nurses are not provided with specific training in working with complex psychological trauma and yet they are required to be in contact with the patient group for longer periods than other professionals in the ward environment, where there is an increased likelihood of the patients 'acting out' their emotional distress. Clearly, this is not limited to nursing staff, but they represent the largest body of mental health practitioners and can be the most disadvantaged in terms of their access to adequate supervision and reflective space during the working day.

The level of disturbance within the childhood of forensic personality disorder patients results in an increased likelihood of early relational patterns being repeated within care-giving relationships. The SFT model is explicit in its consideration of these patterns and actively looks for evidence of these within both the therapy relationship and the wider context. The manifestation of personality characteristics is heavily influenced by contextual factors, yet these are often absent from team discussions. The 'problem' is often seen as being solely located in the patient, rather than being a response to the environment or people within that environment. This can result in a punitive stance being taken towards the patient who 'just doesn't seem to want to change', or a position of tolerance or indifference regarding the known (but not always expressed) difficulties in staff members' provocative interpersonal style. It is only through an open and psychologically informed dialogue that we can hope to make an impact on the relational world of staff and patients in order to provide a 'schema healing' environment that does not reinforce our patients' past experience of abuse and neglect.

Engaging the workforce in a dialogue which requires them to consider their own reactions is not without its challenges. Gordon and Kirtchuk (2008) have described the taboo which exists regarding the outward expression of powerful feelings, suggesting the breaking of this taboo is akin to 'professional suicide'. Reactions such as revulsion, hatred, sexual attraction, fascination and even love are undoubtedly experienced by staff, and yet institutional cultures do not easily sustain a supportive forum where these can be expressed and consequently, like our patients, these reactions are more often manifested through actions. The SFT model represents a way of integrating such conversations into our daily clinical practice. The model gives staff 'permission' to own their reactions to patients, to consider the source of these reactions (self, patient, environment) and how they could manage this differently if conveyed with non-judgemental and respectful curiosity.

Case example: Frank

Frank has a strong defectiveness schema and as a consequence purposefully neglects his self-care through not washing. Some staff react with disgust at having to perform more intimate duties such as searching Frank as he leaves/enters the ward and treat him more harshly as a consequence. In others, Frank elicits compassion and caring, and an urge to protect him from the criticism of colleagues and other patients. There is also a group of staff who physically and psychologically distance themselves from Frank so he has little bearing on their daily working lives.

Staff reaction towards Frank is an example of how our attitudes and experiences interact with those of our patients. Frank's behaviour evokes reactions in others which not only serve to reinforce his sense of defectiveness, but also provide information about why we may choose to reject, reach out to or withdraw from the patients we work with.

The schema mode model as a framework

Staff may recognize these reactions in themselves but may not routinely consider why they react in this way, and how past and present experiences can make sense of them. The schema mode model can facilitate this process. As stated previously, schema modes are the moment-to-moment emotional states and coping responses that we all experience and are triggered by life situations that hold emotional resonance for us (our 'emotional buttons'). Schema modes are grouped into four categories; child modes, coping modes, parent modes and the healthy adult mode. Although it is beyond the scope of a single chapter to provide a full description of how the model can be used in this way, the following provides an overview of the most commonly observed schema modes within a forensic mental health setting.

Child modes

The *vulnerable (practitioner) mode* is taken from the concept of the vulnerable child mode where the person connects with their core fears and unmet needs from childhood and adolescence. In patients, the focus is on early experiences and memories, but in more functional individuals where significant levels of abuse and neglect were not present in their early lives, it is as likely that significant 'schema-forming' events may have occurred later in the person's development. Unmet needs may (or may not) be more subtle in staff, but similarly result from difficulties in trusting others, seeing oneself as worthless, fears that one is isolated or not accepted by others, difficulties in relying on others for emotional support or holding fears that others will leave or reject them. This mode is particularly important as the SFT model suggests that it underpins the coping modes which have developed in order to avoid remaining in this mode.

Case example: Jenny

Jenny, an occupational therapist, had been subject to criticism and occasional threats of complaint by Tom, a patient who was unhappy about her recent assessment report. They had always had a difficult relationship as he perceived that she was responsible for his long wait in accessing the book binders department. He had a history of violence towards female partners, although he had never been violent towards female staff within the hospital. She was fearful of coming onto the ward in case he assaulted her. When she raised her concerns with the clinical team, she felt as though they were not taking her seriously, and that the nursing staff present were particularly dismissive. Some of their comments made Jenny feel that the nursing team resented the prospect of giving additional consideration to her safety when the risks were not overtly present. Jenny had not felt able to raise her concerns again and found she was starting to make excuses not to go onto the ward.

Jenny had suffered significant health problems as a child which resulted in her being absent from school for long periods. This had a significant impact on her friendships at school and she often felt isolated from her classmates. As an adult, she found herself worrying about her health and would take extra precautions to prevent illness and accidents. Jenny's schemas (social isolation, vulnerability to harm) underpinned her vulnerable mode and were activated in this situation.

Tom was working with his psychologist to understand why he struggled so much with Jenny. Tom had a powerful defectiveness schema that was central to his

> *vulnerable child mode. He would frequently flip between self-punishing rumina-*
> *tions (punitive parent mode) for his behaviour towards Jenny and expressing anger*
> *towards her (bully attack mode) as he believed that she viewed him as repulsive*
> *and wanted to punish him for his violence towards his partners. At times it felt as*
> *though she was just like his mother, who would frequently ridicule and physically*
> *chastise him.*

This is an example of schema chemistry. Parallels can be seen between Jenny's childhood experiences and her current situation. Her concerns are valid, but she is also influenced by her fear of harm and her sense of isolation from her colleagues. She tries to cope with this by avoiding the situation. Tom experiences her as abusive and rejecting of him, and his threats of complaint represent an over-compensatory reaction in order to alleviate his experience of vulnerability and humiliation.

The *angry (practitioner) mode* is a representation of the angry child mode where the person acts in anger in response to the needs of the vulnerable mode not being met. When in this mode, the person is responding in a purely emotional way and will often say things 'in the moment' that they later regret. The purpose of the mode is to communicate distress rather than to hurt or attack another.

> ### Case example: Hannah
>
> *Hannah was a young staff nurse who had recently joined the hospital. Her father*
> *had repeatedly expressed doubts about her ability to achieve academically through-*
> *out her life. Hannah often lacked confidence in her abilities (failure), compensated*
> *by working harder (unrelenting standards), but frequently sought approval and*
> *reassurance from others, including her patients (approval/recognition-seeking).*
> *She was struggling to engage with John, a patient who was viewed as difficult by*
> *the nursing team. He tended to treat others with derision, and used his intellectual*
> *capabilities to demean staff, particularly those whom he perceived as less competent*
> *or experienced. He experienced the allocation of Hannah as his named nurse as*
> *an indication that his needs for care and support were being disregarded (emo-*
> *tional deprivation) as he did not think Hannah would be robust enough to tolerate*
> *him and so would withdraw from his care (abandonment). Following yet another*
> *nursing session where John repeatedly pointed out how little faith he had in her*
> *abilities (overcompensating for his schemas), Hannah snapped and told him that*
> *she was not going to put up with his behaviour anymore and was going to request*
> *a change of named nurse.*

Hannah's reaction to John's behaviour is an example of how the angry practitioner mode can manifest. Hannah struggled with being repeatedly exposed to feeling ineffective and so reacted in a way that served to alleviate these feelings. John's schemas resulted in others being 'pulled' into a mode reinforcing pattern which always resulted in him experiencing others as uncaring and ultimately rejecting.

Parent modes

Managers and supervisors can be seen as parent figures within the organization, and colleagues as analogous to siblings, creating an ideal scenario for the enactment of early family dynamics (Bamber, 2006). The primary task of managers is to ensure that staff and patients can interact within a safe environment (Mercer, 2008). When this fails, the organization can be experienced as the invalidating family environment.

In the *punitive parent mode*, the person feels that the self or others deserve punishment or blame for their actions. When a serious incident occurs, staff can experience their managers' or the hospital's actions as punitive.

Case example: Alpha male ward

A particular ward was undergoing difficulties due to the actions of a small group of patients. It had inadvertently developed an identity as the 'psychopath' or 'alpha male' ward due to there being a number of patients who had reputations for being more challenging or subversive. Although there was recognition that a greater number of similar patients were residing together by both the direct care staff and the service managers, it was not explicitly raised as a concern, although the clinical team had made reference to this at a number of meetings.

Ultimately, a number of security incidents took place, which highlighted the difficulties of containing this group of patients together for a sustained period of time, despite the efforts that were made by the clinical team to manage and reflect upon their own clinical practice. The resulting investigations and recommendations for enhanced restrictions and changes in ward procedures resulted in the team feeling as though they were at fault for not being able to prevent the difficulties taking place and that their clinical competence was being called into question by the wider hospital management.

The need to manage and contain serious incidents in forensic mental health settings can be at the expense of the individual's or team's needs. This can be mirrored in patient care in terms of greater restrictions imposed (or existing restrictions imposed more vigorously) in the context of a more 'security-focused' stance, which can sometimes appear to be in opposition to a therapeutic agenda.

At an individual level, a patient's punitive parent mode is often seen in their self-destructive actions, which serve the purpose of punishment for them. The reaction of staff can be frustration and/or repulsion, which can reinforce the patient's sense of being worthy of such punishment. With staff, this mode may not be as readily apparent, as the individual may have developed over-compensatory strategies to cope with this.

Case example: Jackie

Jackie was a nursing assistant who had worked in the hospital for many years. She had experienced a great deal of criticism from her grandmother, who had looked after her whilst her parents were at work and who considered her a nuisance. As

> *a teenager, she had rebelled and dropped out of school. However, her lack of educa-*
> *tion had restricted her job prospects and, as a consequence, she had never fulfilled*
> *her dream of training as a nurse. She did not like to take responsibility at work as*
> *she feared she would make a mistake. One of the patients in particular appeared*
> *to be trying to catch her out and would often comment on the quality of her work.*
> *On one occasion, he observed her leaving the kitchen door open as she was called*
> *away to assist a colleague and informed her he was going to tell the ward manager*
> *when she came on duty. Jackie was so worried about how her manager would react*
> *that she phoned in sick the next day.*

Jackie's self-critical stance and fear of retribution was clearly noted by the patient. His propensity to act in an unforgiving and punitive way towards others was exacerbating Jackie's own schemas to the point where making mistakes was so aversive to her that she chose to avoid the consequences.

In the *demanding parent mode* the individual feels that the 'right' way to be is determined by rules or morals. This could be a desire to keep everything in order, to strive for high status, to put others' needs before one's own or never to express feelings or act spontaneously. The culture of the organization shapes how the demanding parent is experienced by the workforce depending on the opportunities or limitations placed on them. As with the punitive parent, the impact on the individual is also dependent on the familial or societal rules and values they have experienced.

> ### Case example: Daniel
>
> *Daniel, a new psychologist, was keen to take up the opportunities afforded to him.*
> *He was always the first to volunteer for extra tasks and responsibilities and soon*
> *found he was working increasingly long hours in order to keep on top of his workload*
> *(self-sacrifice, approval/recognition-seeking). He was well regarded by patients*
> *and staff as he was seen as committed to the service. However, one of his patients,*
> *Adam, was never satisfied with the frequency of his contact with Daniel, perceiving*
> *that his needs were more important than the needs of his peers (entitlement over-*
> *compensating for emotional deprivation and defectiveness). Daniel knew Adam*
> *had experienced significant abuse and neglect in his childhood and so had extended*
> *his therapeutic limits to try to give him the experience of being cared for. However,*
> *his continuing demands resonated with his experience of both his mother's and*
> *girlfriend's repeated demands on his time and he found that he was extending his*
> *limits further and further in an attempt to pacify Adam and to feel as though he*
> *was a competent psychologist. This was exacerbated by the continual requests by the*
> *nursing staff (sometimes up to five or six telephone calls a day) to 'see Adam for*
> *10 minutes' when he was making excessive demands on them. Daniel was trying*
> *to encourage Adam to build better relationships with his nursing team and so felt*
> *obliged to respond in order to try and maintain their capacity to tolerate Adam.*

Daniel's need to gain approval and live up to the expectations of others was underpinning his ever-increasing workload. Daniel's self-sacrifice schema, which developed out of his mother's over-reliance on him, was activated in his work life generally and particularly within his relationship with Adam. Adam's unmet needs from childhood were so severe that attempts to meet them were likely to result in staff burnout as care-giving was predominately experienced as inadequate or abusive. Daniel was trying desperately to avoid feeling this way himself and to minimize the extent to which his nursing colleagues would have to experience this. This resulted in the team increasingly relying on Daniel to contain Adam's demands, as this alleviated their own distress in having to deal with him.

Coping modes

In the *compliant surrenderer mode* the person acts in a passive, approval-seeking or self-deprecating way with others out of fear of conflict or rejection. Nursing staff in particular become 'compliant' in response to the institutional culture, and where this is supportive of concealing malpractice or inhibiting an alternative way of responding, difficulties can occur.

This may also manifest within patient relationships. Some patients have established interpersonal patterns that manoeuvre staff into boundary transgressions or violations. Staff may transgress boundaries, either with colleagues or patients, due to their need for acceptance or to avoid retribution. Staff members can feel compelled to 'give in' to patients' demands, due to fear or feeling worn down, and quickly find themselves in a position where it is very difficult to re-establish boundaries without a significant reaction from the patient.

Case example: Sharon

Sharon, a staff nurse, had started to bring in a particular type of pudding for Howard which he was not able to access from the hospital shop. She noticed that some of the other patients had started acting in a friendlier manner towards her, which she welcomed as she did not feel that her colleagues liked her (social isolation). It was nice to feel appreciated by somebody for once, which was something she had not felt for much of her life (emotional deprivation). Howard had started to tell her how she would make the 'perfect girlfriend' as she was so kind and understanding. She was aware that he had not received much love and care in his life and so felt that it was important to make him feel special. Sharon was also flattered as men did not normally say these things to her, but knew it was not the kind of conversation that she should be having with a patient. She did not know who to talk to about this and decided that the best thing would be to just carry on bringing him in gifts and hope that no one found out. She knew she was not the only staff member who brought things in for patients, so what harm could it do?

Sharon's lack of emotional nurturance and isolation from her colleagues resulted in her being vulnerable to boundary transgressions. Her emotional needs were limiting her ability to manage her boundaries, despite being aware of them. Her need for care and approval from the patient, coupled with her sense of isolation and rejection from her peers, underpinned her compliant surrender mode.

In the *detached protector mode* the person withdraws emotionally from others, rejects their help and pursues distracting, self-soothing activities in a compulsive way (e.g., drinking alcohol to excess). The staff reaction to the 'raw material' of the patient's experience typically dilutes over time through repeated exposure and can lead to patients being dealt with psychologically at arm's length. There is often an explicit narrative within services regarding the danger of forming close therapeutic relationships with forensic personality disorder patients in particular. The reaction of the organization towards those who are considered to be 'too close' is often more overtly critical than it is in response to those considered to be 'too punitive'. A certain amount of emotional distance is arguably necessary in order to protect one's sense of safety and well-being. However, we need to remain emotionally connected to our patients if we are to effectively modify their emotional worlds.

Case example: Maria

Maria, a trainee nurse, asked to talk to her supervisor, Jake. She reported feeling very distressed and angry about the way staff were talking about patients, often using derogatory and even violent language. When she had voiced her concerns to the nurses concerned, they had laughed it off and informed her that she would 'learn', adding that they used humour to 'get through the day'. Jake was initially irritated, perceiving that Maria had little experience of working in this type of environment and was idealistic and naïve. However, he later reflected on how their conversation reminded him of his own reaction when he first joined the hospital. Jake recognized how removed he had become from his emotional discomfort and wondered whether to raise it in his own supervision, although he was worried that this might be perceived as criticizing his colleagues.

Jake had emotionally detached as a way of coping with the 'toxicity' of the working environment. Emotional detachment is one of the most common experiences of staff in forensic environments and, in the long term, leads to reduced empathy and connectedness to the patient group, paralleling the patient's process of disconnection from their offending and the organization's distance from its individual members. This process is not found exclusively between patients and staff, but can be observed throughout the organization.

> The frontline workers are too caught up in attempting to maintain their self and emotional survival to be able to reflect on what they are caught up in, the rearguard workers 'know' what is going on with a 'clarity of blindness' that comes from never going near the coalface of the workplace and further distancing themselves from the pain by engaging in the all too familiar game of 'them and us'.

(Obholzer, p. ix, in Hinshelwood & Skogstag, 2000)

Policies and regulations which are introduced with little or no warning or consultation are often met with frustration and derision. The patient is ultimately the most affected by policy changes, has limited opportunity to gain a coherent rationale for the decision taken and so often resorts to taking frustrations out on the ward staff, who in turn become desensitized to the patient's distress as they have little power to effect change themselves.

Case example: Albert

Albert had been in the hospital for many years and one of his favourite hobbies was making matchstick models. He had been working on a model of a ship for many months and was delighted when the decision was made to display his model in the hospital reception. This meant the world to Albert as he had felt stupid and worth-less for most of his life and this was the first time anyone had singled him out for his achievements. He proudly told everyone who came on the ward and asked them to look out for the ship when they left that day. A week later, Albert was told that he could no longer use the matchstick cutters unless he was observed by a member of staff. When he asked why, he was told that a patient on another ward, hearing of Albert's achievement, has asked his clinical team if he could make a model. This patient was not considered to be settled enough to use the matchstick cutters and so a change in policy was implemented. When Albert protested, the nurse shrugged their shoulders and replied, 'Don't blame me, I didn't write the policy.'

In the *over-compensator mode*, the person acts as if the opposite of their schemas were true. An example is when the person feels and behaves in an inordinately aggressive, dominant, condescending, exploitative or status-seeking way in response to the underlying schemas associated with their vulnerable mode.

Case example: Mark

Mark, a staff nurse, had recently started working in the hospital. He was very fearful of being assaulted as he had heard many 'horror stories' from the more experienced staff. He felt that the only way to maintain control of the patients was through never showing fear and that patients should be 'tested' to see how they held up to challenge or provocation. This resonated with the messages he had learnt from his father, who would physically assault him when he cried as a young boy until he stopped (mistrust/abuse). He learned from a young age that expressing emotion or vulnerability was wrong (emotional inhibition), and would frequently get into fights with older boys at school in order to win approval from his father. Mark struggled with overt expressions of care or understanding towards patients and would make reference to colleagues who acted in this way as 'wimps' or 'do-gooders'. He also struggled with patients' overt expressions of vulnerability and would tell them to stop whining as they were offenders who deserved no sympathy (punitive-ness). On more than one occasion, this resulted in him being threatened or assaulted by patients.

Mark's difficulty with expressed vulnerability in himself and others resulted in him behaving in ways to negate its expression at all costs. His reaction can be understood as an over-compensatory reaction to his relationship with his father, due to his own needs for support and care being denied. Mark was perceived as an abusive male in authority, representing other abusive males in the early lives of many patients and therefore exacerbated the likelihood of him being the target of their aggression and hostility. This served to reinforce his fears regarding the likelihood of being assaulted and so he tried harder to maintain his 'tough man' front.

Healthy adult mode

The *healthy adult* nurtures the vulnerable mode; sets limits for the angry mode; combats the maladaptive coping modes; and neutralizes or moderates the maladaptive parent modes. This is the 'ideal' mode for us all to be in and can only be achieved through the development of sustained reflective capacities of the individual. The healthy adult recognizes the impact of their own early experiences, the effect of the environment and those in it on their decision-making, and is able to 'step out' of situations where they recognize strong emotional reactions in themselves, or where they are aware of an absence of an emotional response where there should be one.

Case example: Steve

Steve was a young patient with very anti-authoritarian attitudes, due to his experiences of the care system throughout his childhood. He would repeatedly act in aggressive and provocative ways in order to achieve frequent ward moves which paralleled his early experiences and resulted in his alienation from staff and peers alike. A meeting was held at which it was decided that he would no longer be moved, and that strategies would be implemented to support his current ward in containing his behaviour, including the promise of additional nursing support. The clinical team met and agreed a strategy of developing an enhanced care team made up of willing and motivated members who would provide intensive and consistent support for Steve. This included the giving of explicit messages of care and emotional understanding in response to any challenging behaviour at the same time as a clear communication of aspects of his behaviour which were not acceptable. Initially, there was an increase in Steve's attempts to be abandoned and rejected by the team through his escalating behaviour but, with consistent and regular supervision, the team were able to tolerate this and Steve's challenging behaviour slowly started to decrease. Staff reported that being able to talk openly about their emotional reactions to Steve in weekly supervision meetings was crucial to maintaining a consistent approach. Steve's behaviour eventually improved to the point where he was able to move to a medium secure unit. He continued to ring the ward from time to time to let his old team know how he was progressing and tell them know how much he appreciated what they had done for him. The team were also given recognition of their hard work when they received a 'Good Practice' award by the NHS Trust.

Ideally, Steve's case would be an example of standard clinical practice in forensic settings. Clearly, we have a way to go before this is considered the case, but it does highlight what can be achieved when the relational dynamics within organizations are attended to. Forensic services have a duty to attend to the emotional as well as the physical safety of their staff and patients, which necessitates the consideration of the following points:

- It is essential to have an overarching framework which can be used to examine the interpersonal context if staff are to connect the relational worlds of their patients to the relational world of the organization. The schema model represents one such framework which can be used for individual and group supervision, case formulation and critical incident debriefing.
- Effective and consistent supervision for all staff is essential if they are to have the opportunity to develop and maintain their reflective capacities.
- The organization needs to consider how it can actively facilitate and support an emotionally connected staff group. The workforce requires training to develop their reflective capacity and also need to be provided with safe opportunities to use these capacities within their working environment. The organization needs to develop constructive, proactive policies for managing the inevitable boundary transgressions and responding to unacceptable punitive practice in the workplace.

Such measures would be in line with the philosophy of SFT to normalize and not pathologize maladaptive schemas and coping strategies. The benefit for the organization is that such measures are likely to improve staff retention, reduce sickness and most importantly, lead to more effective patient care.

References

Aiyegbusi, A. & Tuck, G. (2008) Caring amid victims and perpetrators: Trauma and forensic mental health nursing. In J. Gordon & G. Kirtchuk (Eds.) *Psychic assaults and frightened clinicians: Countertransference in forensic settings* (pp. 11–26). London: Karnac.

Bamber, M. R. (2006) *CBT for occupational stress in health professionals: Introducing a schema-focused approach.* London: Routledge.

Beckley, K. & Gordon, N. (2010) Schema therapy within a high secure setting. In A. Tennant & K. Howells (Eds.) *Using time, not doing time: Practitioner perspectives on personality disorder and risk* (pp. 95–110). Chichester: Wiley.

Bernstein, D. P., Arntz, A. & de Vos, M. (2007) Schema focused therapy in forensic settings: Theoretical model and recommendations for best clinical practice. *International Journal of Forensic Mental Health*, 6, 169–183.

Campbell, D. (2000) *The socially constructed organisation.* London: Karnac.

Fallon. P. (1999) *Report of the committee of the inquiry into the Personality Unit, Ashworth Special Hospital, V.1.* London: Stationery Office.

Gordon, J. & Kirtchuk, G. (2008) *Psychic assaults and frightened clinicians: Countertransference in forensic settings.* London: Karnac.

Hinshelwood, R. D. (1999) The difficult patient: The role of 'scientific psychiatry' in understanding patients with chronic schizophrenia or personality disorder. *British Journal of Psychiatry*, 174, 187–190.

Hinshelwood, R. D. (2008) Foreword. In J. Gordon & G. Kirtchuk (Eds.) *Psychic assaults and frightened clinicians: Countertransference in forensic settings* (pp. xxix–xxiii). London: Karnac.

Mercer, M. (2008) Bearable or unbearable? Unconscious communication in management. In J. Gordon & G. Kirtchuk (eds.) *Psychic assaults and frightened clinicians: Countertransference in forensic settings* (pp. 63–84). London: Karnac.

Obholzer, A. (2000) Foreword. In R. D. Hinshelwood & W. Skogstad (Eds.) *Observing organisations: Anxiety, defence and culture in healthcare* (pp. ix–x). London: Routledge.

Ruszczynski, S. (2008) Thoughts from consulting in secure settings: Do forensic institutions need psychotherapy? In J. Gordon & G. Kirtchuk (eds.) *Psychic assaults and frightened clinicians: Countertransference in forensic settings* (pp. 85–96). London: Karnac.

Safran. J. & Segal. Z. (1996) *Interpersonal process in cognitive therapy.* New York: Basic Books.

Young, J. E. (1990) *Cognitive therapy for personality disorders: A schema focused approach.* Sarasota, FL: Professional Resource Exchange.

Young, J. E. (2009) Personal communication. 11 August.

Young, J. E., Klosko, J. S. & Weishaar, M. E. (2003) *Schema therapy: A practitioner's guide.* New York: Guilford Press.

Appendix 11.1   Domains and schemas

Disconnection and Rejection Abusive, traumatic childhood, unstable family life, experienced rejection and humiliation, feel different and lacking in some way, long periods of insecurity and inconsistent parenting	**Abandonment/Instability** **Mistrust/Abuse** **Emotional Deprivation** **Defectiveness/Shame** **Social Isolation/Alienation**
Impaired Autonomy and Performance Often over-protected and controlled as children, or neglected and ignored, left alone with no interest shown in their lives, continually undermined and made to feel incompetent, or were encouraged to be dependent on others	**Dependence/Incompetence** **Vulnerability to Harm** **Enmeshment** **Failure**
Impaired Limits Have not developed an internal sense of control, difficulty respecting the rights of others, families lacked boundaries, children did not have rules	**Entitlement** **Insufficient** **Self Control/Self-discipline**
Other Directedness Experience of conditional love (i.e., I will love you only if …), family over-concerned with appearances, parents focused on their own needs	**Subjugation** **Self-sacrifice** **Approval-seeking/** **Recognition-seeking**

Over-vigilance and Inhibition	**Negativity/Pessimism**
Strict control by parents to gain	**Emotional Inhibition**
compliance, learned to be vigilant all the	**Unrelenting standards/**
time, waiting for bad things to happen,	**Hyper-criticism**
frightened to express feelings, severe	**Punitiveness**
punishments	

Appendix 11.2   Schema modes

Child Modes – involve feeling, thinking, and acting in a 'child-like' manner

1. **Vulnerable Child** (abandoned, abused, or humiliated child) – Feels vulnerable, overwhelmed with painful feelings, such as anxiety, depression, grief or shame/humiliation.
2. **Angry Child** – Feels and expresses uncontrolled anger or rage in response to perceived or real mistreatment, abandonment, humiliation or frustration; often feels a sense of being treated unjustly; acts like a child throwing a temper tantrum.
3. **Impulsive, Undisciplined Child** – Acts like a spoiled child who 'wants what he wants when he wants it' and cannot tolerate the frustration of limits.
4. **Lonely Child** – Feels lonely and empty, as if no one can understand him, sooth or comfort him, or make contact with him.

Maladaptive Parent Modes – involve internalized dysfunctional parent 'voices'

5. **Punitive, Critical Parent** – Internalized, critical or punishing parent voice; directs harsh criticism towards the self; induces feelings of shame or guilt
6. **Demanding Parent** – Directs impossibly high demands towards the self; pushes the self to do more, achieve more, never satisfied with oneself

Dysfunctional Coping Modes – Involve attempts to protect the self from pain through maladaptive forms of coping

Avoidance Modes

7. **Detached Protector** – Uses emotional detachment to protect against painful feelings; is unaware of his feelings, feels 'nothing', appears emotionally distant, flat or robotic; avoids getting close to people
8. **Detached Self-soother/Self-stimulator** – Uses repetitive, 'addictive' or compulsive behaviours, or self-stimulating behaviours to calm and soothe oneself; uses pleasurable or exciting sensations to distance oneself from painful feelings
9. **Angry Protector** – Uses a 'wall of anger' to protect oneself from others, who are perceived as threatening; keeps others at a safe distance through displays of anger; anger is more controlled than in angry child mode

Surrender Mode

10. **Compliant Surrenderer** – Gives in to the real or perceived demands or expectations of other people in a anxious attempt to avoid pain or to get one's needs met; anxiously surrenders to the demands of others who are perceived as more powerful than oneself

Over-compensator Modes

11. **Self-aggrandizer Mode** – Feels superior, special or powerful; looks down on others; sees the world in terms of 'top dog' and 'underdog;' shows off or acts in a self-important, self-aggrandizing manner; concerned about appearances rather than feelings or real contact with others
12. **Bully/Attack Mode** – Uses threats, intimidation, aggression or coercion to get what he wants, including retaliation, or asserting a dominant position; feels a sense of sadistic pleasure in attacking others
13. **Conning and Manipulative Mode** – Cons, lies or manipulates in a manner designed to achieve a specific goal, which either involves victimizing others or escaping punishment
14. **Predator Mode** – Focuses on eliminating a threat, rival, obstacle or enemy in a cold, ruthless and calculating manner
15. **Over-controller Mode** (paranoid and obsessive-compulsive type) – Attempts to protect oneself from a perceived or real threat by focusing attention, ruminating and exercising extreme control. The obsessive type uses order, repetition or ritual. The paranoid type attempts to locate and uncover a hidden (perceived) threat

Healthy Adult Mode

16. Serves as an 'executive function' relative to the other modes. In this mode, the healthy adult part of the person helps to meet the child's basic emotional needs. The healthy adult nurtures and protects the vulnerable lonely child, sets limits for the angry child and battles or moderates the maladaptive coping modes.

Chapter Twelve

The Importance of Systemic Workforce Development in High Secure Settings

Andrea Milligan and Neil Gordon

High secure organizations employ staff to work in environments that deliver complex psychological intervention programmes within a risk management framework, with the aim of reducing offending behaviours. Those incarcerated in these environments present a considerable challenge with respect to their psychological vulnerabilities and antisocial personality features. The dialectic between punishment and treatment pervades these systems. Patients in these settings are usually perpetrators – the makers of victims (Morris, 2001) – who have been deemed too dangerous or unacceptable to society because of the crimes they have committed or the threat they pose (Cordess, 1998). As several writers have noted (Cox, 1994; Hinshelwood, 1993; Morris, 2001), the walls of these institutions can serve to exclude those within them from the outside world in order that the painfulness of the internal culture is contained and those who offend society's sensibilities can be put away and forgotten. For those selected to work in day-to-day contact with this disenfranchised group it is particularly important that they demonstrate a degree of self-awareness and an ability to reflect critically on their personal experiences while utilizing interpersonal, therapeutic and self-management skills. Despite the obvious demands of this role, post-employment training and educational inputs aimed at increasing capability and competence remain relatively unsophisticated and poorly organized.

This chapter explores our approach to tackling these problems through the development of a creative, systematic and psychologically informed training programme within the Personality Disorder Service (PDS) at Rampton Hospital. The

Working Positively with Personality Disorder in Secure Settings: A Practitioner's Perspective
Edited by Phil Willmot and Neil Gordon
© 2011 John Wiley & Sons, Ltd.

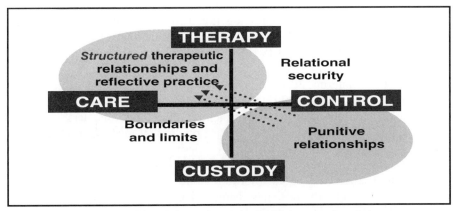

Figure 12.1   Culture change in the high secure hospital

chapter begins by exploring the challenges involved in attempts to change staff culture in this setting before outlining the philosophy, principal features and design of the in-house multidisciplinary educational programme. The following sections discuss the organizational challenge of integrating and embedding this activity effectively (focusing mainly on nurses), with some reflection on the impact these interventions have had on practice. Support for a systemic approach to workforce development is evident in the current National Educational Strategy being implemented for workforces working with personality disorder in health, social care and the criminal justice system (The Knowledge and Understanding Framework: Department of Health, 2009). The educational philosophy underpinning the systemic approach emphasizes the importance of organizationally embedding educational interventions in ways that challenge existing professional cultures, recognizing that it is only through these processes that real changes in clinical practice and patient experience can be realized.

Changing the staff culture in a high secure hospital

Before discussing how we attempted to develop the workforce within our service it is important to reflect on the specific challenges of implementing change in high secure organizations. The high secure hospitals (Rampton, Ashworth and Broadmoor) in England have well-publicized and chequered histories with respect to scandals, accusations of abuse and concerns about a 'negative and oppressive' staff culture. Following numerous attempts to effect change through organizational restructuring with increased external monitoring and control, more recently there has been an emphasis on educational interventions aimed at shifting staff attitudes and behaviour from controlling, punitive and custodial approaches to more therapeutic and treatment-focused practice that recognizes the complex relationship between offending and mental health problems (Figure 12.1).

The reports and inquiries into these institutions during the 1980s and 1990s came to pessimistic conclusions about the possibility of changing what were referred to as insular and resistant staff cultures (Pilgrim, 2007). In a text focusing on Ashworth high secure hospital it was noted that the staff group consistently sabotaged attempts at reform through cynical, and at times threatening, tactics that discredited key reformers in a well-organized 'rearguard action against change' that consolidated vested interests and ritualized practices of the staff group (Kaye & Franey, 1998; Pilgrim, 2007). For some who had struggled to work in these environments (e.g., Pilgrim, 2007) the only solution was to close these institutions and completely rethink management of mentally disordered offenders.

To explore the complex sociopolitical reasons why closure did not happen is beyond the scope of this chapter, but it is relevant to point out that successive Home Secretaries from different political parties consistently avoided making this contentious decision and opted for more strategic approaches to bring about change. More recently the hospitals changed from being managed directly from the *centre* by a Special Hospitals Authority to become part of the NHS in 2001. This represented a strategic attempt to integrate these geographically and professionally isolated environments while bringing them under the direct scrutiny of NHS quality assurance systems. It is clear that the original initiatives focused on changing staff culture in the high secure hospital were *externally* driven, usually by concerned politicians and policy-makers, based on the findings of official inquiries and investigations over a period of years (Fallon, Bluglass, Edwards & Daniels, 1999).

In the official inquiries directed at special hospitals during the 1970s and 1980s, the nursing staff group were often singled out as the resistant 'culture carriers', willing to take extreme measures to maintain the status quo, including, at the most extreme, threatening and intimidating would-be reformers (Pilgrim, 2007). When the authors began working in the organization in 2001 it was clear things had moved on considerably since the 1980s, although attitudes towards the therapeutic goals of the organization remained ambivalent. The staff uniforms (prison blue) and peaked caps had gone and there seemed to be more of a focus on care as well as control. Nevertheless, the organization still seemed to be a long way from recognizing the potential for psychological treatment, and many of the staff group had a tendency at times to be punitive and controlling in their interactions with patients. A simple model (Figure 12.1) we developed (Gordon, 2003) to help us think about the change process was based on the realization that within the organization diverse staff sub-cultures were identifiable. These tended to operate predominantly in one of the four different quadrants in Figure 12.1. In our initial attempts to shape and influence the workforce what became apparent was the powerful influence of particular individuals (situated in the lower-right *control and custody* quadrant) in terms of their capacity to undermine and sabotage the change initiatives. These individuals were particularly antagonistic to the shift to a more therapeutic, relationship-based way of working. A salient lesson for us in this process was the discovery that these attitudes were quite ingrained in a small proportion of our peers within the service who were not supportive of the direction of the culture shift. As is often the case, this resistance from the *shadow side* (Egan, 2002) was rarely voiced in public; rather, it operated through conversations behind closed doors (Shaw, 2002) and the persistent undermining of enthusiastic staff on their return from training events.

The creation of a dedicated development team

It is well recognized that the success of any organization is dependent on the capabilities of its workforce, although within the NHS it is only relatively recently that strategic workforce development has become a feature of organizational planning and service improvement. Within the PDS the Directorate Development Team (DDT), which was created to achieve this more systematic approach to workforce development, had seven members and a remit to replace the more reactive ('doing some training when something goes wrong') or osmotic ('they will pick it up on the job') approach to training that preceded it. The team managed in-service development programmes, such as mandatory training, ranging from introductory courses to advanced clinical skills development (e.g., group work and specific therapeutic interventions). Team members were also involved in environment-specific, ward-based initiatives, including the introduction of a reflective clinical supervision culture and increasing the psychological health and inter-professional collaboration skills of multidisciplinary teams. The team members maintained their credibility as educators by remaining clinically active, delivering individual and group therapies, and conducting audit and research activity related to monitoring clinical improvements.

The team operated across the organization in close liaison with heads of discipline (psychology, social work, nursing, medicine and occupational therapy) and ward managers to assess and improve the capabilities of the workforce in response to national policy guidelines on managing and treating personality disorder (Department of Health, 2003). The team also facilitated the hospital's engagement with NHS service modernization and national workforce development initiatives such as *Agenda for Change* (Pay Modernization), *The Ten Essential Shared Capabilities* (Department of Health, 2004a) and the *Knowledge and Skills Framework* (KSF) (Department of Health, 2004b). The DDT represented the organization's local investment and commitment to nationally driven workforce development and service improvement through capability enhancement. This integrated team approach achieved significant organizational cultural shift, particularly in terms of enhancing ethical and psychologically informed, patient-centred care among members of a forensic mental health workforce that is noted for its capacity to resist change (Kaye & Franey, 1998). In terms of 'cultural impression management' the DDT became a valued local symbol of the organization's engagement with the modernization agenda and reinforced the view that effective organizational redesign aimed at achieving meaningful change is dependent on developing the capabilities of the workforce.

The philosophy, underpinning values and design of the training strategy

The training strategy that was developed was conceptualized as a skills escalator, with a particular focus in the early stages on addressing the needs of frontline staff who had limited knowledge of personality disorder and, at a higher level,

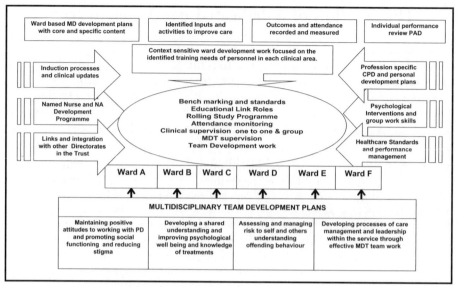

Figure 12.2   Training and development strategy

concentrating on group work skills and intervention strategies or specific develop-ment for identified professional groups, such as named nurses. The team had four full-time staff working under the leadership of the Nurse Consultant in Personality Disorder and reporting to the clinical leads. The team had specialist qualifications and skills in teaching and training, personality disorder, substance misuse, suicide prevention, team development and psychotherapy. The team's work focused on developing the skills and knowledge of the clinical workforce, using the experience and expertise of senior clinical staff in lecturing and supervision roles. This included the creation and implementation of personality disorder-specific educational pro-grammes and facilitating access to mandatory training. The practice development and audit dimension of the role involved improving clinical practice and supervi-sion systems, while the team and ward development function related to improving team skills and MDT working.

All team members facilitated clinical supervision groups and provided individual supervision to practitioners across the service. Team members were also involved in the delivery of key treatment programmes and training initiatives across the Trust. The development strategy, outlined in Figure 12.2, evolved from consultations with clinical leads and managers and was designed to promote and maintain a suitably skilled and knowledgeable work force. The plan was based on the core agenda of educational work reflecting national initiatives and policy guidance – *No Longer a Diagnosis of Exclusion* (Department of Health, 2003); *Breaking the Cycle of Rejection* (Department of Health, 2004b) – which needed to inform our organizational approach while recognizing that the 'local needs' of individual clinical areas should develop their own context-sensitive programmes, based on the needs of the individuals within the clinical team. The educational philosophy informing this strategy focused on creating a staff group who were able to reflect critically on their experiences and practices. For example, rather than create more formal induction and development programmes the whole organization embarked on a programme of practice development and effective team work; shifting the ownership of these activities to their rightful place within the clinical team.

The role of the professional leads, ward managers, educationalists and clinical development leaders was central in this plan, as they had the responsibility for working with the DDT in specific clinical environments to create training plans, while also working with the Senior Management Team (SMT) to ensure the plans were integrated with service development agendas and individual performance reviews. As the left-hand side of Figure 12.2 indicates, there were core developmental inputs across the service including mandatory training, named nurse and nursing assistant development programmes and more advanced specialized training (e.g., group work skills) to support the development of core treatment interventions. As these inputs were a recurrent feature of the development agenda, they were programmed on an annual basis. This was coordinated and integrated with individual and discipline-specific Continuing Professional Development. Multidisciplinary team work and clinical supervision were further core elements of development in each clinical environment. The training programme and development agenda at ward level were organized around the seven pillars of clinical governance (McSherry & Pearce, 2002).

At the bottom of Figure 12.2 the core training inputs identified reflected the Personality Disorder Capability Model (Department of Health, 2004a) which informed the national agenda on education about personality disorder (Department of Health, 2004b). This model emphasized the importance of developing ethical practitioners who have a well-developed knowledge base and the appropriate therapeutic skills to deliver care effectively using evidence-based treatment interventions. This development strategy aimed to ensure that all staff joined the organization with access to a skills escalator (Department of Health, 2004b) which provided them with opportunities for life-long learning.

The initial stage of this process involved ensuring that staff had the foundational knowledge and professional attitudes required to practise effectively with personality disordered individuals in a high secure setting. This input was based on the assumption that, to be effective, all staff require a clear understanding of the core tasks of the service, the treatment pathway and its rationale, and the importance of effective teamwork and supervision systems. The training plans developed by each ward were based on an annual programme of events and activities, with input from key personnel within the service with specialist knowledge. As indicated in Figure 12.2, the material covered in these development plans also informed individual performance reviews, with staff being encouraged to develop and maintain a portfolio of evidence that demonstrated their familiarity with core concepts and theoretical perspectives related to personality disorder. The training strategy was conceptualized using the skills escalator developed by the Sainsbury Centre for Mental Health (2000). It provided a model that described the skills and knowledge required of staff working within the service. It outlined the training and developmental opportunities available to staff in-house and externally to the service. The skills escalator framework offered an organizational tool that informed personal development plans and provided a 'whole system' approach to training and development. The goal was to move us towards being a learning organization (Senge,

1990) which encouraged reflective practice and facilitated optimism about treatability and change in a patient group that has traditionally been viewed with stigmatizing and negative attitudes.

The national strategy on education about personality disorder, *Breaking the Cycle of Rejection* (Department of Health, 2004b), emphasized the importance of continual training which adopted a whole team approach and involved recurring training inputs focused on clinical developments embedded within and supported by sound organizational planning. This PDS workforce strategy represented a local response to this national agenda ensuring that staff at all levels could work positively with patients and their issues. This development required us to think more critically about the way we had developed and educated our staff in the past. By creating organization-wide processes and educational activity, we demonstrated that we were a learning organization (Senge, 1990). The PDS also recognized the importance of clinical supervision for all staff who work with personality disordered patients, and we therefore committed significant resources to the development of a supervision culture within the PDS. This included the establishment of nursing assistant supervision groups on each ward within the PDS and a series of supervision workshops for specific staff groups and clinical teams to prepare staff for the role of supervisee and supervisor, using individual and group supervision methodologies (see this volume, Chapter 13).

The Directorate Development Team (DDT) were also core members of the Courses and Conference Committee, which was responsible for allocating the annual training budget to best meet the needs of the organization. This committee was made up of DDT staff, professional leads from psychology and social work and the Clinical Development Leaders. This group made decisions on all applications to attend training or conferences from nursing, psychology, social work, occupational therapy and ancillary staff within the PDS. The team also assisted ward managers and clinical leads to facilitate staff access to mandatory training, while maintaining a database detailing the mandatory training records of all staff. This database was accessible to all team leaders, ward managers and clinical leads within the PDS. The DDT developed a training strategy that aimed to equip the workforce with the knowledge, skills and attitudes required to work with this challenging patient group. It was decided initially to focus particularly on the skills of the nursing staff, as they had no identified developmental pathway to build on their existing knowledge and skills. Nursing staff were also the group who spent the most time in direct contact with patients and had the potential to affect patient behaviour and ward dynamics, either positively or negatively, through their attitudes and behaviour. A brief outline of some of the key nursing programmes is offered below.

The core development programmes

The 'Introduction to Personality Disorders' three-day programme ran monthly throughout the year and evolved from an earlier one-day 'Personality Disorder Induction' programme. It was primarily aimed at new staff joining the PDS. However, there was an expectation that all existing staff should also complete this training. A programme of this nature was essential for promoting positive attitudes among staff, particularly as most staff joining the service had limited experience of working with the complexities of the diagnosis of personality disorder, and acknowledging the specialist nature of the service we provide was critical in supporting and maintaining the workforce.

The course aimed to provide staff with a basic understanding of personality disorders and the challenges of working with this patient group. Key themes within the introduction programme included:

- what personality disorder is and what factors influence its development;
- clusters of personality disorder and the strengths and limitations of classification systems;
- treatment pathways for personality disordered patients and the PDS's approach to organizing treatment;
- The importance of clinical supervision and staff support, including what can go wrong;
- legal aspects of detention in a high secure setting and proposed changes to mental health legislation;
- challenges, dangers and potential risks when working with forensic patients diagnosed with personality disorder; and
- the value and importance of teamwork and developing a shared understanding of personality disorder.

The programme was considered as a foundational element of working within our service as it provided staff with essential clinical information that helped them understand personality disorder and the specialist nature of the work within the service. The programme provided a starting point for ongoing development work through mentorship relationships provided by the DDT.

The next steps on the escalator acknowledged the specific skills required from both qualified and non-qualified nursing staff. It was acknowledged by service managers that staff could be working in a supermarket one week and providing care in a high secure personality disorder environment the next. This led to the development of the 'Nursing Assistant Development' programme, aimed at providing specialized, 'foundation' knowledge and understanding for unqualified staff within the service. It aimed to develop further and validate the clinical experience, knowledge and skills of this particular group. It covered a range of key issues related to working with personality disorder and reflected the guidelines issued in recent policy developments. It used teaching and learning strategies that helped individuals apply new learning and their existing skills to the ward environment, while acknowledging the value of sharing and reflecting on their practice within a wider educational forum. The planning process was informed by a needs analysis with key staff, pre- and post-course evaluation, and module evaluation with the participant group it was designed for. It was initially delivered over three consecutive days every month. However, over time some modules were delivered in a flexible format to facilitate the release of staff from their wards. To ensure the credibility of the training, this programme was developed and delivered by nursing assistants under the supervision of a member of the DDT.

The educational philosophy underpinning the programme emphasized taking learning away from the classroom and into the ward environment. As a consequence, the delivery took many forms to ensure it met the needs of the staff it was targeting. The main aim was to explore the role of the nursing assistant in caring for this patient group by asking them to identify what types of behaviour they would be observing, and thinking why patients might be behaving in this way. The programme encouraged nursing assistants to move away from pejorative terms like 'attention-seeking' and 'manipulative' and think more psychologically about behaviour. This was an essential element of culture change as it was the nursing assistants on the 'shop floor' who often set the tone of the interpersonal environment by the way they responded to patient distress and offered therapeutic and containing relationships.

The 'Named Nurse' programme was a two-day, classroom-based programme designed to explore and clarify the role of the named nurse. It was recognized that training within this area had been neglected. Traditionally, the model of learning for nurses embarking on this role had typically been a 'pick it up as you go along' apprenticeship model. The amount of time spent with experienced nurses and the quality of the mentorship usually influenced the confidence and competence nurses experienced in their role. The DDT felt it was important to focus on this area of training as nurses spent the most time with patients and could therefore have the greatest impact, either positive or negative, on patients through their attitudes and behaviour. It was important to design a programme that would positively influence patient care by challenging attitudes towards working with this complex patient group as well clearly outlining the behavioural expectations of the role.

The programme was designed and delivered by nurses who were recruited to the programme, based on their credibility, expertise and enthusiasm for the role. They were asked to consider what was required within the service that would help clarify and standardize named nursing practice. Those who were selected to deliver the training had a range of experiences, and involvement was not dependent on years of qualification. A number of development days introduced the idea of developing an educational programme and an implementation strategy was developed by this core group, identifying what was required to effectively develop named nurses and improve the capacity to contribute to patient care. The development days were used to identify the key elements of the role and to describe exactly what the organization expected from staff in relation to their work with patients.

The DDT had begun the process by auditing current practice to identify the key elements of the role and the variance in its implementation. At this time within the organization there were no standardized job descriptions or document templates for named nurses. There was evidence of many different types of nursing care plans, the quality of nursing reports for CPA was inconsistent and face-to-face contact (named nurse sessions) with patients was unpredictable, with some patients having very little face-to-face contact with their named nurse. In designing the programme, existing good practice needed to be built upon, but it was also important that practice was standardized so that all patients were receiving good quality named nursing interventions. The increased scrutiny of what named nurse nurses actually did highlighted gaps in knowledge and helped identify further development. The programme was therefore designed to bring about real behavioural change, improving and standardizing practice in the following key areas:

- the structure and process of the named nurse one to one session;
- the quality of the nurses contribution to the Care Planning Approach process; and
- the quality of the contribution to multidisciplinary communication and teamwork.

The programme initiated a real cultural shift for the service as it encouraged named nurses to think about the therapeutic potential of their role while ensuring that the patient was now at the centre of what they did. This was supported by further audits of practice, including patient evaluations of the role. This initiative helped to shift many nurses from traditional custodial practice to new, patient-centred ways of working (Figure 12.1), increasing their understanding of personality disorder and enabling them to make more of a contribution as therapeutic agents.

At an organizational level all qualified nurses had the programme identified within their annual appraisal document with an expectation they would attend the two-day classroom programme. This ensured that the workforce had access to the relevant knowledge, skills and attitudes to enable them to fulfil the demands of the named nurse role. However, as with many new initiatives in this cultural context, this was not without its challenges. Programme evaluation through the audit process highlighted the difficulties of achieving behavioural change and sustaining changes in practice. The initial audits confirmed that limited change had been achieved in terms of standardizing named nurse practice, with evidence suggesting that even something as simple as using a nursing care plan template continued to be resisted at ward level.

The DDT identified that there had been a lack of standardized training in group facilitation for all disciplines within the service and this led to the development of the 'Working with Challenging Personalities in a Group Setting' programme. As group work is an essential part of the treatment pathway provided by the personality disorder service it was considered important that the next step on the escalator addressed this. This programme was developed to foster a multidisciplinary approach to develop the competence, confidence and knowledge needed to deliver effective groups. This training initiative recognized that individuals may need different levels of theoretical input and skill development. This five day-curriculum was divided into learning units that allowed staff to access at the appropriate level. The programme encouraged the learners to be active participants, reflecting on their own experiences as the focus of skill development to build on their confidence in delivering the range of group work within the service. Although this programme met the needs of staff from all disciplines, it was specifically focused on group facilitators and nurses who had limited inputs in their professional preparation related to managing group dynamics and developing facilitation skills.

The selected core programmes described above were implemented alongside a range of multidisciplinary, team-focused development initiatives and attempts to develop a sustainable supervision culture. With respect to the latter, it is interesting to note that despite several years of concentrated development work it was not until supervision became identified as a service performance management target that organizational commitment to these essential support systems became fully evident.

Conclusion

Organizational change theories often make spurious assumptions about a discernible organizational culture capable of being unfrozen, worked on and shaped into a new form (Grey, 2005). These theories often fail to engage with the meaning of change for individuals and misrepresent the complexity of human social experience and the many factors that influence it. Through the work of the DDT over the last five years we have at times struggled to come to terms with the slow pace of change and felt frustrated with peers who appeared cynical about the capacity to change this insular organization. More sophisticated theoretical accounts of the change process based on ideas such as the learning organization and complex adaptive systems have helped us deal with the paradoxical nature of this experience and refocus our efforts with particular organizational sub-cultures and professional groups. It is clear that some positive changes in professional practice have occurred particularly for individuals who, in Prochaska's (1984) terms, had already moved from the pre-contemplative (not thinking about change and have no sense of the need to change) to the contemplative (needing and wanting change). We have no doubt that the training and development agenda within our service achieved some degree of cultural shift, particularly in the capacity of the nursing staff to work more positively with the challenges of personality disorder. However, we are also aware that, throughout the organization at all levels, there remain covertly hostile and resistant forces with arguably more investment in the past than in the future. This mixed bag is perhaps the paradox of attempts to change complex organizations. We remain optimistic that, with persistence over time, the *stickiness factor* (Gladwell, 2000) within the core messages of the DDT and the important role of external NHS influences will gradually move us towards the organizational *tipping point*, and the therapeutic potential of the high secure milieu will be fully realized.

References

Cordess, C. (1998) The multidisciplinary team: An introduction. In C. Cordess & M. Cox, (Eds.) *Forensic psychotherapy: Crime psychodynamics and the offender patient* (pp. 95–97). London. Jessica Kinglsey.

Cox, M. (1994) A supervisor's view. In C. Cordess & M. Cox (Eds.) *Forensic psychotherapy: Crime psychodynamics and the offender patient*, Vol. 2 (pp. 199–224). London: Jessica Kingsley.

Department of Health (2003) *No longer a diagnosis of exclusion: Policy guidance on the care and treatment of people diagnosed with a personality disorder*. London: NIMHE.

Department of Health (2004a) *The ten essential shared capabilities of the mental health workforce*. London: NIMHE.

Department of Health (2004b) *Breaking the cycle of rejection: The personality disorder capability framework*. London: NIMHE.

Department of Health (2009) *The knowledge and understanding framework*. London: Department of Health.

Egan, G. (1994) *Working the shadow side: A guide to positive behind-the-scenes management*. San Francisco, CA: Jossey-Bass.

Egan, G. (1988) *Change-agent skills: Managing innovation and change.* San Diego, CA: University Associates.

Fallon, P., Bluglass, R., Edwards, B. & Daniels, G. (1999) *Report of the committee of inquiry into the personality disorder unit, Ashworth Special Hospital.* London: Stationery Office.

Gladwell, M. (2000) *The tipping point: How little things make a big difference.* London: Abacus.

Gordon, N. (2003) Rampton Hospital Personality Disorder Directorate: Workforce development plan. Unpublished. Nottinghamshire Healthcare Trust.

Grey, C. (2005) *A very short, fairly interesting and reasonably cheap book about studying organizations.* London: Sage.

Hinshelwood, R. D. (1993) Locked in a role: A psychotherapist within the social defence system of a prison. *Journal of Forensic Psychiatry,* **4**, 427–440.

Kaye, C. & Franey, A. (1998) *Managing high security psychiatric care.* London: Jessica Kingsley.

McSherry, R. & Pearce, P. (2002) *Clinical governance: A guide to implementation for healthcare professionals.* Oxford: Blackwell Science.

Morris, M. (2001) Grendon Underwood: A psychotherapeutic prison. In J. Williams Saunders (Ed.) *Life within hidden worlds: Psychotherapy in prisons* (pp. 89–112). London: Karnac.

Pilgrim, D. (2007) *Inside Ashworth: Professional reflections of institutional life.* Oxford: Radcliffe Publishing.

Prochaska, J. (1984) *Systems of psychotherapy.* Homewood, IL: Dorsey Press.

Sainsbury Centre for Mental Health (2000) *The capable practitioner.* London: Practice Development & Training Section, The Sainsbury Centre for Mental Health.

Senge, P. (1990) *The fifth discipline.* New York: Doubleday.

Shaw, P. (2002) *Changing conversations in organisations: A complexity approach to change.* London: Routledge.

Chapter Thirteen

Establishing a Supervision Culture for Clinicians Working with Personality Disordered Offenders in a High Secure Hospital

Andrea Daykin and Neil Gordon

Introduction

This chapter focuses on how the supervisory needs of multidisciplinary staff working in the context of a high secure hospital are met. It begins by exploring the unique nature of this environment, highlighting the complexity of the issues the workforce must deal with and respond to. Practitioners working with personality disordered offenders in this setting are constantly exposed to challenging and potentially disturbing interpersonal dynamics. Consequently, it is essential that they have access to professional support and supervision systems that help them maintain their psychological health and reflective capacities. Those working in day-to-day contact with this disenfranchised group need dedicated space to reflect on their motivations and attitudes regarding their patients, to help protect themselves and those in their care from distorted and destructive unconscious dynamics.

A range of individual/group supervisory and support processes are discussed, as well as the challenges of establishing a culture and system of supervision in this context. We illustrate this by drawing on the key elements of best practice in this area. There is a particular focus on managing the emotional demands of clinical work with some analysis of how different therapeutic perspectives can inform the approach taken. In addressing the complexity of professional roles and the contribution of wider organizational and systemic influences, the chapter demonstrates the importance of creating different modes of professional support and supervision

Working Positively with Personality Disorder in Secure Settings: A Practitioner's Perspective
Edited by Phil Willmot and Neil Gordon
© 2011 John Wiley & Sons, Ltd.

that can be integrated effectively to address what Proctor (2000) describes as the practitioner's normative (managerial), restorative (supportive) and formative (educational) needs. The chapter also explores some of the recurrent themes in this unique context which can result in personal distress and undermine psychologically informed clinical practice.

The nature and context of working with personality disordered offenders in a high secure hospital

As we have highlighted throughout this book, those detained in conditions of high security often have complex offending histories, combined with acute and long-term mental health and personality difficulties. The violent and sexual nature of the offences these individuals have committed confronts the professionals who attempt to help them with the emotionally challenging experience of working therapeutically with a vulnerable person whilst managing their own psychological discomfort about the damage and hurt this person may have caused. Managing such ambivalence is no easy task, as this high risk group, who by definition pose a risk to others, are also some of the most emotionally deprived and socially disenfranchised people in our mental health system. Following a typically abusive, traumatizing and rejecting childhood with long periods of institutionalization and incarceration, the individual arriving in the Personality Disorder Service (PDS) finds himself in another potentially rejecting environment where the relationships he creates with his carers can quickly lead to a re-enactment of earlier maladaptive patterns of relating. The implications of this for the approach taken when supervising staff needs to be understood as it is common for professionals who experience such re-enactments to develop ambivalent views about those they work with. At one extreme the patient may be perceived as unworthy of help and deserving punishment as opposed to care, with these perceptions being fuelled by feelings such as anger, anxiety and frustration. Alternatively, the professional may feel pulled into a protective, rescuing role to compensate for the deprivation and hurt the individual has experienced. This fundamental split, although an oversimplification, is often at the heart of many interpersonal and inter-professional conflicts in these contexts.

These complex emotional responses can be further illuminated with reference to the psychodynamic concept of *psychic assault*, as articulated by Gordon and Kirtchuk (2008), who use this term to describe the potential negative consequences involved in the emotional labour of working with the *raw material* of human beings who have committed acts of violence against others. They refer to the 'gnawing anxiety' commonly experienced by multidisciplinary forensic staff. This anxiety, they believe, emerges from knowing that, when someone has acted on an impulsive or distorted belief resulting in them damaging another person catastrophically, there can never be an absolute reassurance that this behaviour will not be repeated. As Foster (2001) observes, faced with this kind of persistent anxiety, workers may need to split off part of their emotional experience to preserve their own mental health and maintain their capacity to provide a service to the patient group. Foster goes on to suggest that psychologically defending oneself in this way represents what she terms 'normal splitting'.

At one level these defensive manoeuvres can help to numb the awareness of danger and destructiveness, protecting the worker from overwhelming anxiety and pain. It should be stressed that while the tendency of professionals to deny and minimize may have a positive effect in the short term by facilitating the development of a non-judgemental and collaborative alliance, it can lead to difficulties if the therapist loses a sense of what the individual has done or experienced. Cox (1994) provides a dramatic analysis of the potential difficulties in dealing with the demands of this patient group by deconstructing the view that our problems with such patients are 'hung up with our keys at the gate' (1994: 447). As he eloquently puts it, therapists in this setting are in constant contact with experiences 'that bad dreams are made of'. Therapists who each day interact with patients struggling with their propensity for violence and feelings of fear are therefore always in need of high quality supervision to help them process and manage their vulnerabilities and psychological reactions to their clinical work.

Managing emotional demands: psychological implications of working with personality disordered offenders

Part of the role of supportive supervision in the high secure setting involves helping individuals to protect themselves from the inevitable corrosive effects of being exposed to the narratives of patients who have committed violent and sexual offences and who have themselves experienced various levels of physical and sexual abuse. As Ryan and Lane observe, 'professionals who interact with dysfunctional populations are at risk personally, socially and professionally' (1997: 457). These risks stem from the realities, beliefs and attributions of each individual and how they meet the challenge of integrating these experiences into their personal world-view. Part of the process of protecting oneself from and integrating these extremes of experience is to become *desensitized* to the horror of the story being told, as one of our therapists observed in a recent supervision group; much as a soldier in the front line becomes hardened to the idea of death and killing in order to survive the horrors of war, the worker can become dehumanized and insensitive to the actual horror of the pain and damage those we are working with have perpetrated against others.

A further negative psychological implication of working with personality disordered patients in this context has been discussed by Morgan (1979) using the evocative phrase 'malignant alienation'. This term describes the patient's deteriorating relationships with others, leading to a loss of sympathy and support, and an increasing tendency by professionals to construe the patient's behaviour as provocative, unreasonable or over-dependent. Indeed, such negative feelings can be evoked when patients do not appear to be making progress or are perceived to be placing extra demands on an already stretched clinical team. This state of affairs can be reduced by encouraging a culture where staff can openly reflect on and acknowledge their feelings (both negative and positive) towards their patients. In some situations, staff may develop fantasies that the clinical team will make the decision to transfer the patient to another ward, a response that can be perceived by those least affected as punitive and simply moving the 'problem' elsewhere. However, from the patient's point of view, such actions simply serve to reinforce earlier interpersonal dynamics whereby they are rejected and their care is passed on to someone else. In stark contrast, working with personality disordered patients can also be a rewarding experience, in that the particular nature of a high secure hospital and working with the challenge of rehabilitating society's most damaged individuals can become infused with therapeutic optimism that treatment interventions will enable the patients to lead more fulfilling and less destructive lives.

Whatever the stance of the professional working in this setting and with this particular client group, the establishment and maintenance of boundaries is crucial to the provision of care. When working with this client group, boundary maintenance helps maintain safety for unregulated feelings (Adshead, 2004) and it is with this in mind that a safe and supportive place is important for the clinician to explore these feelings. In this context, it could be argued that boundary violations are inevitable (see this volume, Chapter 8 on boundaries) and clinical supervisors have to be mindful and alert to signs that these might be occurring, and be willing to explore the wider meanings of these interpersonal processes in relation to the therapeutic task. Supervision should ensure that these issues are explored and addressed. A further complicating factor highlighted by Kurtz (2005) is that professionals working in a multidisciplinary team (MDT) may not always have a common sense of purpose about the aims and goals of their work. In our experience we have noted how easy it is for teams to become fragmented and conflicted about how patients should be managed and their needs responded to. This highlights how the process and functioning of the MDT working is in itself an essential area to attend to when supporting professionals in this context.

It could be argued that a necessary feature of working with high risk men who have harmed others is the psychological capacity to protect oneself from the overwhelming horror associated with some of the offences they have committed. Therapists and ward-based staff in individual and group supervision settings will readily share how they find themselves minimizing and avoiding thinking about what the person had done as a way of maintaining capacity to work with the individual. This struggle is further supported by Straker and Moosa's (1994) reflections on working with victims of trauma where they explore the concept of 'vicarious traumatization' of therapists associated with hearing accounts of torture and violence in everyday clinical work. This concept has some resonance within our setting where therapists recognize and acknowledge how their experiences over time (and personal levels of energy) can impact on their capacity to hear (and listen to) offence narratives or accounts of the abuse that these men have experienced. A number of colleagues have alluded to their struggle to comprehend the accounts of the patients that seemed so alien to their own understandings of human behaviour and experience.

Obstacles to supervision: Individual, organizational or both?

Given this agenda, traditional models of supervision do not necessarily always fit. Indeed, from a supervisory point of view, our experience has been that organizational demands and situational factors can influence whether supervision takes place at all, either directly or indirectly. Factors such as managing seclusions, staff sickness and consequent reduced staff numbers on the ward can dictate whether supervision can go ahead. However, these factors may equally be used as an active means of avoiding supervision, a common practice when working within the culture of a high secure hospital where some staff may have anxieties about being perceived as weak if they enter into the supervision arena. In addition, the anxiety or fear of being perceived as incompetent by those supervising, and subsequently by the organization, can hinder supervision, the same process that can result from working with personality disordered offenders. Finally, some staff may perceive that supervision is organized to simply 'tick the organizational box' and not because the organization genuinely cares about its workers. We have observed how the organization can become the focus of blame or be perceived as the root of the problem, a view shared by Kurtz (2005: 417), whereby frustration with patients is displaced onto 'external, concrete issues'. For example, it is common in clinical supervision narratives for staff to avoid exploring their difficulties working with patients by displacing their feelings of frustration and anxiety onto external sources such as the organization. This then avoids addressing and reflecting on difficult emotions the practitioner may be struggling with (Kurtz, 2000).

Within the unique context of a high secure hospital there is scope to be flexible in the approach adopted in the supervisory relationship, as prescribed models and frameworks do not always fit with the supervisee population. As such, the various approaches adopted in our therapeutic work with patients in this setting mean that the process of supervision can adopt similar modalities (i.e., individual or group) and that supervisors can apply a specific model to meet the needs of the supervisee who may be working within a particular theoretical framework (e.g., schema focused therapy or dialectical behaviour therapy). In other contexts, supervisors can apply supervision models to structure their session, such as Hawkins and Shohet's (2000) process model, they may have to respond to need at a time of crisis for example, by facilitating a critical incident debrief.

Hinshelwood (1999) highlights that, as professionals, we may develop personal reactions and feelings about particular patients we come into contact with, particularly those who are deemed to be difficult: 'Difficult patients create reactions in the staff members who care for and treat them' (1999: 187). The way we as professionals react can in turn cause more difficulties for the patients and ultimately for the services we run. As our reactions impact at different levels in a range of interpersonal contexts (individual, group, MDT) our supervisory responses need to be both systemic and individualistic, to respond meaningfully to the different dimensions of the care context and professional activities. It is essential that such approaches are not prescriptive as although adhering to one particular supervisory model or framework may mean the 'organizational box' is ticked, many of the important processes that need our attention can be overlooked.

Working in a high secure setting can present professionals and the organization with specific challenges where supervision is concerned. In our experience, resistance to receiving supervision can be present in qualified and unqualified staff. A common distortion we have found among staff with anxieties about attending supervision is the notion that requiring access to supervision is a sign of their inability to manage the demands of the job and a fear of being judged as weak by peers.

For those professionals who are ward-based, meeting another professional for supervision on the ward where they are based can mean that they remain unhelpfully attendant to the ward atmosphere whilst supervision is taking place. Many voice a preference for support to be provided in a less open, more neutral supervision space The common occurrence of extended family groups (sometimes several generations of the same family) working together in this context can also lead to concerns about confidentiality and the boundaries between the personal and professional. This boundary can be further complicated by those who view the processes of supervision as being too closely aligned with personal therapy, and rather than see it as creating the opportunity to reflect critically on practice, they fear it will be psychologically invasive and exposing of their vulnerabilities.

Evershed, Tennant, Boomer, Rees, Barkham and Watsons (2003), in looking at the particular challenges facing those working with personality disordered offenders, emphasize the importance of constantly revisiting motivational issues and recognizing that this patient group is particularly prone to engaging in therapy interfering behaviours, leading to disengagement and rejection of the therapist. Part of this issue relates to the personality disordered individual's tendency to turn to impulsive and self-destructive interpersonal behaviour. As Morris (2001: 97) points out, personality disordered individuals' 'psychopathology is expressed in their relationships'. Whereas a psychotic person's psychopathology is usually manifest in their mind in the form of delusions and hallucinations, it is within the therapeutic encounter itself that much of the personality disordered person's distress emerges and has to be responded to and made sense of. This is further complicated in high secure contexts by the increasingly litigious culture where patient complaints and the involvement of solicitors are becoming more common. Therapists have a difficult line to tread in maintaining the individual's commitment and engagement with therapy while expecting periods of disenchantment and withdrawal as an inevitable feature of their work. Being prepared for this helps the therapist manage his or her own vulnerability and encourages a complex formulation of the patient's behaviour that does not become overly personalized and detrimental to the practitioner's self-esteem.

Developing the supervision culture: a brief review of our models of practice

When faced with the challenge of developing a supervision culture within our service there were several key issues that had to be addressed. First, the multidisciplinary workforce, with a few exceptions, had a limited understanding of what supervision was and why it was an essential element of effective practice with this client group. Secondly, for some professional groups, and particularly unqualified staff, there was great deal of resistance to the idea because it was seen as a potentially invasive 'Big Brother' initiative to extend what was perceived as judgemental organizational surveillance. Milligan and Gordon (this volume, Chapter 12) explore how this was addressed educationally through a systematic training and organizational development programme; whereas this chapter explores the different systems that were established and their underpinning rationale.

It is useful when thinking about supervision and support to focus on the range of delivery methodologies that can be deployed. The best known methods are represented by one-to-one supervision and group interactions which have a well-developed supporting literature and evolving evidence base (Carroll, 1997; Hawkins & Shohet, 2000; Holloway, 1995). Team and multidisciplinary supervision processes have, surprisingly, received far less attention. As Beckley (this volume, Chapter 11) illustrates, paying attention to team dynamics and communication is an essential element in maintaining effective practice and managing the inevitable interpersonal and inter-professional tensions that emerge in this work setting. In addressing the challenges for practitioners at an individual and team level, the supervision philosophy informing developments within the service adopted a systemic multi-level approach focused on six main areas:

1. *Profession-specific, one-to-one supervision*, which was well established in certain disciplines such as psychology and social work, but less developed in nursing and other professional cultures. The key role of frontline nursing staff in creating and maintaining the therapeutic milieu made this a priority for attention. This involved creating a structured training programme for 10 selected senior nursing staff (ward managers and team leaders) and training them in supervision skills using an adapted version of the Hawkins and Shohet (2000) process model. These individuals then each took on a group of four supervisees and received 'supervision on their supervision' experiences. This cascade model increased access to supervision for nursing staff, but was quite difficult to sustain due to the time commitment involved from an already stretched group of senior nurses and ambivalence from some of the potential supervisees. Despite the limitations of this initiative it did raise awareness in many staff and facilitated several high-quality staff to see supervision as an essential part of their practice and to seek out regular supervision.

2. *Supervision groups for unqualified nurses* aimed at improving the psychological mindedness (Egan, 1996) of frontline staff and increasing their awareness and understanding of the interpersonal demands of working with patients with personality disorder. A huge amount of time was invested in this process as it was believed that this group of staff tended to be the 'culture carriers' (Goffman, 1961) in ward environments and therefore their attitudes and behaviour with patients significantly contributed to the potential therapeutic milieu, both positively and negatively. This initiative struggled at times, with staff not turning up or not being released to attend although, again, a significant number of motivated individuals became regular attendees and feedback from the groups was very positive. The supervisors selected to deliver the groups were given an initial training programme and then had regular group supervision of their supervision work with senior clinical staff. The focus on nursing staff in these initiatives was part of a deliberate strategy as this was the group which had the least developed systems for supervision and probably also the greatest resistance to the idea, holding negative views about the purpose of supervision and how it could be helpful to them in their practice. In addressing this the service also organized a series of workshops for unqualified staff to help explain what supervision was (and what it was not), acknowledging

that many people had negative experiences of supervision, or more commonly, that they held negative assumptions that it involved being managed, monitored and controlled.

3. *Therapy-focused supervision* concentrating on psychological therapies was also a priority, and involved establishing dialectical behaviour therapy consultation processes (Linehan, 1993) and schema focused therapy supervision groups to support individual therapists in their one-to-one work and group facilitator roles. These approaches were organized to parallel the core concepts and principles of the therapeutic model the therapists were operating within, encouraging staff to conceptualize and apply the model in an analysis of their own behaviour and emotions. This type of theoretically congruent supervisory strategy helps the practitioner develop their therapeutic skills in the safety and containment of the supervisory relationship while enhancing self-aware and reflective practice regarding therapeutic interventions and their impacts.

4. *The multidisciplinary team supervision* we developed was designed to enhance team effectiveness and help teams resolve conflict and disagreements. This involved staff from different disciplines taking protected time in a group setting to reflect on their shared experiences of patient work and the work context. It involved exploring the team's experiences with patients, their working relationships and their current approaches to clinical practice and team tasks. The key aim of this reflective process was to support, develop and improve communication between team members with the goal of enhancing the quality of the care experienced by the patient group. The structure and process of these meetings were integrated into existing meeting processes. The supervision process was based on having an external facilitator managing the supervision time by encouraging detailed discussion about challenging patients to clarify and commit to a consistent team approach while discussing ethical and professional issues related to patient care. This approach reduced professional isolation and improved information-sharing around risk assessment and management. The facilitated meetings also created space to explore within the team problematic feelings and attitudes towards patients and address issues of conflict that may have been leading to team splitting. This not only supported individuals with the stress arising from their practice, it also exposed them to the perspectives and approaches of other disciplines and improved their understanding of different roles. The aim was to maintain the effectiveness and healthy functioning of the team and improve decision-making processes and working relationships.

5. A further area of development was *incident debriefing*, which involved supportive reviews of practice following a difficult team experience related to particular patient (or group of patients) behaviours and their impact on the team. These interventions were used to good effect in a range of contexts following individual and team trauma, adopting a clear structure to encourage both individual and group reflection on the event and its consequences for those involved. It was essential that these interpersonal processes were facilitated in a non-judgemental and emotionally sensitive way in order to help teams feel contained and to avoid the creation of a blame culture withn the

organization. The aim of these incident debriefs was to assist the team with processing their distress and also identifying what had been learned from this series of events.

6. *Team-focused formulations* provided detailed working hypotheses of individual patient presentations, effectively assisting treatment planning. However, there are several other important functions associated with this type of collaborative activity. When individual team members are required to articulate their understanding and interpretations about an individual patient, it encourages them to be more explicit about their own values and theoretical approach, and assists others with understanding different professional philosophies and alternative conceptual frameworks. The associated dialogue emerging in these exchanges encourages people to learn more about their colleagues and be clearer about what they can contribute to the team. It also enables the team to develop a shared understanding of the patient and his problems or alternatively facilitates the creation of different models of intervention that can inform the team's clinical work.

This multi-level approach ensures that a practitioner's needs are met at the levels proposed in Proctor's model – namely, restorative, normative and formative. In particular, developing a supervision culture and a system for supervision within the context of a high secure hospital means that not only are an individual's needs fulfilled, but the flexibility of the model means that supervisory needs can be accommodated according to team, organizational and situational demands that may be operating at a given time.

Conclusion

This chapter has highlighted how the high secure hospital is a unique setting where the complexity of the patient group does not lend itself to a one-size-fits-all supervisory framework. The supervision needs of professionals in this setting are diverse, with unqualified staff working very closely with patients, requiring exposure to developmental opportunities to help them understand the traumatic roots and interpersonal nature of personality difficulties For those working therapeutically who are qualified, supervisory needs may be informed by a particular theoretical model, such as schema focused therapy or dialectical behaviour therapy. At times there will be a need for a debrief following an incident, and team functioning is so important that multidisciplinary team supervision needs to be a core element of practice. Supervisory interventions in this setting should fulfil the needs of the individual, the team and the organization, and ultimately the needs of the patient to be treated and contained in a therapeutic environment where earlier damaging ways of relating are made sense of and modified.

References

Adshead, G. (2004) Three degrees of security. attachment and forensic institutions. In F. Pfafflin & G. Adshead (Eds.) *A matter of security – the application of attachment theory to forensic psychiatry and psychotherapy* (pp. 147–166). London: Jessica Kingsley.

Carroll, M. (1997) Clinical supervision: Luxury or necessity? In I. Horton & V. P. Varma (Eds.) *The needs of counsellors and psychotherapists: Emotional, social, physical, professional* (pp. 135–151). London: Sage.

Cox, M. (1994) A supervisor's view. In C. Cordess & M. Cox (Eds.) *Forensic psychotherapy: Crime psychodynamics and the offender patient* (pp. 199–224). London: Jessica Kinglsey.

Egan, G. (1996) *The skilled helper, a problem management approach to helping.* Pacific Grove, CA: Brooks Cole.

Evershed S., Tennant A., Boomer D., Rees A., Barkham M., & Watsons, A. (2003) Practice-based outcomes of dialectical behaviour therapy (DBT) targeting anger and violence, with male forensic patients: A pragmatic and non-contemporaneous comparison. *Criminal Behaviour and Mental Health*, **13**, 198–213.

Foster, A. (2001) The duty to care and the need to split. *Journal of Social Work Practice*, **15**, 81–90.

Goffman, E. (1961) *Asylums: Essays on the social situation of mental patients and other inmates.* New York: Anchor Books.

Gordon, J. & Kirtchuk, G. (2008) *Psychic assaults and frightened clinicians: Countertransference in forensic settings.* London: Karnac.

Hawkins, P. & Shohet, R. (2000) *Supervision in the helping professions.* Buckingham: Open University Press

Hinshelwood, R. D. (1999) The difficult patient. The role of 'scientific psychiatry' in understanding patients with chronic schizophrenia or severe personality disorder. *British Journal of Psychiatry*, **174**, 187–190.

Holloway, E. L. (1995) *Clinical supervision: A systems approach.* London: Sage.

Kurtz, A. (2002) A psychoanalytic view of two forensic mental health services. *Criminal Behaviour and Mental Health*, **12**, 68–80.

Kurtz, A. (2005) The needs of staff who care for people with a diagnosis of personality disorder who are considered a risk to others. *The Journal of Forensic Psychiatry and Psychology*, **16**, 399–422.

Linehan, M. (1993) *Cognitive-behavioural treatment of borderline personality disorder.* New York: Guilford Press.

Morgan, H. G. (1979) *Death wishes: The understanding and management of deliberate self harm.* Chichester: Wiley.

Morris, M. (2001) Grendon Underwood: A psychotherapeutic prison. In J. Williams Saunders (Ed.) *Life within hidden worlds: Psychotherapy in prisons* (pp. 89–112). London: Karnac.

Proctor, B. (2000) *Group supervision: A guide to creative practice.* London: Sage.

Ryan, G. & Lane, S. (1997) *Juvenile sexual offending: causes, consequences and correction.* San Francisco: Jossey Bass.

Straker, G. & Moosa, F. (1994) Interacting with trauma survivors in contexts of continuing trauma. *Journal of Traumatic Stress*, 7, 457–465.

Section Five

Outcomes

Chapter Fourteen

An Individual Approach to Assessing Change

Jason Davies

Developing and implementing approaches to evaluation and outcome assessment are as important as providing the services and the interventions themselves. Inevitably, evaluating change carries a cost in terms of time and money. However, when providing care to people, knowing what impact the care has had should be seen as part of the duty of care to the individual. Many resources exist which provide guidance for assessing outcomes (e.g., Bergin & Garfield, 1971; Ogles, Lambert & Fields, 2002; Ogles, Lambert & Masters, 1996; Sperry, Brill, Howard & Grissom, 1996), however, for many years and in many services, an idiosyncratic and subjective approach to determining change has been the norm. Often judgements have relied on the opinion of a single individual or a clinical team, with little reference to objective measurement. Due to changes in the health and prison services, emphasis is again being placed on outcome data and cost-effectiveness, resulting in the promotion of evidence as a cornerstone for practice. This provides the foundation for practitioners to turn their attention and some resources to the pursuit of individual change measurement.

The level of evidence required from practitioners to support their views in relation to individual change, especially when such information might help others' decision-making, is becoming more demanding. Two examples of statutory obligations in forensic mental health practice are (i) the requirements to review need, progress and care as part of the Care Programme Approach (Department of Health, 2008); and (ii) the requirement to provide evidence to aid in the decision-making processes in relation to detention under the Mental Health Act (Department

Working Positively with Personality Disorder in Secure Settings: A Practitioner's Perspective
Edited by Phil Willmot and Neil Gordon
© 2011 John Wiley & Sons, Ltd.

of Health, 2008) in managers' hearings or Mental Health Review Tribunals. However, equally important is the need to understand individual change in order for the clinical team to determine the appropriateness of the care being offered and the opportunities for care to be offered elsewhere (e.g., in conditions of lesser security). Such decisions need to be based on robust evidence concerning the level and nature of need and of change.

In recent decades, research in forensic mental health and personality disorder services has become dominated by a paradigm that seeks to describe change at the group level. Inevitably, this has influenced the questions being asked by services, researchers and commissioners. As a result, the 'what works?' agenda has become focused on the question that can be answered by group-based research (i.e., 'what might work for this *type of need*?') rather than addressing the questions faced by practitioners working with individuals (i.e. 'has change taken place in *this individual*?'). Clearly, these questions are complementary. However, research and evaluation specialists have not developed mechanisms for routinely answering this critical second question. This is important given Slade and Priebe's comment: '[i]f care is to be provided on the basis of evidence, then it follows that equal opportunity should be available for all types of relevant research evidence to be gathered and considered' (2001: 286).

The limitations of the randomized controlled trial (RCT) approach in psychotherapy outcome research, forensic and personality disorder services have been discussed elsewhere (e.g., Davies, 2005; Davies, Howells & Jones, 2007; Sperry *et al.*, 1996). Some key problems with RCTs in forensic services are:

1. Although the approach of the RCT may function to manage some threats to internal validity, external validity (generalizability) is often poor due, for example, to the selectivity of those providing or receiving the treatment (see Black, 1996).
2. The variation in individual responses to the same treatment means that the assumption of a 'universal response' is likely to be inappropriate where interventions have long, complex causal pathways, or where such pathways can be affected by a multitude of things (see Victora, Habicht & Bryce, 2004).
3. The difficulties with conducting randomization and in identifying control conditions (e.g., who to use as the control group and what to provide them with) mean that many studies use comparison groups or non-control conditions, so weakening their design.
4. The heterogeneity of the sample is generally hidden, masked by the reduction of individuals in a group to a basic single factor (e.g., a common diagnostic label). Factors such as age, coexisting problems, differences in coping styles, variations in challenging or offending behaviours, substance use history, prior treatments and personal history, are typically overlooked, even though these variables are likely to introduce important differences. The use of diagnosis as a grouping variable itself raises many issues, as each diagnostic label is 'pseudo-homogeneous' (i.e., has multiple possible presentations contained within it).
5. The failure to account for the beliefs about change held by the individual, their wishes and the attitudes, training and supervision of the professionals

introduces significant variance, which is generally overlooked: 'the effectiveness of the intervention depends on the subject's active participation, which in turn depends on the subject's beliefs and preferences' (Black, 1996: 1216).

6. Evidence from large-scale studies and RCTs often takes many years to be published so that treatments may have to be used before the evidence is available or treatments have evolved since they were manualized for a research trial. This can be seen in relation to offender treatment programmes in the UK (Nagi & Davies, 2010). Added to this, the conditions of the trial invariably differ from the practice setting in which the approaches which have been evaluated are being used.

It is important to remember that group-based research typically hides the reality that whilst, 'on average', treatment may have had a positive impact on many in the group, it is highly likely that some have not changed and some may have been 'made worse' by the intervention. Overlooking adverse effects is a hidden problem (Jones, 2004).

This chapter considers approaches to assessing change at the individual level. In particular, consideration is given to techniques for determining whether change has taken place, how much change has occurred, how stable the change is and what might have caused it.

Throughout this chapter the approaches to evaluation that are presented are 'change theory'/'therapy approach'-neutral. This is essential if the approaches are to be useful in various settings using different interventions. However, readers are encouraged to consider how they might use each approach as it is acknowledged that some principles may be easier to slot into particular approaches to treatment.

Before outlining general approaches to evaluation based on the individual, it is essential to consider the universal concerns of reliability and validity. In group-based evaluation, the use of psychometrically robust measures and 'manipulations' such as randomization, control or comparison groups are typically stated as the means by which reliability (and validity) are managed. However, in assessments of change at the individual level, these techniques are of limited use – if they can be applied at all. Therefore, alternative approaches are included to enhance reliability and minimize the threats to validity. Work by Turpin (2001) and Bloom, Fischer and Orme (2006) highlights the various threats to validity and how these might be managed in practice. The main principles of these are highlighted next.

Reliability in individual measurement

Questions such as 'Does the selected measure accurately measure anything?' 'If nothing has changed, do I get the same (or more likely very similar) reading on the measure each time I use it?' use very much the same approach as the group-based counterparts. In individual measurement, factors that aid reliability are:

- the use of well-researched/evidenced psychometric measures;
- clear anchor points for all scale-based measures; and
- review of inter-rater reliability between observers.

Validity

The issue of validity addresses questions such as 'Does the measure assess what I say it does?', 'Is change on the measure caused by what I say it is?' (internal validity), and 'Is the change observed in this individual likely to be replicated in others or in other situations by this individual?' (external validity or generalizability). However, a number of procedures need to be in place to manage it.

The most common threats to validity for individual evaluation can be summarized as 'history' – extraneous events that lead to change (e.g., developing a romantic relationship); 'maturation' – the natural course of change over time; 'testing' – the impact of measurement and monitoring (e.g., diary keeping as an intervention rather than a benign assessment); 'instrumentation' – change related to the 'error of measurement' contained within the tool used; 'regression to the mean' – the tendency for extreme responses to be less extreme on repeat measurement; and 'bias' (i.e., therapist (rather than therapy) variance). Although these threats are not unique to individual measurement, they require specific attention through:

- careful recording of all known intended and incidental interventions and life events;
- the use of multiple measures (including the assessment of factors that are expected not to change as well as those that are);
- multiple data points (i.e., recording data on many occasions);
- replication of an apparently successful intervention with another individual;
- the maintenance of change in different settings and over time;
- the use of measures with low face validity but good construct validity; and
- the use of indices such as the Reliable Change Index and Clinical Significance (e.g., Jacobson & Truax, 1991) to set appropriate thresholds for the level of change required.

General approaches to individual evaluation

Practitioners working in personality disorder services rely on a formulation approach to understanding strengths and needs. This should enable practitioners to predict (hypothesize) what might change and how it might change. In forensic contexts this can include the assessment and formulation of offence paralleling behaviour (OPB) and the inclusion of this in aspects of what is being measured (Davies, Jones & Howells, in press). Thus the starting point for individual measurement is a formulation that includes what *needs* to change (e.g., in order for the individual to move to conditions of lesser security) and what *should* change, based on the individual formulation (e.g., increased skills use when distressed as the result of participation in a dialectical behaviour therapy (DBT) (Linehan, 1993) distress tolerance skills module. Therefore, the most robust individual change measurement will be based on a formulation of change; the selection of appropriate measures; the use of multiple approaches to measurement, repeated measurement over time; and, where possible, across settings.

Broadly, individual change measurement can be clustered into two groups: infrequently repeated measures (not more than every three months) and frequently repeated measures (e.g., monthly, weekly or daily). Most services using structured approaches to evaluating change will use both approaches, and, where possible, multiple sources and types of data should be collected. Collecting information on dynamic factors that are not expected to change is also important. Further considerations when measuring change are: who will gather the data (e.g., self-report, observer ratings); what scales will be used (e.g., commercially available, developed within the service); what form the data will take (qualitative or quantitative); and the nature of the data (subjective, e.g., mood ratings; or objective, e.g., time spent off the ward).

The following sections consider a range of strategies for assessing change. Each of the strategies discussed is described in brief and an example given to outline the use of the specific approach. Although ideographic data might also be used to answer questions at the group or service level, the methods for undertaking this, including some of the principles for transforming and presenting data, are outside the scope of this chapter.

Infrequently repeated measures

Many tools used in services can be repeated over time to allow changes to be assessed. This section considers four techniques for gathering data using infrequently repeated measures.

Pre-/post-psychometric assessment. Many services make use of formalized self-report assessments to collect data at the start and end of a period of intervention. This approach has been incorporated into some group-based interventions (e.g., sex offender treatment programmes) and can enable individual scores to be compared with 'group norms' at the start and end of treatment. This approach can be used with little resource demand in most circumstances. A detailed discussion of the use of psychometric tests for treatment planning and outcome evaluation can be found in Maruish (1994).

The most robust way to use pre-/post-psychometric data is to assess both the reliability and clinical significance of change (e.g., Davies, Jones & Howells, in press). A detailed review of the clinical significance approach (Ogles, Lunnen & Bonesteel, 2001) shows multiple approaches available to the practitioner and researcher. One method (based on Jacobson & Truax, 1991) combines assessing statistically reliable change, as measured by the Reliable Change Index (RCI), with the movement of an individual from the 'dysfunctional' population to a 'functional' population score. Calculations for reliable and clinically significant change can be found online (see www.psyctc.org/stats/rcsc.htm; www.leeds.ac.uk/lihs/ psychiatry/courses/dclin/research_products/RCI_Tramline_Display/Reliable

_Change_Index_background_info.html) and through their associated links. An example of the use of pre-post psychometric data is shown below.

Case example: Use of pre-/post-psychometric assessment

Andrew is a 32 year old who has been participating in an anger management intervention for the last nine months. Andrew completed a range of psychometric measures at the start of treatment which were repeated when the treatment group came to an end. His scores on one of the measures, STAXI-II (Spielberger, 2000), a measure of anger, are shown in Table 14.1. As can be seen, Andrew's scores indicate a number of areas where change has taken place; however, use of the RCI reveals that on four scales the change recorded may not be reliable. Therefore, the team decided to report no change on these scales. On the other eight scales, the various 'clinical significance indices' provide different pieces of information. For example, although the level of change on AC-I is modest on the index using s.d. change and falls below the expected end score, the score on this scale has moved into the normal population range. In contrast the AX-O shows large change (> 3) on the s.d. index, and is of an expected level but does not fall within the normal range. As these indices use different 'metrics' it is unsurprising that they show different levels of results. However, this example shows the importance of measuring the extent of change with a range of different approaches. The clinical team must then use their skills and judgement to reach the most appropriate conclusion.

Clinical/professional judgement methods. Clinicians can use various methods to build evidence through clinical judgement. However, for the purposes of individual evaluation, structuring the judgements being made is critical. Structured professional judgements provide clear anchor points for the ratings being made and potentially provide information for other raters to compare against. In this simple approach to evaluation, clinicians use the structured rating at various points in time, with change being evidenced through differences in ratings. One established and widely used structured clinical judgement scale for violent mentally disordered offenders is the HCR-20 Version 2 risk assessment tool (Webster, Douglas, Eaves & Hart, 1997). Whilst the Historical (H) scale concerns static information, the Clinical (C) and Risk (R) scales are made up of items that can vary over time, influenced by factors such as changes in context and changes in the individual's presentation. The data from the C & R scales, when used for outcome assessment, could be plotted to show estimated risk level (high, medium or low), actual risk score (ranging from 0 to 20) or the number of items increasing and decreasing over time (see case example below). As with pre-/post-psychometric assessment, it is possible to set thresholds required for change to be meaningful at the outset. An example is provided below.

Table 14.1 Review of pre-/post-intervention STAXI-II data for Andrew

Scale	Score at start of treatment	Score at end of treatment	Published mean, standard deviation and α**	Reliable Change (>1.96) (RCI)	Number of s.d. change**	Expected score at end of treatment*	Change greater than expected	Movement into 'normal' population range***
SAng	51	34	18.43 (5.63) α .91	Yes	>3	32	No	No
SAngF	20	14	6.95 (2.76) α .84	Yes	>2	14	Equal	No
SAngV	18	12	6.06 (2.10) α .78	Yes	>2	12	Equal	No
SAngP	13	8	5.40 (1.30) α .77	Yes	>3	9	Yes	No
TAng	28	25	16.80 (4.24) α .78	No	<1	26	Yes	No
TAngT	12	10	5.76 (1.82) α .75	No	>1	11	Yes	No
TAngR	16	15	8.08 (2.52) α .69	No	<1	13	No	No
AX-O	29	20	14.22 (2.84) α .55	Yes	>3	20	Equal	No
AX-I	28	25	15.10 (3.84) α .73	No	<1	23	Yes	No
AC-O	13	24	24.65 (4.96) α .84	Yes	>2	27	No	Yes
AC-I	15	22	22.70 (5.70) α .89	Yes	>1	28	No	Yes
AX Ind.	77	47	30.36 (12.68) α .69	Yes	>2	65	Yes	No

* The clinical team derived this score from the T = 60 score on Table B9 (Normalized T-scores for male psychiatric patients ages 18 years and older).

** Using Tables 4 and 5 – Normal adult male 30 years and older.

*** Defined as within the 25 and 75 percentiles of the normal population (Table A7: Normal males ages 30 Years and older).

> **Case example: Use of structured professional judgement – an HCR-20 example**
>
> *Dave is a 24-year-old who has been in the service for just over a year. Soon after his admission the HCR-20 was completed by his clinical team. As can be seen in Table 14.2,[1] he was considered to be a high risk at that time, with high scores (2) on many of the clinical and risk items. When his clinical team repeated this assessment last week, their overall judgement of his risk had reduced (from high to moderate) and the scores on six of the ten items were found to have reduced. One item (C5) was found to have increased. From this assessment the clinical team concluded that Dave is now less of a risk in the current setting than he was at the point of admission.*

Table 14.2 Dave's scores on the HCR-20 C and R scales at two points in time (current and at admission)

	C1	C2	C3	C4	C5	R1	R2	R3	R4	R5	Risk score	Risk category	Increase/ decrease*
Score one year ago	2	1	2	2	1	1	2	2	2	2	17	High	
Score this week	1	0	1	2	2	1	2	1	0	1	11	Moderate	+1 −6

* Number of items that have increased or decreased.

Although not undertaken for this example, the next step might be to scrutinize those items that have changed against the individual formulation and documented evidence in case notes to identify (i) the importance/relevance of the areas that have changed against needed and expected change for risk reduction to be meaningful; (ii) the possible cause(s) of change; (iii) areas that were expected to change but have not done so; and (iv) the possible reasons for this.

Construct-based methods.   A cluster of methods based on repertory grid techniques, including traditional grids, multiple card sort and Q-Sort approaches, allow data to be collected from individuals and analysed to reveal relationships between and patterns contained within the specific facets considered through the production of a 'plot'. Most typically, the data are derived from comparing or rating a range of individuals (actual and role-based), known as elements, on a

[1] Only the dynamic scales (C and R) have been included in this example.

number of factors, known as constructs. These techniques can be used to compare an individual plot against a 'normative' or 'reference' group plot or to review the plots derived from an individual at two (or more) points in time (e.g., pre-/post-intervention). In order to strengthen the validity of the interpretations made, based on the plots, a formulation should be used to make predictions about the ways in which a plot would be expected to be affected if change had taken place. One method commonly used is to review the 'element plot' over time to reveal the relationship between 'self now' and other elements (e.g., ideal self; self when offending; best friend). Although a potentially useful technique that may have the benefit of low susceptibility to dissimulation, it requires knowledge of the approach and familiarity with the tools used to analyse the data in order to use it effectively. An example of this approach is shown below.

Case example: A card sort assessment of change[2]

Peter is a 50-year-old who has been receiving treatment for drug misuse. Peter completed a card sort at the start and the end of treatment. The elements for the card sort (i.e., the cards) were: 'self now' (SN); 'self when using drugs (SD); 'self when offending' (SO); 'ideal self' (IS); 'friend 1' (F1) – his co-defendant for index offence; 'friend 2' (F2) – who Peter often took drugs with; 'sister' (ST); 'honest person' (HP) – who he identified as his ex-girlfriend; and 'a non-drug user' (ND). He used a range of constructs (e.g., 'friendly', 'kind', 'abusive', 'threatening', 'copes well') to sort the cards. The data were analysed to produce a plot of the relationships between the elements. As can be seen (plot 14.1 & 14.2) by the end of treatment 'self now' had moved relative to a number of the other elements. The clinical team had predicted that if treatment were successful, then self now would become distanced from the SD, SO, F1 and F2 cluster and move towards SI, HP and ND. It was also expected that the distance between SN and IS would reduce.

As can be seen in comparing element plot 14.1 (completed before treatment) and element plot 14.2 (completed after treatment), although there are some minor differences in the location and distance between several of the elements, the only notable move is of 'self now', which has moved in accordance with the initial predictions. Although not shown here, a plot of the labels (constructs) used to undertake the sorts suggested that cluster 1 was associated with 'abusive', 'threatening', 'reckless' and 'needy', whilst cluster 2 was associated with 'happy', 'kind', 'able to cope' and 'friendly'.

Clinical assessments. Often, clinical assessments can be repeated in order to evaluate change. One example of this in relation to interpersonal functioning is the use of the Interpersonal Adjectives Scale (IAS) (Wiggins, 1995). At the simplest level, an individual's profile on the scale at two time points can be

---

[2] Thanks to Sean Hammond for the basis of this example.

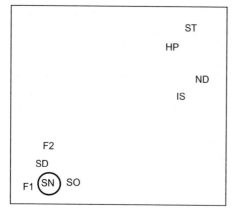

Plot 14.1   Start of treatment   **Plot 14.2**   End of treatment

compared to reveal changes in self-perception. Where the clinical team makes predictions about the nature and extent of likely change based on the individual formulation and the likely impact of the intervention, this predicted outcome can be compared with the actual output. However, this assessment can also be completed as an 'observer report' by others who know the individual well. These observer reports can be used as part of the change assessment. This range of configurations of assessment can be used to explore the following questions:

- Does self-perception change over time, in terms of the most prominent interpersonal style or the degree of flexibility in interpersonal style?
- Does how others perceive the individual change over time?
- Is there congruence between self-perception and the observer ratings and, if not, do self and observer ratings converge over time?
- Does the nature and degree of change conform to predictions of change?

A basic example of the use of this approach is shown below.

Case example: Use of IAS to assess interpersonal style

Bill is a 35-year-old who has been treated in the service for 18 months. The IAS was completed as part of the assessment of his personality style/functioning after he had been admitted to the service for three months and was repeated last week. On both occasions Bill completed it himself, as did his key worker (who has remained the same throughout). For the purposes of this example only the most basic summary information produced using the IAS is presented.

Plots 14.3 and 14.4 show in summary form 'angular location and vector length', which provide information on the most prevalent/characteristic interpersonal style at the first and second assessments. As can be seen, over time the self and observer reports have converged – both have become less extreme (as shown by the length of the line) and both have moved towards the warm/agreeable octant.

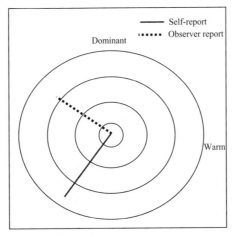

Plot 14.3 Plot showing the 'angular location' and 'vector length' of the self-report and observer report information at initial assessment

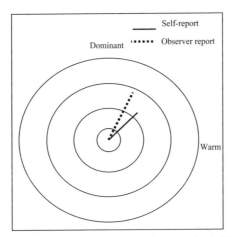

Plot 14.4 Plot showing the 'angular location' and 'vector length' of the self-report and observer report information at recent assessment

Frequently repeated measures

Undertaking measurement on a regular basis enables change to be reviewed, along with its extent. Frequent measurement is also much more likely to help in identifying when change occurred and therefore what the likely cause of the change is. Davies, Howells and Jones (2007) have outlined arguments for the use of such methods in forensic settings and in services for those with personality disorder, as well as some of the basic considerations for using this approach.

Essentially, all frequently repeated measurements make use of the time-series approach, although depending on the sophistication of the measurement, the number and nature of measures taken, and the control exerted over the nature and timing of the intervention(s), it may be possible to undertake a more rigorous 'single-case experimental design' outcome assessment. For the purposes of this chapter, the general principles of the time-series approach are outlined. Those wishing to pursue this or undertake a more thorough single-case experimental study should refer to Bloom, Fischer and Orme (2006), Petermann and Müller (2001) or Ottenbacher (1986).

In mental health settings, the time-series approach originated in behavioural research and has a long history of use in developing clinical approaches and assessing change (e.g., Bloom, Fischer & Orme 2006; Long & Hollin, 1995; Turpin, 2001), although the techniques have been widely used in other settings and date back to 1662! (Klein, 1997). The paradigm uses repeated measurement over time to create a pool of data to be analysed. Depending on what is being recorded, measurement may be at the nominal, ordinal, interval or ratio level. This can have implications for the ways in which the data are analysed and reported.

Sources of data. In personality disorder services many forms of data are collected repeatedly, or could be. *Self-report* methods are well established for the collection of data in single-case and time-series psychotherapy research and can take many forms. Scaling techniques can be used to make a rating of any experience or judgement – 'strength of a belief' through to SUDs (subjective units of distress), which are ratings of emotional experience (e.g., anxiety or anger). Scaling techniques require a fixed scale (e.g., 0–5), with points along the scale being clearly identified and the use of the scale 'calibrated' regularly to ensure that the user continues to use the scale as originally defined. Diary cards, such as those used in dialectical behaviour therapy (Linehan, 1993) allow the user to record information easily (e.g., experience ratings – see above; frequency information – e.g., use of skills; the duration of an event, or data such as number of hours slept). Usually, diary cards are completed at a set minimum interval (e.g., daily) and supplementary information is often collected to help understand factors that might affect or influence what is recorded.

Observer reports are usually based on behavioural data and may also use scales or diaries as with self-report. Common examples include Daily Behavioural Rating Scales (e.g., Beeley & Hogue, 2006), frequency counts of skills use, ratings of types and quality of interactions, objective data (e.g., time off the ward) and goal attainment scales (Kiresuik, Smith & Cardillo, 1994). The Global Review Form (Davies & Maggs, 2009) presented below is based on principles derived from goal attainment scaling. Although used infrequently, data may also be collected from sources such as tapes of individual therapy sessions with information analysed and the frequency of particular themes plotted to reveal how these change over time (e.g., if providing an intervention for low self-esteem, the frequency of positive self-statements might be recorded as an index of change).

Physical data are used less often in forensic mental health care, but may also be appropriate for measuring change over time. Drug urine screening, gaze, skin conductance and penile plethysmograph measures all fall into this group.

Data analysis.   Data can be reported in their 'raw' form, however, more commonly they are subjected to graphical or statistical analysis. There is a wide variety of tools and techniques for assisting with this (e.g., Bloom, Fischer & Orme, 2006; Morley & Adams, 1989, 1991; Ottenbacher, 1986). Graphical analysis is typically the starting point for analysis. There are many factors to consider when presenting data graphically in order to ensure clarity (e.g., use of a line graph; time along the X axis; time spanning a baseline and other periods; limited number of factors per graph) and minimizing potential bias and distortion of the data (e.g., ensuring the scale on the Y axis is appropriate). Features such as trend lines, annotations and summary scores can all be used to help clarify the presentation of the data. Some of the pitfalls and principles in presenting data graphically are shown in Figures 14.1a, 14.1b and 14.2.

Statistical analysis can be used to augment graphical analysis when there is a need to know whether or not the level of change observed is statistically significant. This can be particularly helpful when there is large variance in the data, when even a small change may be important to be able to note with some confidence or when it is important to establish that an apparently large change is statistically significant.

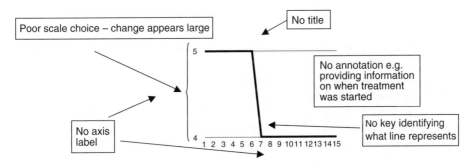

Figure 14.1a   Example of a poorly presented graph

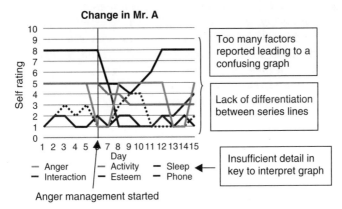

Figure 14.1b   Example of specific graph presentation problems

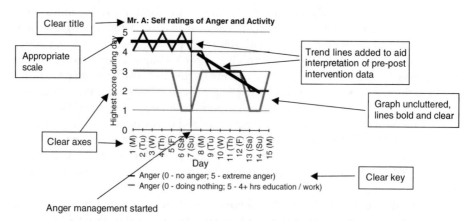

Figure 14.2   Example of some principles for presenting a clear graph

---

Case example: Graphical analysis of simple time-series data

Liam is a 45-year-old with an extensive history of substance misuse who has pro-gressed, over a number of years, from high to low secure care. Liam's progress has been monitored by the team using the Global Review Form (GRF), which is based on goal attainment principles.[3] Four of the factors monitored are detailed in Table 14.3 and a plot of Liam's progress over the last six months on the GRF is shown in Figure 14.3. As can be seen, there is a huge amount of information com-municated within the graph and the annotations help highlight points of interest and possible important events. Figure 14.3 enables hypotheses to be made and tested, as well as the possible relationships between the factors monitored to be iden-tified. For example, the increase in symptoms (weeks 5 and 6) correspond to three recent events: (i) increased autonomy with medication (hypothesis – non-compliance causes increased symptoms); (ii) commencement of unescorted leave (hypothesis – stress or other factors associated with leave cause increase in symp-toms); and (iii) illicit drug use (hypothesis – drug-taking has caused an increase in symptoms). Following the graph over time allows hypothesis (iii) to emerge as the most likely explanation for symptoms becoming more evident; self-medication is constant throughout whilst symptoms vary and eventually improve; unescorted leave occurs over a number of weeks (11–13; 18–24) without a deterioration. A second encouraging piece of information from the graph is the gradual engage-ment with treatment and eventually the development of a 'relapse plan' in rela-tion to drug misuse.

---

[3] Further information on the GRF is available from the author.

Table 14.3 The GRF rating scale used to monitor Liam's progress

	Medication	Treatment	Drug and alcohol use	Symptoms
+ 3	Manages own medication with no prompting	Has detailed relapse plan. Seeks out MH treatment as necessary *Stage of change*: maintenance	No drug and alcohol misuse history OR has a well-developed plan to manage use and recognizes/proactively manages warning signs	No obvious symptoms. Manages symptoms/distress effectively. Seeks support on the limited occasions needed
+ 2	Manages own medication with limited (occasional) staff involvement	Actively engaged in formal treatment. Evidence of clear benefit from interventions. Awareness of relapse signature. Developing relapse plan. *Stage of change*: Action	Has a well-developed misuse management plan which can be used with support	Occasional but well-managed symptoms
+ 1	Manages own medication with staff support/reassurance	Engages in formalized treatment. Evidence of benefit not confirmed. *Stage of change*: Action	Has developed a management plan which can be used with support, some limits to recognition of relapse indicators	Regular symptoms which are generally managed through use of skills/strategies/medication. May use some PRN medication

Table 14.3 (*Continued*)

	Medication	Treatment	Drug and alcohol use	Symptoms
0	Compliant with staff administered medication	Engages in formalized treatment – planning/exploring treatment possibilities *Stage of change:* Preparation	Is developing a management plan/understanding or risk factors	Experiences regular symptoms which can be managed with regular medication, staff-directed support and occasional PRN medication
−1	Compliant with medication with prompting	Engages in some structured discussions re: treatment. MotInt approach used *Stage of change:* Contemplation	Some awareness of risk factors and of management, but lack of motivation to develop this further OR No awareness of risk factors, but not actively seeking opportunities to acquire drugs	Experiences regular symptoms which can *sometimes* be managed with regular medication supplemented by support/PRN medication
−2	Variable compliance with medication. Often requires much prompting	Engages in few structured discussions re: treatment. MotInt approach being used *Stage of change:* Pre-contemplation	Seeking opportunities to acquire drugs. Regular cravings	Experiences regular symptoms which can *occasionally* be managed through support/PRN medication
−3	Non-compliant with medication	Not willing to engage in conversations with staff *Stage of change:* Pre - contemplation	Misused alcohol/drugs since last rating. Dealing or attempting to deal	Experiences regular, significant symptoms/distress that are difficult to manage

The GRF uses a 'traffic light' system (not shown) of red (−3 and −2); amber (−1, 0, +1) and green (+2, +3) to allow simple review of strengths and areas needing urgent attention.

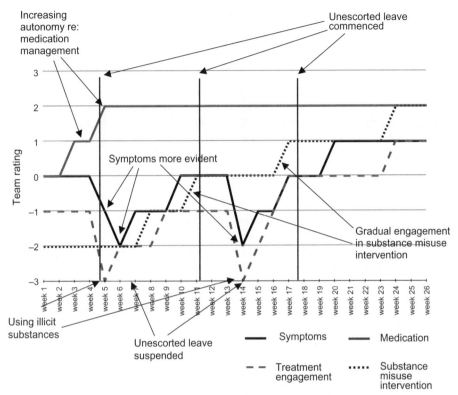

Figure 14.3   Plot of Liam's progress monitored using the GRF on a weekly basis over six months

Conclusion

If services are to be able to show that they provide effective treatment and care, and demonstrate to others the nature and degree of change made by an individual, robust systems for individual measurement need to be routinely incorporated into practice settings. Demonstrating the impact of care is important, not only to justify expenditure, but also to address ethical issues, such as whether some individuals are harmed by services and, if so, whether we can notice and address this; whether we can provide evidence of the level of change made by an individual to help inform their care; whether we can support our decisions about care with appropriate evidence; and whether we are continuing to provide some individuals with treatments that provide them with no discernible benefit. This chapter has considered a range of methods for beginning to approach the measurement of individual change. Clearly, this represents only a sample of possible approaches; however, the key challenge is for practitioners is to consider how they will build evidence of 'what works for this individual' even when this pursuit occasionally presents workers with the less welcome evidence of 'what isn't working for this individual'.

Author's note

All the case examples in this chapter are fictitious.

Acknowledgements

Thanks to Sean Hammond, John Hodge, Todd Hogue, Kevin Howells, Lawrence Jones and Graham Turpin for fuelling my interest in idiographic measurement of change and for exploring with me, over the years, many of the ideas outlined in this chapter.

References

Beeley, C. & Hogue, T. E. (2006) Daily behaviour rating scale: Monitoring risk and clinical need. Paper presented at DSPD conference, Leeds, June.

Bergin, A. E. & Garfield, S. L. (1971) *Handbook of psychotherapy and behavior change.* New York: John Wiley & Sons.

Black, N. (1996) Why we need observational studies to evaluate the effectiveness of health care. *British Medical Journal,* **312**, 1215–1218.

Bloom, M., Fischer J. & Orme, J.G. (2006) *Evaluating practice: Guidelines for the accountable professional,* 5th edition. Boston, MA: Allyn & Bacon

Davies, J. (2005) Accountable practice: Using single case methods in forensic services. Paper presented at Division of Forensic Psychology Annual Conference, Aston.

Davies, J., Howells, K. & Jones, L. (2007) Using single case approaches in personality disorder and forensic services. *Journal of Forensic Psychiatry and Psychology,* **18**, 353–367.

Davies, J., Jones, L. & Howells, K. (in press) Evaluating individual change in forensic settings. In M. Daffern, L. Jones & J. Shine (Eds.) *Offence paralleling behaviour: An individualized approach to offender assessment and treatment.* Chichester: Wiley & Sons

Davies, J. & Maggs, R. (2009) Measuring individual change in a new low secure service: systems for individual and service evaluation. Paper presented at International Association of Forensic Mental Health Conference, Edinburgh.

Department of Health (2008) *Refocusing the care programme approach: Policy and positive practice guidance.* London: DoH.

Jacobson, N. S. & Truax, P. (1991) Clinical significance: A statistical approach to defining meaningful change in psychotherapy research. *Journal of Consulting and Clinical Psychology,* **59**, 12–19.

Jones, L. (2004) Offence paralleling behaviour (OPB) as a framework for assessment and intervention with offenders. In A. Needs & G. J. Towl (Eds.) *Applying psychology to forensic practice* (pp. 34–63). Chichester: Wiley-Blackwell.

Kiresuk, T. J., Smith, A. & Cardillo, J. E. (Eds.) (1994) *Goal attainment scaling.* Mahwah, NJ: Lawrence Erlbaum Associates.

Klein, J. L. (1997) *Statistical visions in time.* New York: Cambridge University Press.

Linehan, M. M. (1993) *Cognitive behavioral treatment of borderline personality disorder.* New York: Guilford Press.

Long, C. G. & Hollin, C.R. (1995) Single-case design: a critique of methodology and analysis of recent trends. *Clinical Psychology and Psychotherapy,* **2**, 177–191.

Maruish, M. E. (Ed.) (1994) *The use of psychological testing for treatment planning and outcome assessment.* Mahwah, NJ: Lawrence Erlbaum Associates.

Morley, S. & Adams, M. (1989) Some simple statistical tests for exploring single-case time-series data. *British Journal of Clinical Psychology*, **28**, 1–18.

Morley, S. & Adams, M. (1991) Graphical analysis of single-case time-series data. *British Journal of Clinical Psychology*, **30**, 97–115.

Nagi, C. & Davies, J. (2010) Addressing offending risk in low secure mental health services for men: a descriptive review of available evidence. *The British Journal of Forensic Practice*, **12**(1), 38–47.

Ogles, B. M., Lambert, M. J. & Fields, S. A. (2002) *Essentials of outcome assessment.* New York: John Wiley & Sons.

Ogles, B. M., Lambert, M. J. & Masters, K .S. (1996) *Assessing outcome in clinical practice.* Boston, MA: Allyn & Bacon.

Ogles, B. M., Lunnen, K. M. & Bonesteel, K. (2001) Clinical significance: History, application, and current practice. *Clinical Psychology Review*, **21**, 421–446.

Ottenbacher, K. J. (1986) *Evaluating clinical change: Strategies for occupational and physical therapists.* Baltimore, MD: Williams & Wilkins.

Petermann, F. & Müller, J. (2001) *Clinical psychology and single-case evidence.* Chichester: John Wiley and Sons.

Slade, M. & Priebe, S. (2001) Are randomised controlled trials the only gold that glitters? *The British Journal of Psychiatry*, **179**, 286–287.

Sperry, L., Brill, P. L., Howard, K. I. & Grissom, G. R. (1996) *Treatment outcomes in psychotherapy and psychiatric interventions.* New York: Brunner/Mazel.

Spielberger, C. D. (1999) *State-Trait Anger Expression Inventory – 2.* Psychological Assessment Resources Inc.

Turpin, G. (2001) Single case methodology and psychotherapy evaluation: From research to practice. In C. Mace, S. Moorey & B. Roberts (Eds.) *Evidence in the psychological therapies: A critical guide for practitioners* (pp. 91–113). Hove: Brunner-Routledge.

Victora, C. G., Habicht, J.-P. & Bryce, J. (2004) Evidence-based public health: Moving beyond randomized trials. *American Journal of Public Health*, **94**, 400–405.

Webster, C. D., Douglas, K. S., Eaves, D. & Hart, S. D. (1997) *HCR-20 Manual (Version 2).* Lutz, FL: Psychological Assessment Resources Inc.

Wiggins, J. S. (1995) *Interpersonal adjective scales: Professional manual.* Lutz, FL: Psychological Assessment Resources Inc.

Chapter Fifteen

Patient Experiences of Therapeutic and Anti-therapeutic Processes

Phil Willmot

'Never allow a crisis to go to waste.'

Rahm Emanuel

People with a diagnosis of personality disorder are often characterized as being difficult to treat and responding slowly to psychological treatments (e.g., Bender, Dolan, Skodol, Sanislow, Dyck, McGlashan, Shea, Zanarini, Oldham & Gunderson, 2001; Critchfield & Benjamin, 2006). Clinicians who work with this patient group, however, may recognize that the picture is more complex than this. At times they respond very well to treatment and make rapid progress. However, at other times they appear to be standing still in therapy or can even appear to be deteriorating. Jones (2007) described how patients in this group tended to have long histories of unsuccessful interventions and described various ways in which interventions could be harmful to them.

This chapter describes a study of patients' experiences of therapy in a forensic personality disorder service. While service users' perspectives are now regularly considered in other mental health services, within forensic mental health settings they continue to receive relatively little attention. The reasons for this are not well researched. While there is some evidence that forensic patients under-report their problems and risk (e.g., Duggan, 2004; Milton, McCartney, Duggan, Evans, Collins, McCarthy & Larkin, 2005), the lack of attention to patients' perspectives may also in part reflect wider societal attitudes which stigmatize and marginalize both offenders (Funk, 2004; Maruna, LeBel, Mitchell & Naples, 2004) and people with a diagnosis of personality disorder (Department of Health, 2003).

Working Positively with Personality Disorder in Secure Settings: A Practitioner's Perspective
Edited by Phil Willmot and Neil Gordon
© 2011 John Wiley & Sons, Ltd.

The research took place in the Personality Disorder Service at Rampton Hospital. All participants had completed a significant amount of psychological therapy. (For a description of the treatment pathway in this service, see this volume, Chapter 5.) The participants were nine men detained under the Mental Health Act 1983 with a primary diagnosis of personality disorder and undergoing psychological treatment who were interviewed about their experiences of therapy. The transcripts of theses interviews was then subjected to a grounded theory analysis (Glaser & Strauss, 1967; Strauss & Corbin, 1994) to explore their individual experiences of therapy and to develop a theory about the processes affecting therapeutic change among patients.

Positive therapeutic processes

Although all participants had completed at least one lengthy course of therapy; dialectical behaviour therapy (Linehan, 1993) and/or schema focused therapy (Young, Klosko & Weishaar 2003); none mentioned therapy itself as a factor in their therapeutic progress. Instead, they all made reference to interpersonal interactions and specific relationships as the critical factors that had promoted change.

Most participants spoke about individual therapists who had been influential. The most widely mentioned therapist quality was persistence, both in the sense of 'hanging on' to the therapeutic relationship, sometimes in the face of great hostility from the participant, and persistence in pursuing the goals of therapy and not allowing themselves to be sidetracked.

'She was not going to give in, no matter what, and we did fall out on numerous occasions. I did say some horrible things to her, but she was a strong person, so carried on.' (P8)

'He stuck around, he kept coming back, week after week, stuck in there; he basically stayed until the work was done.' (P3)

Another frequently mentioned quality was that of non-judgemental acceptance by the therapist.

'My opinion of myself was that nobody found me worthwhile, but here is a person sitting in front of me that's spent week after week, hour after hour with me saying that I am worthwhile, then there must be some truth in it.' (P10)

I'd always felt instinctively that women would dislike us. So having two women that are actively supporting you and helping you and believing in you was a big help.' (P2)

Other important characteristics included believing in the possibility of therapeutic change, being supportive, caring and allowing participants to work at their own pace.

Participants also described incidents when other patients' behaviour had promoted change; these included other patients advocating therapy when they were ambivalent, working collaboratively with and feeling accepted by other patients and feeling similar to other patients after hearing their self-disclosures, as well as receiving critical feedback from other patients.

Critical incidents

The process of change was generally not gradual or linear. Several participants described having been detained for many years without apparently making any progress or even deteriorating. These participants all described key incidents which had been a turning point for them. These incidents fell into two categories, which were termed 'crises' and 'fresh starts'.

Crises

Crises were generally interpreted by the participant at the time as being detrimental, for example, being secluded after committing a serious assault, being returned from a medium secure unit to a high secure hospital after a placement had failed, experiencing psychotic symptoms and a deterioration in behaviour and not being discharged by a Mental Health Review Tribunal after expecting a positive outcome.

Crises such as these were generally not unusual for these individuals, whose lifestyles were often extremely chaotic. Participants described how, in previous similar incidents, the responses of people in authority had seemed entirely punitive; they had typically been moved to another ward or hospital, leading to a sense of resentment and that they had been rejected by their clinical team at a time of crisis. What appeared to be different about these critical incidents was the response of the team and of individual staff members. Even when a participant was moved as a result of their behaviour, a key person, usually a therapist, stayed in touch and continued to provide contact and support. Indeed, the crisis often prompted the therapist to intensify their efforts, or at least to reassure the participant that he or she would continue to support them. These critical encounters appeared to create cognitive dissonance for the participant, providing clear disconfirming evidence for previously strongly held and dysfunctional, therapy-interfering beliefs.

Case example: Mark

When Mark was in prison he was extremely violent. This led to him being transferred numerous times. When he arrived in a new prison he would feel isolated and vulnerable because he did not know anybody. In order to cope with these feelings of vulnerability he would deliberately get into conflict with the prisoner he saw as the biggest threat on the wing and end up seriously assaulting him. This generally resulted in Mark being transferred to another prison, where the cycle would quickly repeat itself.

Eventually Mark was transferred to Rampton, where he was very quickly involved in a serious assault on another patient and placed in seclusion. He expected to be returned to prison, but instead his named nurse came to talk to him about what sort of help he needed to help him control his violent behaviour. When interviewed several years later for this study Mark said that this was a turning point for him because it felt like the first time in his life that people had not immediately rejected him because of his violence, but instead were offering him a way out of his cycle of violent behaviour.

Fresh starts

Several patients described how a change of environment had allowed them to change dysfunctional patterns of behaviour. A number of the participants in this study had transferred from other high secure hospitals. All described a similar pattern of engagement in therapy, where they had made little or no progress in their previous hospitals before transferring to this service, but had then made relatively rapid progress within a few years of transferring.

Case example: George

George had been detained in another high secure hospital for 15 years before being transferred to Rampton. In that time he had made very little progress in treatment and both he and his clinical team felt hopeless about his prognosis. On occasions he had tried to change his behaviour. For example, he recognized that he was often demanding and abusive to nursing staff when he perceived that they were not acting as quickly as they could to meet his requests, and that this behaviour generally led to his requests taking even longer to be met. On several occasions George tried to approach staff in a more polite and assertive manner but this was generally met with suspicion; staff accused him of being 'manipulative' or 'trying to prove something' and did not respond any faster to his requests. George would quickly become discouraged and revert to his old pattern of being demanding and abusive, which felt more comfortable for him and for staff, and which was just as effective as being polite and assertive.

When he was transferred to Rampton, George decided to try his polite and assertive approach again. This time, because the staff did not know him so well they did not question his behaviour but responded positively to his appropriate behaviour. This encouraged him to continue with this behaviour and to build more positive and less mutually suspicious relationships with his clinical team.

Anti-therapeutic processes

All the participants described behaviour by staff that had interfered with their therapeutic progress. Anti-therapeutic processes fell into several categories:

- *Overt abuse*: Participants described incidents of bullying, intimidation, threats and physical violence by nursing staff in hospitals and by prison officers. None of the participants mentioned this behaviour occurring in hospital in the last

20 years, though some said they had experienced it more recently in prison. Such behaviour made them feel unsafe and unwilling to be open with staff. Participants generally recognized that such behaviour by staff generally resulted in cycles of mutual abuse and suspicion between staff and patients/ prisoners.

- *Staff responding angrily or punitively to participants' hostile or aggressive behaviour, which tended to reinforce or perpetuate such behaviour*: Some participants recognized that their own behaviour had been provocative and could understand why staff sometimes reacted to them in angry or punitive ways. Nevertheless, even when they could understand the staff member's response, they still felt that such behaviour undermined their trust in that individual.
- *Stigmatizing and stereotyping attitudes towards personality disorder*: A number of participants felt that they were judged more harshly, particularly by mental health professionals, because of their diagnosis of personality disorder, as a result of which they felt that some staff were always suspicious of their motives and expected them to be devious, underhand and manipulative.
- *Therapists leaving*: It was inevitable among a group of patients who had been engaged in long-term psychological therapies that participants would all have many experiences of therapists or other key workers leaving. Particularly where this was done in an unplanned or sudden manner it tended to have a detrimental effect on the participant, prompting feelings of abandonment or rejection and leading them to disengage from therapy altogether, or to be distrustful of the next therapist to work with them.
- *Feeling that therapy was not collaborative or was being imposed*: Although participants saw the therapy process as being led and structured by the therapist, their positive experiences of therapy generally involved a sense of collaboration and negotiation about the goals of therapy and the pace of change. Where participants felt that goals were being imposed without consultation or that therapists were not being responsive about the pace of treatment, they tended to feel distrustful and to disengage.

All of these staff behaviours were anti-therapeutic because they reinforced participants' old perceptions of others, particularly of people in authority as abusive, rejecting or ignoring their needs.

As well as these interpersonal factors, participants also identified a number of intrapersonal factors, which they felt hindered change. These included fear of other people's reactions if they did change, fear of change itself or of having to explore unpleasant aspects of themselves, and focusing on less important goals such as education or physical fitness.

Schemas of self, others and relationships

Participants were asked to describe how the way they saw themselves and others had changed since they had begun to engage in therapy. Prior to therapy, participants' perceptions of themselves and others, and of relationships in general, were overwhelmingly negative. Participants saw themselves as being stigmatized, different, disliked and unwanted. They saw other people as being hostile and abusive and relationships as being transitory, painful and exploitative. Although some participants drew specific links with their childhood experiences of being abused or rejected by carers, the sense of alienation generally applied to society as a whole.

'I was not worth bothering with, unlovable, unworthy to be around people. I thought people always hated me.' (P4)

'I was on my own and it was just one big frightening battle.' (P3)

'I felt like a milk bottle that doesn't belong to anybody and is just passed around from doorstep to doorstep.' (P1)

'I was frightened of closeness and affection, or very mistrusting of it because it left me vulnerable being close to people.' (P9)

Following therapy, participants all had more balanced views of themselves and others.

'I feel wanted. People are talking to me or asking about things; they really want to know things or value my views.' (P5)

'I feel like other people.' (P5)

'I suppose I see people as being more trustworthy and being more honest and genuine with me than I ever had before. I suppose more receptive of me too, rather than just someone might just pay lip-service, or somebody might have an agenda, a hidden agenda.' (P9)

'I can go up to people and say whatever I have to, and know it's not going to be used in ways that's going to be detrimental to me.' (P2)

Participants' beliefs about relationships had also changed and closeness to others was seen as being intrinsically worthwhile and rewarding rather than threatening and aversive.

'I understand how important relationships are. It's easier for me to be able to get involved with somebody and for me to work with myself and with them to better the friendship or relationship.' (P9)

'Friendship is particularly important; it's part of being human.' (P1)

Why are therapeutic relationships so important with this user group?

While the therapeutic relationship is important across a range of client groups (Martin, Garske & Davis, 2000), a review of psychotherapy research with clients with personality disorder by Critchfield and Benjamin (2006) suggested that it is particularly important because of the particular problems of interpersonal functioning that people with personality disorder experience. Clients with personality disorder are more likely to drop out or disengage from therapy so a strong therapeutic relationship is important to keep them engaged and motivated (Horvath,

2001). Critchfield and Benjamin suggested that the therapeutic relationship with clients with personality disorder also provides a valuable means through which the client can learn effective interpersonal skills. Safran, Muran, Samstag and Stevens (2002) found that clients with personality disorder dropped out significantly less and showed better outcomes at end of therapy and follow-up if the model of therapy specifically addressed ruptures in the therapeutic alliance: 'The relationship ... has a dual role. The relationship is the vehicle through which the therapist can effect the [dialectical behaviour] therapy; it *is* also the therapy' (Linehan, 1993: 514; emphasis in the original).

This study provides further evidence for the importance of a strong therapeutic relationship in treating people with personality disorder and offers an insight into how much this patient group values positive therapeutic relationships. It also suggests a mechanism for therapeutic change.

Many of the interpersonal problems associated with forensic clients with a diagnosis of personality disorder can be understood in terms of their extremely negative schemas about themselves, others and relationships, which typically reflect developmental experiences characterized by insecure attachment, abuse and rejection. The beliefs that other people are generally abusive, rejecting, hostile and selfish, and will exploit any weaknesses they see in others, appear common among forensic patients with a diagnosis of personality disorder and are important in understanding the aggressive, exploitative and suspicious behaviour that many of these individuals display in the community and in institutions. Unfortunately, those patterns of behaviour often elicit a hostile response from peers and punitive or rejecting behaviour from people in authority, which generally reinforces the perception that others are hostile and rejecting.

Similarly, these individuals tend to come into therapy with very negative views of themselves, which generally stem from childhood and are reinforced by repeated experiences of rejection and abuse.

The experiences of participants in this study suggest that being in a long-term secure therapeutic relationship provides consistent disconfirming evidence for these negative beliefs about the self, others and relationships. Where previously others were seen as abusive and rejecting, the therapeutic relationship showed that others could be caring and dependable. Where, previously the rejecting and hostile behaviour of others reinforced patients' beliefs that others saw them as detestable and unworthy, the consistent, non-judgemental acceptance within the therapeutic relationship showed that others could see them more positively. Where previously relationships had been adversarial, abusive or exploitative, the therapeutic relationship showed how relationships could be collaborative, supportive and intrinsically rewarding.

The significance of crises

The lives of people with personality disorder can often be chaotic and marked by frequent crises, so it was significant that among participants in this study therapeutic progress had often been triggered by crises. The previous experience of these participants in times of crisis had generally been that, at the point when they most needed help and support, they had experienced support being withdrawn – partners and friends had left them, professional agencies had told them they could no longer work with them or had referred them to other agencies, or they had been moved to a different ward or institution. These experiences had reinforced their sense of themselves as failing and incompetent, their sense of others as rejecting and uncaring, and their sense of relationships as fragile.

In contrast, a consistent feature mentioned by all the participants who described a crisis as a turning point in their therapeutic progress was consistent support by another person which helped them through the crisis; the relationship had not only survived, but also had often been strengthened by the mutual experience of the crisis. These positive experiences provided strong disconfirming evidence for participant's previous negative beliefs and this may explain why persistence was rated as such an important therapist characteristic by participants.

Discussion

Various authors have suggested links between insecure patterns of attachment, personality disorder (e.g., Bartholomew, Kwong & Hart, 2001; Meyer & Pilkonis, 2005) and offending (e.g., Fonagy, 2003; Rich, 2006) and the findings of this study can be interpreted in terms of concepts from attachment theory.

The therapist as 'secure base'

Although Bowlby (1977) conceptualized the therapist as a 'secure base', Farber and Metzger (2009) have suggested that, since exploration in therapy tends to occur before the secure base is established, the therapeutic relationship should more accurately be described as a 'good enough base' (2009: 48). Farber and Metzger have also proposed that the qualities of a 'therapist as a secure base' went beyond Rogers' (1957) necessary and sufficient conditions for therapeutic change by including the ability to respectfully challenge the internal working models of their insecurely attached client.

Internal working models

Internal working models (IWMs) are another key concept in attachment theory and consist of beliefs about the self and others and the relationships between them. Bowlby (1988) suggested that while IWMs were generally stable, they were also amenable to change in the light of new experiences, and that they changed more rapidly under certain circumstances. The results of this study provide evidence of changes to the IWMs of the participants in this study as a result of psychological therapy, though it is not clear from these results how stable or generalized these changes are. Nevertheless, this is a significant finding since Cobb and Davila (2009) reported that there has been relatively little published evidence of change in IWMs resulting from psychological therapy.

Cobb and Davila suggested three alternative models of change of IWMs. The life stress model (Davila & Sargent, 2003) suggests that IWMs are most likely to change when the person's interpersonal environment is changing. Davila and

Sargent found that change in adult attachment was more affected by the meanings that people ascribed to events rather than the events themselves. According to the life stress model the mechanism by which therapy leads to more secure attachments is by helping the client to develop new understandings of earlier experiences or to provide new experiences that they can use to change IWMs.

The social cognitive model (Baldwin, Keelan, Fehr, Enns & Koh-Rangarajoo, 1996) proposes that people have a range of alternative sets of IWMs with one dominant model which can be superseded by another subordinate model as result of interpersonal circumstances that increase the availability of that model. According to the social cognitive model, the key mechanism of effective therapy is the way it enables clients to form and maintain healthier IWMs.

The individual differences model (Davila & Cobb, 2003) proposes that individuals with histories of adverse interpersonal experiences, life stressors and psychopathology may develop unclear and unstable IWMs, leading to fluctuations in their view of self and others, and chaotic, confusing interpersonal experiences. This presentation is most likely to be seen in individuals with a disorganized attachment style and borderline personality traits. According to the individual differences model the mechanism of therapy would be to help clients to develop more integrated and balanced IWMs.

These three models are not necessarily mutually exclusive; the individual differences model is likely to apply only to those individuals with the most chaotic IWMs and borderline interpersonal style. There also appears to be some overlap between the other two models. Since all the participants in this study had histories of extreme adverse interpersonal experiences and life stressors, and a number had formal diagnoses of borderline personality disorder, it might be expected that their experiences of therapy would most closely match the individual differences model. However, their accounts of the change process appear more in line with the life stress model or the social cognitions model, while the significant impact of critical events appears to be most consistent with the life stress model. The variety of different models and the different therapy goals associated with each model raises the possibility that attachment-informed therapy with this client group will lead to different goals and approaches depending on the structure and organization of the IWMs of the individual client. Thus, for clients with more stable but dysfunctional IWMs, corresponding to anxious or avoidant attachment styles, the goal of therapy would be to help them form and maintain healthier IWMs, whereas for clients with more unstable IWMs, corresponding to a disorganized attachment style, the primary goal of therapy would be integrate their IWMs before developing more positive models.

Conclusions

This study shows the value of qualitative research methods with patients in forensic mental health settings. Qualitative research is concerned with understanding the lived experience and how people make sense of their experiences. Despite increased interest in patient perspectives in mental health research in recent years, the stigma and suspicion surrounding forensic patients, and particularly those with the added stigma of a diagnosis of personality disorder, mean that little qualitative research has been carried out with this group. This study demonstrates the richness of the qualitative data that this previously under-researched group can provide. The length and intensity of psychological therapy which these clients undergo means that they have much to tell us about the processes of therapeutic change, which may well have applications outside the narrow field of forensic personality disorder.

References

Baldwin, M. W., Keelan, J. P. R., Fehr, B., Enns, V. & Koh-Rangarajoo, E. (1996) Social-cognitive conceptualizations of attachment working models: Availability and accessibility effects. *Journal of Personality and Social Psychology*, **71**, 91–109.

Bartholomew, K., Kwong, M. J. & Hart, S. D. (2001) Attachment. In J. W. Livesley (Ed.) *Handbook of personality disorders* (pp. 196–230). New York: Guilford Press.

Bender, D. S., Dolan, R. T., Skodol, A. E., Sanislow, C. A., Dyck, I. R., McGlashan, T. H., Shea, M. T., Zanarini, M. C., Oldham, J. M. & Gunderson, J. G. (2001) Treatment utilization by patients with personality disorder. *American Journal of Psychiatry*, **158**, 295–302.

Bowlby, J. (1977) The making and breaking of affectional bonds: II. Some principles of psychotherapy. *British Journal of Psychiatry*, **130**, 421–431.

Bowlby, J. (1988) *A secure base: Parent–child attachment and healthy human development*. London: Routledge.

Cobb, R. J. & Davila, J. (2009) Internal working models and change. In J. H. Obegi & E. Berant (Eds.) *Attachment theory and research in clinical work* (pp. 209–233). New York: Guilford Press.

Critchfield, K. L. & Benjamin, L. S. (2006) Integration of therapeutic factors in treating personality disorders. In L. Castonguay & L. Beutler (Eds.) *Principles of therapeutic change that works* (pp. 253–271). New York: Oxford University Press.

Davila, J. & Cobb, R. J. (2003) Predicting change in self-reported and interviewer-assessed adult attachments: Tests of the individual difference and life stress models of attachment change. *Personality and Social Psychology Bulletin*, **29**, 859–870.

Davila, J. & Sargent, E. (2003) The meaning of life (events) predicts changes in attachment security. *Personality and Social Psychology Bulletin*, **29**, 1383–1395.

Department of Health (2003) *Personality disorder: No longer a diagnosis of exclusion. Policy implementation guidance for the development of services for people with personality disorder*. London: DoH.

Duggan, C. (2004) Does personality change and, if so, what changes? *Criminal Behaviour and Mental Health*, **14**, 5–16.

Farber, B. A. & Metzger, J. A. (2006) The therapist as secure base. In J. H. Obegi & E. Berant (Eds.) *Attachment theory and research in clinical work* (pp. 46–70). New York: Guilford Press.

Fonagy, P. (2003) Towards a developmental understanding of violence. *British Journal of Psychiatry*, **183**, 190–192.

Funk, P. (2004) On the effective use of stigma as a crime-deterrent. *European Economic Review*, **48**, 715–728.

Glaser, B. G. & Strauss, A. (1967) *The discovery of grounded theory: Strategies for qualitative research*. Chicago: Aldine.

Horvath, A. O. (2001) The alliance. *Psychotherapy*, **38**, 365–372.

Jones, L. F. (2007) Iatrogenic interventions with personality disordered offenders. *Psychology, Crime and Law*, **13**, 69–79.

Linehan, M. M. (1993) *Cognitive-behavioural treatment of borderline personality disorder.* New York: Guilford Press.

Martin, D. J., Garske, J. P. & Davis, M. K. (2000) Relation of the therapeutic alliance with outcome and other variables: A meta-analytic review. *Journal of Consulting and Clinical Psychology,* **68**, 438–450.

Maruna, S., LeBel, T., Mitchell, N. & Naples, M. (2004) Pygmalion in the reintegration process: Desistence from crime through the looking glass. *Psychology, Crime & Law,* **10**, 271–281.

Meyer, B. & Pilkonis, P. A. (2005) An attachment model of personality disorders. In M. F. Lenzenweger and J. F. Clarkin (Eds.) *Major Theories of Personality Disorder,* 2nd edition (pp. 231–281). New York: Guilford Press.

Milton, J., McCartney, M., Duggan, C., Evans, C., Collins, M., McCarthy, M. & Larkin, E. (2005) Beauty in the eye of the beholder? How high security hospital psychopathically-disordered patients rate their own interpersonal behaviour. *Journal of Forensic Psychiatry and Psychology,* **16**, 552–565.

Rich, P. (2006) From theory to practice: The application of attachment theory to assessment and treatment in forensic mental health settings. *Criminal Behaviour and Mental Health,* **16**, 211–216.

Rogers, C. (1957) The necessary and sufficient conditions of therapeutic personality change. *Journal of Consulting Psychology,* **21**, 95–103.

Safran, J. D., Muran, J. C., Samstag, L. W. & Stevens, C. (2002) Repairing alliance ruptures. In J. C. Norcross (Ed.) *Psychotherapy relationships that work: Therapist contributions and responsiveness to patients* (pp. 235–254). New York: Oxford University Press.

Strauss, A. & Corbin, J. (1994) Grounded theory methodology: An overview. In N. K. Denzin and Y. S. Lincoln (Eds.) *Handbook of qualitative research* (pp. 273–285). Thousand Oaks, CA: Sage.

Young, J. E., Klosko, J. S. & Weishaar, M. E. (2003) *Schema therapy: A practitioner's guide.* New York: Guilford Press.

Chapter Sixteen

Looking to the Future

Neil Gordon and Phil Willmot

This book has provided an account of our work in a high secure setting over the last ten years, touching on the different stages of our patients' journey from admission to eventual discharge to conditions of lower security. We have illustrated the challenges we face as practitioners working with a marginalized and often severely traumatized group of men, showing how we have developed our understanding of their needs and adapted our approach to meeting these through treatment interventions and workforce development. Undoubtedly the narrative we have created is infused with hope about the potential difference that well equipped and psychologically informed services can make to the lives of those who find themselves incarcerated in this setting. We have also emphasized the central role of public protection and risk management in this context, arguing that this is most effectively addressed through understanding and working with psychological needs, in conjunction with a focus on offending and high risk behaviours.

When discussing how we would end the book we identified some key issues we felt it would be important to mention as a way of drawing the narrative to a close, while also looking forward to potential future developments in this type of service. It is readily acknowledged in current national policy initiatives related to personality disorder that we have reached a potential 'tipping point' (Gladwell, 2002) in terms of service provision and practice in this specialist field. As highlighted in the preceding chapters several key elements have pushed us to this point. The new NICE guidelines on antisocial and borderline personality disorders were launched in 2009 and, although some have pointed out that they did not state anything particularly new or radical, they have highlighted the key elements of best practice

Working Positively with Personality Disorder in Secure Settings: A Practitioner's Perspective
Edited by Phil Willmot and Neil Gordon
© 2011 John Wiley & Sons, Ltd.

and emphasized the importance of containing therapeutic relationships, high functioning inter-professional teams and multi-agency working. The new Mental Health Act provides a further impetus to reframing our understanding of the needs of those given the diagnosis of personality disorder and limits the capacity of treatment providers to exclude those with high levels of distress who do not fit neatly into categorical psychiatric classification systems. At the policy level new guidelines on commissioning services for those with personality disorder address the complex nature of this service user group and highlight the need to respond effectively to medical, social, and psychological distress through the creation of integrated care pathways that dissolve the unhelpful and often rigid boundaries between health, social care and criminal justice systems (Department of Health, 2009). The existing taxonomies and classification systems that we have been using to frame our clinical work are also under review, partly in recognition of their limitations and also because of the increasing emphasis on articulating more clearly the relationship between Axis I and Axis II disorders.

As we have highlighted throughout this book, those who operate on the therapeutic front line or what have been called the swampy lands (Schön, 1983) of practice in high secure settings, inhabit a world shaped by what Pilgrim refers to as 'ephemeral government social policy priorities' (2001: 263). An ambivalent societal attitude towards mentally disordered offenders, those Prins (1995) describes as 'the people that nobody owns', has meant that clinical, research and treatment agendas have become increasingly politicized. For those who have contributed to this book who work in these settings, the competing agendas of risk management and therapeutic treatment permeate their day-to-day therapeutic experiences. Cordess (2001) has argued that effecting change in this system is further complicated by demoralization and neglect, arising from societal ambivalence towards the roles and tasks of such organizations. He highlights how the tension created by the therapy vs. custody dynamic has a tendency to 'skew off balance' with the creation of increasingly bureaucratic systems and rigid practices that act as defensive manoeuvres to combat fear and anxiety and can create resistance to change and development.

High secure psychiatric services are the last resort for patients who have typically spent the first twenty or thirty years of their lives shuttling between abusive and neglecting families, overstretched and under-trained agencies and professionals, and a criminal justice system that often increases their sense of resentment and alienation. If a child repeatedly failed to get appropriate treatment for an ingrowing toenail until they were in their twenties and then needed to be admitted to intensive care to have their leg amputated, there would be understandable outrage at the needless distress and expense incurred. Outrage would turn to disbelief if the government's response to such systemic failure was to focus mainly on building new and better intensive care units, yet in the field of personality disorder this effectively has been the response. Many millions have been sunk into DSPD services for a tiny number of the most damaged patients, while fewer and fewer resources have been allocated as the focus moves along the spectrum to medium and low secure services and non-forensic services. Prevention and early interventions with children have struggled to even find a place on the agenda.

Colleagues from less secure services are understandably envious of the resources and time that are available in high secure services. However, such services serve a vital function, not just as a treatment provider of last resort, but also, as this book shows, as somewhere that has the space and the resources to innovate and develop not just new treatment techniques, but all the essential ancillary systems of governance, supervision, training and evaluation. Just as, in the last twenty years, the prison service has been able to develop, pilot and evaluate new correctional programmes which are now widely used in probation and community forensic mental health services, so high secure forensic services have a vital role to play as the source of innovation and practice development in the treatment of personality disorder.

These are exciting times to be working in the field of personality disorder and the next few years are likely to see many new and exciting innovations. We would like to highlight a few:

- Clinicians working with personality disorder now have a widening range of therapeutic models to choose from, all of which have many features in common and appear to be of similar effectiveness. What is also clear is that, probably more so than with other client groups, the process of therapy is often more important than the content. Various chapters in this volume have highlighted how factors such as attachment style, the therapist's own schemas and therapeutic style and team dynamics can all affect the therapeutic process. For the therapist to consider all of these factors, even before they start to consider the patient's own personality and motivations is a virtually impossible task. An important focus of future research, therefore, should be to develop a better understanding of the process of therapeutic change with this client group in order to refine our therapeutic techniques.
- Given the many factors that the therapist needs to bear in mind, it is not surprising that even the most experienced clinicians can sometimes get it wrong, resulting in treatment outcomes that harm the patient, and most personality disorder services will be littered with the consequences of such harmful interventions. Jones (2007) has highlighted the importance of studying adverse treatment effects just as much as successes. The medical profession takes seriously its obligation to do no harm in a way that mental health professionals working with personality disorder would do well to consider.
- While 'service user involvement' has become a nearly all-pervasive mantra in the health service in recent years, one area it has not penetrated has been forensic personality disorder services. The old stigmas and myths, that these patients are untrustworthy, manipulative and self-serving, live on, and so researchers and service managers are still reluctant to give these patients a real say. We hope that the chapters in this book that have included a patient 'voice' will help to undermine these myths and demonstrate the clear insights that these patients can provide, particularly in giving clinicians clear feedback about what works and what does not.
- Sue Evershed (this volume, Chapter 8) highlights the yawning chasm between the ethical frontier territory inhabited by clinicians working with forensic personality disorder and the ethical standards and regulations that organizations and professional bodies impose, as well as the conflict between the increasingly defensive and risk-averse organizational culture we work in and the fact that therapy with this client group inevitably involves risk. Because we are a small group, drawn from various different professions and generally marginalized

within those professions, we cannot rely on our professional bodies to take the lead in setting the ethical agenda. Instead clinicians in the field need to take the lead in beginning a dialogue about these issues.

As the editors of this text it has been a privilege to gather the experiences of professional colleagues who demonstrate such high levels of commitment to improving services for this patient group. We began the book reflecting on the importance of 'finding a voice' to communicate to others our struggles and successes during ten years of change and innovation in a unique context. We hope the insights and accounts of our practice we have provided can help others in frontline services to continue responding positively and creatively to the challenges of personality disorder.

References

Cordess, C. (Ed.) (2001) *Confidentiality and mental health*. London: Jessica Kingsley.

Department of Health (2009) *Recognising complexity: Commissioning guidance for personality disorder services*. London: The Stationary Office.

Gladwell, M. (2002) *Tipping point: How little things can make a big difference*. New York: Little, Brown.

Jones, L. F. (2007) Iatrogenic interventions with personality disordered offenders. *Psychology, Crime and Law*, **13**, 69–79.

Pilgrim, D. (2001) Disordered personalities and disordered concepts. *The Journal of Mental Health*, **10**, 253–265.

Prins, H. (1995) *Offenders, deviants or patients*. London: Routledge.

Schön, D. A. (1983) *The reflective practitioner: How professionals think in action*. Aldershot: Ashgate.

Index

Index compiled by Terry Halliday